GARDENING
MONTH-BY-MONTH

The Collingridge Handbook of
GARDENING
MONTH-BY-MONTH

PATRICK JOHNS

COLLINGRIDGE

Acknowledgements

The Editor would like to thank Pat Brindley, Patrick Johns, Robert Pearson, and Michael Warren of Photos Horticultural for providing the photographs used in this book.

Line drawings by Patricia Capon

Published by Collingridge Books
an imprint of Newnes Books
a division of The Hamlyn Publishing Group Limited
84–88 The Centre, Feltham, Middlesex, TW13 4BH
and distributed for them by
The Hamlyn Publishing Group Limited
Rushden, Northants, England

ISBN 0 600 36890 4

Printed in England

CONTENTS

Introduction

I meet many people each year during the course of my work, not all directly face to face but often through the medium of gardening radio programmes when the telephone lines are open for questions; others make good use of the question session after a talk at their horticultural society meeting, and, of course, there are many other opportunities for all who are interested to talk gardening. Some are new to the hobby, others have been enthusiasts for many years and yet not one of them could honestly say that they know everything there is to know about gardening. That is one of the fascinations of the subject – there is always something new to learn, another type of plant to grow or the perfect technique to be found for growing those we know so well.

This handbook attempts to answer many of the questions that gardeners, whether beginners or experienced practitioners, often ask. It also contains a good deal of information that seldom, if ever, crops up in question time. In fact anyone who has not put spade to soil before will find the essential details necessary to grow good plants, while those well versed will find much of interest.

Most of us feel a great sense of satisfaction when we sit back to admire a job well done, when the plants are blooming as they never have before and crops we have grown have that extra bit of flavour. But do not be too impatient to set everything in motion: seeds and tender young plants can hardly be expected to flourish when they are set out in the garden before the weather is favourable.

Each season varies slightly from year to year: spring may be a week or two early one year and the following year be two or three weeks late. In the end most things catch up and so nothing is lost, except for those tender plants that have been put out too soon. Guidelines to sowing and planting times have been given through the book, but they really can only be a guide, as, in addition to seasonal changes from year to year, different localities are 'early' or 'late', as the case may be. Generally the southern half of the British Isles tends to be warmer than the north so the growing season gets under way sooner, although there are sheltered areas in the north-west which may well be warmer on average than exposed localities in the south-east. The various dates suggested for carrying out the different tasks in the 'month-by-month' section of the book relate to the Midlands and South; the sowing or planting of particular plants may need to be delayed by two weeks or so in the North, where the growing season is rather shorter.

The gardener who can keep on top of the work all the year round is most fortunate; there are times when the weather makes life difficult, especially for those who can only garden at the weekend. Do not lose heart if you find that you are falling behind the monthly guide; gardening should be fun and a few days either way, or even a week or two in some cases, may not make that much difference in the end.

Much time and effort can be saved by using weedkillers and growth regulators, and these aids have been dealt with in some detail. With their use perhaps more time could be made available for propagation, or some of the other aspects of gardening discussed in the following pages. But however that maybe, there is much pleasure to be gained from gardening. Few pursuits are more satisfying.

Patrick Johns

January

FLOWERS, TREES AND SHRUBS Make the most of every opportunity to catch up on outdoor work during the month because each week that passes produces an extra few minutes of daylength and before long there will be many jobs to be done.

Plant bare root trees and shrubs Provided the soil is in a fit state – on no account should heavy wet soil be trodden on or be tampered with otherwise the resulting poor structure will hamper plant growth – deciduous bare root plants can be planted. Unlike trees and shrubs established in a plastic pot or other container, those which have been lifted from the nursery with bare roots should be transplanted at this time of year when they are completely dormant, otherwise a severe check to growth will result, probably causing the death of the plant.

Should the plants arrive when the ground is stiff with frost or is in other ways unsuitable for working, the plants can be 'heeled in' by opening up a shallow trench, inserting the roots and then covering them with soil. Alternatively, the plants may be stored in a frost-free place for a few days provided they are not allowed to dry out.

Dig the planting hole large enough to accommodate the roots without buckling. The top soil should be kept separate from that taken from below so that it can be replaced properly at the surface. Fork over the bottom of the hole and incorporate some bulky organic material like garden compost, peat or composted bark; a sprinkling of general fertilizer worked into the soil will assist establishment of the plant. The same ingredients can be mixed with the soil to be replaced around the roots.

Should a support stake be necessary, drive it into position before inserting the plant to avoid damaging the roots. Now the plant can be set in position so that it is at the same level as it was before lifting from the nursery. The level can be determined by the soil mark on the stem. Fill in the soil and gently lift the plant up and down so that the soil trickles between the roots. Really firm planting is necessary and the replaced soil should be well trodden in, taking care to avoid damaging the roots. Finally, a tree tie can be applied if a stake was used and the soil surface raked over to give a tidy finish.

Firm soil after frost and wind Frosty weather has the tendency to loosen soil around newly planted subjects and it is worthwhile checking those recently planted, by treading around the root zone to ensure firmness. Check tree ties at the same time to make sure they are firm but not tight enough to strangle the plant and inhibit growth during the following season. Many a plant has been maimed for life due to a tree tie cutting into the stem and the tell-tale groove can be seen for evermore.

Autumn and winter gales sometimes rock plants so that a gap is left around the stem base at soil level. This may fill with water which is unable to escape and so sets up neck rot. Refirm the soil as necessary and secure stakes that have become unsteady.

Shake snow from branches Heavy snow can do untold harm weighing down branches or worse still even snapping them off. Use a broom or rake to shake the plants to remove the snow, starting with the lower branches and working upwards. Evergreen plants are particularly susceptible to damage, not only from snow but also from cold winds and protection can be provided by attaching polythene or sacking to wooden or cane supports placed around the plant. Tender plants can be safeguarded by packing bracken between the branches and then tying it in place with soft string.

Collect up leaves Fallen leaves, dead stems and other debris around plants provide shelter for slugs and other pests and every opportunity should be taken to remove rubbish, particularly from the herbaceous border and rock garden. Stone chippings should then be topped up around deserving alpine plants in the rock and sink garden. At the same time tender young shoots need to be protected from slugs.

Control weeds Any weeds present should be dealt with before they get out of hand because many continue growing throughout winter and some, like chickweed, even germinate during milder winter weather. Contact weed-killers are much more effective than hormone types at this time of year; care should be taken to keep them away from cultivated plants, or a hoe may be used to remove the weeds provided the soil is not too wet and sticky.

Wintertime provides a good opportunity to remove weeds from paths and other hard surfaces, especially those with cracks that are so effective in encouraging weed growth. Such surfaces can be very slippery in areas subject to slime moulds, algae and moss growth. Walls and flat roofs often support such growth and the application of a tar oil winter wash preparation usually solves the problem, at least temporarily until regrowth appears next year. Although these formulations when mixed with water are unlikely to damage such surfaces, it is prudent to treat a small trial area first because certain light colours may be stained.

Prune plants Wisteria is a glorious plant when laden with its chains of flowers in summer. It does tend to become rather straggly unless kept within bounds; ideally the current season's shoots should be cut back to five leaves during summer and any long stems that are not required to fill gaps may now be cut back to two buds from the old wood. Dead and over-congested wood should be removed at the same time. Winter-flowering ericas can be pruned as soon as the flowers have faded. This is best done with a pair of shears, clipping over the plant to remove the flowering stems and two-thirds of the previous season's growth.

Feed bulbous plants Potted bulbs that are nearing the end of their flowering cycle will be all the better for being fed with liquid fertilizer. They often respond well to foliar feeding which encourages the bulbs to develop properly for planting out in the open garden when the foliage dies down. Treated properly in this way the bulbs often flower again during the first season out of doors.

Check stored tubers and corms Tubers and corms overwintered in frost-free conditions are, never the less, subject to rot and should be checked over to ensure all is well. Remove any that show signs of infection and dust the remainder with a fungicide.

LAWN Turf maintenance is just as important during mid-winter as it is at any other time of the year. Much can be done now to correct any faults in drainage and other problems, so that the lawn will have time to re-establish before summer. On no account should work proceed during frosty weather otherwise the grass will be damaged by snapping and bruising the leaves: simply walking over frosted grass will leave foot prints that turn brown.

Brush away snow One of the biggest threats to the well being of any lawn is the layer of snow that may persist at this time of year. Conditions under the snow are ideal for the development of certain turf diseases and moss often spreads at an alarming rate, so that subsequent mowing is made difficult due to the spongy texture of the moss; the uneven patchwork colour caused by moss is unattractive and the growth is apt to smother and inhibit the vigour of the grass sward. Snow should be brushed away at every opportunity.

Remove leaves Fallen leaves can have much the same effect, especially when they remain for any length of time, and even a thin layer will restrict the amount of light reaching the grass plants: ideal conditions, especially when associated with short days, for the onslaught of moss. Worms tend to pull the leaves partially into the ground which makes their removal rather frustrating, and so there is much to be said for raking the leaves up as soon as they fall. They make an excellent addition to the compost heap, which may eventually be used as top dressing for the lawn.

Apply top dressing It is fair to say that the vast majority of garden lawns never receive any form of top dressing and yet the response by the grass can be outstanding. Professional greenkeepers know the value of a thin layer of bulky organic material worked into the surface from time to time to stimulate root action; provided the dressing is applied correctly, small undulations are levelled out simultaneously.

Top dressing in this context should not be confused with the application of fertilizer, although it will undoubtedly contain some plant food by nature of its composition. Basically, a top dressing consists of a mixture of soil with other additives in the form of sphagnum peat, garden compost, farmyard manure, composted tree bark or leafmould. Special mixtures can be purchased from garden centres or landscape gardeners or the dressing may be mixed up at home.

Any one of the bulky organic materials like peat or leafmould used on its own tends to create a spongy surface to the lawn. This may cause too much absorption of moisture leading to root death and disease; peat used on its own may cap the soil so that it becomes difficult to wet during dry spells. The use of farmyard manure or garden compost and, to a certain extent, soil, may bring problems in the form of weeds but these are usually the annual species and once mowing starts they soon succumb to the clipping; even more pernicious weeds are not too much of a nuisance because they can be controlled by the use of a selective weedkiller during the summer.

Applying a top dressing to the lawn.

The proportion of each of the components used in a top dressing depends on the type of soil in the lawn: heavy soil would benefit from the addition of lime-free sand, which can be left out of the mixture for sandy soils. Generally a well mixed top dressing consisting of one part by volume loam and two parts each of sand (not builder's sand) and organic material works well. Any stones or other inappropriate matter should, of course, be removed and there is much to be said for passing the material through a sieve before application.

Top dressing can be scattered over the lawn surface by hand or with a shovel but, whichever method is used, it is important to work the material thoroughly in around the grass plants. This is done by using a besom broom or the back of a garden rake; if a large area is to be treated, the use of a lute has much to commend it so that the dressing is spread evenly. No more than ¼in (6mm) depth should be applied to the surface otherwise weak grass growth will result. As a rough guide, 1 ton of dressing including soil would be sufficient for approximately 500 sq yd (418m²) of lawn area but much depends on the evenness of the surface to be treated.

Repair edges Neat and tidy lawn edges enhance the appearance of the garden and where part of the edge has been damaged or worn, renovation may be carried out during the month provided the ground is not frosted or too wet. The simplest way to repair the lawn edge is to cut out the worn piece so that it is approximately 1½in (4cm) thick and replace it with another turf. Alternatively the worn piece can be turned round so that the new edge is made good and the worn area filled in with compost and sown with seed.

Check machinery Motor mowers should be started up and run for a few minutes to keep the contact breaker points and other parts in good working order. Service departments are not so busy now and so it is a good idea to send machinery in for service so that the equipment will be ready for use at a later date.

POND The garden pond is inclined to be forgotten during the dormant winter months but it is so important to keep the water level topped up, otherwise fish and plants will be damaged should the shallow water become frozen solid.

Prepare for ice Place a large rubber ball on the water surface so that when ice does form, the ball can be removed leaving a hole to allow the escape of gases. A piece of sacking draped over the hole will help to keep it free from ice. Alternatively an empty container stood on the ice and filled with hot water will melt a hole. On no account should the ice be cracked with a heavy object, because the fish will be harmed by shock waves and the overall temperature of the pool will drop as the ice mixes with the water.

Feed fish during mild weather Mild weather will keep the fish active and a small portion of food may be given to sustain them if this is the case.

FRUIT Garden hygiene is always important and much can be done now to help prevent any build up of pests and diseases that would attack the plants when they return to activity next spring. Fallen leaves harbour all kinds of potential problems often difficult to see now that the green colour has disappeared; they should be collected up and added to the compost heap where they will rot down and may then be used to dig into the vegetable plot at a later date. Leaves sticking to grease bands should also be removed otherwise they may act as a bridge for insects crawling up the tree trunk.

Spray winter wash Certain pests and diseases overwinter on the trees and bushes and now that the plants are completely dormant, a winter wash of tar oil can be used to control them. A forceful mist-like spray of fine droplets applied from a pressure sprayer is ideal, so that the liquid will penetrate the crevices in the bark to reach the eggs and spores. Choose a still day to carry out the work otherwise most of the spray will be wasted by being blown away without contacting the branches. Grass or other plants growing below the trees should be covered over with polythene sheeting because tar oil spray will scorch green leaves and make them unsightly, although grass usually greens up again as the weather improves during spring.

Winter wash is best applied every alternate year because, although it controls algae, moss, lichen and overwintering pests and diseases, it does have a tendency to reduce some of the beneficial predatory insects.

Check stakes and ties Tree stakes and the soil around newly planted subjects may need refirming, particularly when the weather has been frosty, due to the expansion and contraction of the soil.

Check tree ties, which are liable to become detached during windy weather, and adjust them if necessary so that the stem has room to expand during the following growing season. Polypropylene string and other weatherproof materials used for securing stems and branches often cut into the plant and restrict growth. Now that the leaves have fallen the ties are easy to see and replace if necessary.

Set out bare root plants This is a good time to plant bare root plants provided the soil is not too wet or frosted (see page 9). The plant is likely to be in the ground for a number of years and it is worth taking trouble to prepare the area properly. In the case of plants like raspberries that are set out in rows, the ground should be dug over and bulky organic material like garden compost or farmyard manure incorporated as cultivations progress. Any weeds present may be turned in, although perennial weeds, especially those with a tap root like dock and dandelion, should be removed completely.

Soft fruit bushes like gooseberries and currants benefit from planting in bare ground and although fruit trees often look attractive with grass growing below, for preference they should be planted in ground devoid of grass and other plants that would compete with them during the early years of establishment.

The technique used for the tree planting is given on page 9. Fruit bushes should be planted so that the roots are just below the surface of the soil. Trees are usually grown on a special rootstock and it is most important that the union where the stem meets the rootstock, often seen as a small bulge, is kept well above the ground. Deep planting of grafted trees so that the union is placed below soil level will encourage the scion to produce roots and eliminate the dwarfing or other advantageous effect of the special rootstock. When a large hole needs to be dug, a garden cane or straight length of timber placed over the hole when the plant has been positioned will indicate if the union is at the correct height.

Prune after planting when necessary Some plants are pruned immediately after planting. Black currants, for example, are pruned to almost ground for growing in trenches to mature during the winter. Cultivars for growing on level ground to mature during late summer include 'Golden Self Blanching' and 'American Green'.

Sow summer cabbage and cauliflower Summer cabbage 'Hispi' sown in trays in the greenhouse, or 'May Express' in a cold frame, will provide plants for transplanting out of doors later to mature in June and July. Cauliflower 'All The Year Round' and 'Snowball' may be treated in the same way.

Prick out onions Onion seed sown last month should be pricked out as soon as they can be handled, spacing the seedlings 2 by 2in (5 by 5cm) in the tray. Keep them shaded for a day or two so that they establish quickly.

Sow bedding plants This is a very busy month for sowing flower seeds, and bedding plants due to go in include ageratum, aster, *Begonia semperflorens*, bedding dahlias, dianthus, heliotrope, lobelia, marigold, mesembryanthemum, nemesia, nicotiana, pansy, petunia, *Phlox drummondii*, rudbeckia, salvia, tagetes and verbena. Sow the seed thinly and cover the receptacles with glass and brown paper or black polythene; the glass should be turned daily to clear the condensation and as soon as seedlings appear, the glass and shading material are removed. Prick out the seedlings as soon as they can be handled.

Sow seed of flowering pot plants Plants to grow on and decorate the greenhouse can be sown now including balsam, calceolaria, canna, celosia, coleus, begonia, mimulus, streptocarpus and schizanthus; morning glory makes a fine plant for this purpose too. Try to maintain a temperature of 60°F (16°C).

Take cuttings Geranium plants that were rooted last summer and autumn and kept growing during winter should now be at the stage where the tops can be used as cuttings; these should be approximately 2in (5cm) long and prepared by removing the lower leaves. No time should be lost in taking mid-season and late-flowering chrysanthemum cuttings; early flowering chrysanthemum and dahlia cuttings may be taken towards the end of the month.

Start tubers Gloxinia and begonia tubers may be started now by planting them in moist peat at a temperature of 60°F (16°C). The same applies to achimenes, which can be potted up and spaced at a density of one to each 1in (2.5cm) size of pot used; 5 plants would occupy a 5in (12.5cm) pot.

Rest freesias after flowering Gradually reduce water when freesias finish flowering. This will encourage food in the leaves to be translocated to the corms for the resting period.

Prune plants Several plants require pruning during the month: shortly after the true flowers fade and fall from the bracts, *Beloperone guttata*, the shrimp plant, will benefit from cutting back to active shoots. This will encourage the shoots to grow and produce the next flush of flowers. Ivy-leaved geraniums tend to grow rather straggly unless they are trimmed back to an active bud. Gardenia, fuchsia, passion flower and plumbago can all be pruned now by cutting back to two buds from old wood.

March

FLOWERS, TREES AND SHRUBS Now that the hardest of weather is behind us shrubs and trees should be inspected for winter damage; twigs and shoots showing signs of die back and those broken by the weight of snow or high winds should be cut back to healthy buds.

Prune shrubs Many subjects that flower on the current season's wood should now be pruned. Shrubby potentillas are due for pruning – cut back any weak growth to soil level so that strong growth is encouraged. *Spiraea* 'Anthony Waterer' and 'Goldflame' benefit from cutting back hard at this time so that fresh sturdy growth will produce flowers on the current season's shoots during summer. The same treatment is given to hardy fuchsias which produce new shoots from buds at or just below soil level and so all of the bare stems can be cut away to within an inch or two (2.5 to 5cm) from the soil. Caryopteris is yet another shrub that is much more attractive during its growing season following hard pruning by removing last year's stems to soil level towards the end of the month.

The flowers of *Hydrangea paniculata* are even more spectacular if the shrub is moderately pruned during this month: cut back last year's growth by at least half and remove any weak stems. *Hydrangea macrophylla* should not be cut back other than to remove old flower heads and weak shoots. Final pruning should now be completed on *Buddleia davidii* by reducing the shoots to two buds from the old wood.

Much depends on local weather conditions so far as the timing of rose

A flowering cherry with tulips and daffodils in a spectacular spring garden.

pruning is concerned: large-flowered hybrid tea bushes are often pruned during early winter in favoured areas whilst rose-growing enthusiasts in other areas cut the stems only one-third back at that time to avoid wind-rock and leave the main pruning until spring. Either way, the bushes should now be pruned by cutting out unwanted growth completely and the stronger shoots back to half length. Cluster-flowered floribundas can also be pruned during the month.

Chaenomeles growing as a free-standing bush rarely needs pruning other than to keep it within bounds, although it does pay to thin out the growth of those plants growing on a wall. This is best done as soon as the flowers fade, beginning with shoots that are growing straight out from the wall which should be cut back to within 2 or 3 leaves.

The low-growing hebes like 'Autumn Glory' are often overlooked so far as pruning is concerned and whilst annual pruning may be unnecessary, an occasional clipping helps to keep the plant compact and attractive, as it does with the hypericums, which are more attractive when the dead shoots have been removed.

Layer magnolias and heathers Magnolias are easy enough subjects to grow provided the soil is not too alkaline; their lower shoots can be induced to root by layering (see page 155) and when sufficient roots have formed, the new plant is cut away to grow elsewhere, or perhaps to replace the parent which has outgrown its situation. Heathers are other plants that can be layered now by pegging down the outside stems.

Sow seeds of trees and shrubs Seeds of trees and shrubs that have been stratified over winter can now be sown in a nursery bed; remove any weeds already germinated and sow the seeds in straight drills so that subsequent weed control is made easier.

Finish planting bare root subjects Bare root deciduous trees, shrubs and hedge plants should be planted in their final quarters by the end of the month together with any that need to be moved from one part of the garden to another for any reason. Bare root evergreens can be planted in favoured areas at the end of the month and it is as well to protect them from cold winds by using hessian or polythene supported on stakes. Excessive water loss from the plant can be reduced by spraying the leaves with S600 solution which can be obtained from garden centres and stores. Bare root deciduous hedging plants are often pruned back to within 6in (15cm) from the ground after planting to encourage branch development low down, but this treatment should not be necessary with well grown container plants. Avoid topping conifers until they have become well established, in fact they may be left to grow on until they have reached their desired height.

Keep newly planted trees and shrubs moist at the root Newly planted trees

Above: A colourful group of deciduous azaleas. *Below*: Alyssum, tulips and aubrieta make an attractive feature of this dry wall.

and shrubs should not be allowed to dry at the root; it may be necessary to water them during dry spells, and a surface mulch of bulky organic material will do much to prevent soil moisture loss and suppress competing weeds at the same time.

Protect from frost Take care to protect camellia flowers from frost and spray them over with clear water before the sun reaches them after a frosty night; they will be less susceptible when the plant is growing on a north or west wall.

Watch for pests Inspect plants for an early attack of greenfly and apply an insecticide if necessary. Diseases like blackspot and mildew on roses are far easier to prevent than to cure once they have become established and an application of systemic fungicide will help to keep the plants healthy. Rose fertilizer, which can also be applied to other shrubs and trees, will encourage healthy growth during the growing season.

Apply fertilizer Polyanthus and primroses are among plants that benefit from a fertilizer dressing and then, after a week or two, established plants can be lifted and divided if the beds have become congested; take the opportunity to remove any perennial weeds that may be present. Thrift, sedum and *Polygonum vaccinifolium* can also be divided now.

Sow flower seed The first hardy annual seed can be sown, provided soil conditions permit, to produce flowers from July onwards. Proprietary seed dressing powder shaken up with the seed in the packet will assist germination by preventing pests and diseases from attacking the seed once it is sown. Seed sown thinly produces the best type of plant without the need to thin out and waste so many seedlings at a later date. There is still time to sow sweet peas and they can be sown in their final quarters 1in (2.5cm) deep spaced 3in (7.5cm) apart in rows 1ft (30cm) apart. Sweet pea plants sown earlier should be stopped by removing the growing point to encourage side shoots to develop; these tend to produce more flowers on a longer stalk compared with those arising from the main stem.

Plant hardy bedding Spring-flowering bedding plants like pansies, violas and bellis are available in garden centres now; Canterbury bells, forget-me-nots, wallflowers and others not yet planted should be lifted from the nursery bed and planted without delay.

Divide herbaceous perennials This is a very good month to lift and divide herbaceous perennials that have remained in their quarters for three or more years. Lift the clumps and then remove healthy offsets from the outside of the mass; the older, less vigorous central portion can be discarded, because there is normally more than sufficient outside pieces for replanting. These are best pulled off by hand where possible although it may be necessary to split the clump by using two garden forks back to back using one against the other as a lever. Plant up 3 to 5 offsets in each group and remember to label each group with the correct name if possible. Plants purchased locally or those arriving from orders placed earlier should be taken from their packing and watered if necessary; the plants will, no doubt, be in polythene

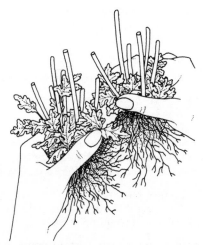

Dividing herbaceous perennials
into small clumps.

pots but if not, they should be boxed up or heeled in. Set the plants out in their final quarters as soon as possible and be on the guard for slugs.

Plant bulbs and corms A range of bulbs and corms can be planted during the month starting with snowdrops, which should preferably be transplanted before the leaves die down. New snowdrops could be purchased now from specialist bulb nurseries, but most producers sell them during autumn together with other sorts. Gladioli corms are best planted over a period of three weeks or so to provide a succession of flowers during summer. The large-flowered hybrids are planted in informal groups spaced 6in (15cm) between each corm, or they may be planted in rows at the same spacing but with the rows 1ft (30cm) apart. The species and miniature cultivars can be planted closer at 3in (7.5cm) spacing. Plant them all 3in (7.5cm) deep in heavy soil or up to 6in (15cm) deep in light sandy soil.

Montbretias are colourful flowers; although dry corms can be bought they are often slow to grow away when planted in that condition and it is better to purchase actively growing plants in polythene pots from a local garden centre now. Set them out so that they are at the same depth as they were in the pot, or in the case of dry corms, 2in (5cm) below soil level.

'Prepared' Dutch iris bulbs can be purchased now and planted 4in (10cm) apart and 3in (7.5cm) deep in well prepared soil and they will flower during the summer.

Discard diseased tulips Tulip bulbs that produce leaves and flower buds with brown marks and distortion should be lifted and discarded: the plant is most likely infected with the disease tulip fire, which could easily spread to other plants.

Tend alpines The sheet of glass or other material protecting alpines in flower can now be removed and stored away unless persistent heavy rain is likely. Remove by hand any weeds that grow through chippings and top up with more chippings where necessary. Slugs can often be active at this time and precautions should be taken before they cause damage.

LAWN Control moss if that has not already been done but on no account rake the lawn until the moss has been killed, as this will only spread the problem even further.

Firm after frost Frosty weather may have lifted the turf and a light rolling will be beneficial unless the ground is wet.

Stale seed bed The stale seed bed technique is useful for sites to be sown with grass seed or turved later: allow weed seeds to germinate after final soil preparation and deal with them by applying a herbicide which becomes inactivated as soon as it touches the soil. Perennial weeds are better dug out complete with root at this stage because it is too soon to apply hormone type weedkillers and they often take several weeks to be effective.

Top grass The grass should be topped before it grows too long; setting the cutting height to 1in (2.5cm) will protect the turf from subsequent frost and yet allow sufficient light transmission to avoid yellowing of the leaf base.

Scatter worm casts Cast-forming worms can still be active and the casts should be scattered at every opportunity when the surface is dry. Apply a worm killer if necessary and a leatherjacket or wireworm insecticide may also be required.

Apply fertilizer The application of a spring fertilizer dressing with high nitrogen content will set the turf off to a good start for the season and promote vigour to sustain growth during later dry spells. It is essential to apply fertilizer uniformly to avoid scorching the grass and special lawn spreaders are available for this purpose.

Scarify lawn Once the grass has started growing, it often pays to scarify the lawn to remove any dead moss and thatch that may have built up during the winter months. This can be done by using a lawn rake, or a mechanical scarifier for large areas.

Renovate bare patches Established lawns showing wear and bare patches can now be renovated by sowing grass seed or by removing the bare patch and laying new turf. Grass seed can also be sown at the rate of 1 to 1½oz per sq yd (50g per m²) to make a new lawn. Germination usually takes place within two weeks at this time of the year and although fungal diseases are not often a problem, any that occur should be controlled by using a fungicidal spray suitable for new lawns. When the grass is approximately 3in (7.5cm) high, lightly crop to remove ½in (13mm) of growth with hand shears or a mower. On no account should a mower be used when the soil is wet otherwise skid marks and a surface pan will result, especially on the heavier soils. Weed seeds may have germinated by now but they are not often a problem because they usually disappear as mowing proceeds.

Tidy lawn edges Ragged lawn edges can spoil the effect of a good lawn and they should be shaped and straightened by using a half moon and board.

POND Life is stirring all around the garden now not least in the pond: plants and fish will become more active as the temperature rises towards the end of the month. Fresh water will help to create a healthy environment and it is a good policy to remove up to three-quarters of the water and replenish with clean.

Remove blanket weed Take the opportunity to remove blanket weed and other encroaching plants but watch out for water snails which help to keep the poolside clean. *Iris pseudacorus* 'Variegata' can be divided by cutting the fleshy rhizome and replanting, as can the water poppy (*Hydrocleys*) and pickerel weed (*Pontederia*). Top growth of marginal plants should be removed to avoid decomposition leading to stagnation and tender plants removed for the winter can now be returned to the pool.

Install fountain Moving water adds much interest to the garden and when the water level is reduced, a submersible electric pump and fountain could be installed. It is worthwhile fitting a small immersion heater at the same time so that a hole will be kept open in the ice during subsequent winters. This will allow air exchange to take place and reduce the level of toxic gases that tend to build up under ice.

Feed fish Fish activity will make them search for food and their rations can be increased to an amount that they clear in 15 to 20 minutes.

FRUIT Birds are often attracted to developing buds and whilst a fruit cage solves the problem, replacement of the top net needs critical timing because snow fall can still occur in some areas. Individual plants can be protected by black cotton or proprietary deterrents but when old net curtains or similar material are used, be sure to leave access for bees. Peach and nectarine trees draped during the winter to keep the wood dry so that peach leaf curl is controlled should be opened up for the same reason.

Protect from frost Frost can cause much damage at blossom time especially to plums and other early blossom: spraying over the plants with clear water before the sun reaches them helps and this is achieved effectively by installing a lawn sprinkler or other device amongst the plants.

Complete pruning There is little time left for pruning gooseberries, red and white currants but it is still worthwhile to open up the centre of the bush in case of a wet spring. This will allow better air circulation and help to control diseases.

Pest and disease control Diseases are far easier to prevent than eradicate once they have become established and those plants due for fungicidal spraying now include raspberries and loganberries against spur blight and cane-spot; apples, currants and gooseberries for mildew control and apples and pears against scab. Some pests will already be active including greenfly, especially on strawberries and plums; towards the end of the month, however, a watch should be kept for them on other fruit trees and bushes. Capsid bugs, caterpillars and apple sucker often make an appearance now.

Control grass and weeds Competition from grass and weeds growing around fruit plants can cause considerable loss of potential crop and research work has established that 49 per cent of an apple crop can be lost due to competing weeds. Many plants have roots growing close to the soil surface which would be damaged by using a hoe: in this case weeds may be controlled by using a herbicide that becomes inactivated as soon as it touches the soil. Where grass growth is desired around fruit trees, it should be mown short and the clippings allowed to fly so that they return to the turf to replace plant foods and to act as a mulch: both fertilizer, especially nitrogen, and soil moisture is taken up by grass at the expense of tree growth.

Whether grass is growing around trees or not, fertilizer should be applied now. A soil test will determine just how much nitrogen, phosphate and potash should be applied but if in doubt red and white currants, gooseberries, cane fruits and strawberries like a high potash fertilizer; black currants should be given a fertilizer with high nitrogen content as should fruit trees growing in grass. Top fruit trees growing in cultivated ground will require a general balanced fertilizer but much depends on tree growth vigour during the last growing season, previous fertilizer application, soil type and rainfall – hence the need for a soil test to be sure.

Mulch plants Mulching the soil surface with a bulky organic material like garden compost, well rotted farmyard manure or composted bark has much to commend it to maintain general soil health, so that beneficial soil organisms become more active, the soil retains moisture during periods without rain and weed growth is suppressed. The only exceptions are strawberries, cranberries and other fruits lying on the surface; in their case mulching should be carried out by using straw or special mats made for the purpose.

Plant strawberries The ideal time to plant strawberries is during late summer and early autumn although, if for some reason they were not planted then, plants can be set out during this month. It is always worthwhile obtaining plants certified by the Ministry of Agriculture as being virus tested, otherwise much expense, time and effort will be wasted in growing inferior plants that do not produce a satisfactory crop.

Thorough preparation of the ground is necessary both to incorporate bulky organic material and to remove weeds. This is best done at least one month before planting (another good reason for planting in late summer) so that the soil settles. General fertilizer should be raked into the surface of the soil a few days before planting. Set out the plants 18in (45cm) apart in rows spaced 30in (75cm) apart. A hole large enough to take the root system without crumpling should be made so that the crown of the plant is at soil level when it has been firmed in; deep planting often causes disease infection within the plant as does very wet soil. This can be avoided to a certain extent in heavy soil by planting on small ridges to facilitate drainage away from the crown of the plant.

No fruit should be allowed to develop during the summer following spring planting so that the plants have a chance to establish properly. Remove any runners that develop before the small plant grows at the tip. Weeds should be controlled at an early stage otherwise they would compete for food and moisture; they are also inclined to harbour pests like greenfly and red spider mite.

Strawberry plants can be propagated at home during the summer. Select mother plants now with the best trusses of flower, true to type and free from pests and diseases, especially virus. Small pots filled with potting compost can be sunk into the ground underneath developing runners so that the small plants at the tips can root into them. The most vigorous daughter plants are produced from mother plants which have been deblossomed to prevent fruit developing on them.

Graft top fruit Top fruit can be propagated this month by grafting (see page 159) and established trees that do not do well in the garden due to altitude, susceptibility to late frosts or for some other reason can be cut back and grafted with a more suitable variety.

Train figs Fig shoots bundled together during the winter and covered for frost protection should now be uncovered and tied in to supporting wires. Remove diseased and damaged wood together with weak growth and crossing branches. Do not cut away tips of healthy vigorous growth because these will produce fruit to ripen in late summer.

Tie in berry canes Blackberries and hybrid berries should now be untied from the bundle and spaced out along the horizontal wire supports, leaving a space above the crown for new canes to grow this year. Old fruiting canes should, of course, have been cut out after harvest last autumn and any remaining cut out before tying in the young canes to fruit this year.

Plant bare root trees and bushes There is still time to plant bare root blackberries, fruit trees and bushes but try to get them in before the middle of the month. Those planted last autumn or during the winter should be checked and refirmed if necessary. Do not allow the soil to dry out around the roots.

VEGETABLES AND HERBS With hedgerow plants coming into leaf it is a sure sign that the soil is warming up and final preparations can be made for sowing a wide range of plants. Do not attempt to work the soil if it is still wet and sticky – more harm than good will be done to the soil structure and the hope of a fine spring tilth will be lost if a heavy clay soil is involved. Lightly fork or rake general fertilizer into the soil surface, preferably a few days before sowing or planting.

Sow seeds of onions and spinach Onions can be sown during the early part of the month; make the drills ½in (13mm) deep and space them 1ft (30cm) apart. Spinach to mature during summer can be sown at the same spacing but slightly deeper.

Sow carrots Carrot seed requires a very fine tilth for successful germination and under those conditions drills ¼in (6mm) deep can be made with a seed label or by pressing the edge of a straight piece of timber into the ground. Sow the seed very thinly to avoid thinning out the seedlings later. Stump rooted cultivars are better for stony soil because they are less likely to become deformed. Early and maincrops can be sown during the middle of the month but delay sowing if the soil is unfit.

Sow leeks Leeks are often sown in trays in the greenhouse but there is no reason why seed should not be sown out of doors this month. Shallow drills are necessary and thin sowing essential for the best transplants.

Sow peas and dwarf broad beans With the advent of restricted space in the smaller garden, peas are often given a miss to provide room for more space-effective crops; many gardeners, however, look forward to the first picking of early peas and a row sown during the middle of the month will undoubtedly be worthwhile. Where space permits, successional sowing every fortnight will provide continuity and possibly some for the freezer if necessary. Broad beans come into the same category so far as space is concerned and the dwarf cultivars are most useful with the added advantage that they do not require supporting.

Sow other seeds Other vegetable seeds due for sowing include Brussels sprouts for transplanting later, chives, endive, kohl-rabi, lettuce including cos types now that the days are getting longer, late summer cabbage, parsnip, parsley, scorzonera, salsify, spinach beet and turnips.

Okra can be sown outside in favourable areas during the middle of the month, although it does better when raised under cloches; northern gardeners would be more assured of a reasonable crop by growing the plants in a greenhouse. The fruits are cut when they are young, cut in half and fried and they have a pleasant nutty flavour. When space is limited it is a good idea to grow decorative vegetables like Ruby Chard in the flower border.

Protect seed beds and seedlings Seed beds attract cats and birds; when necessary protect the area by placing netting or cloches over the ground. Birds can also cause much damage to seedlings unless they are kept away from the area. The flea beetle attacks seedlings of brassicas like cabbage, sprouts and particularly turnip, making small holes in the young leaves: protect the plants by dusting or spraying with insecticide just before the seed germinates.

Thin out seedlings Seedlings should always be thinned out as soon as they can be singled without the possibility of damaging adjacent plants; use a small onion hoe or the fingers: the remaining plants left standing will be more sturdy and will mature more quickly.

Support peas Insert pea sticks along rows of seedlings before they grow too tall and topple over. Should suitable twiggy sticks be difficult to obtain, pea and bean netting is relatively inexpensive and easy to erect.

Propagate herbs Various herbs can be sown at the end of the month in a sunny border. They are best sown a pinch at a time for continuity or if required for drying then sow sufficient to make the process worthwhile. The various kinds that may be sown include parsley, basil, borage, chervil, coriander, Florence fennel, sorrel and sweet marjoram. Mint roots can be lifted, divided and then replanted, preferably in a container sunk into the ground. Another plant that should be contained because it is very invasive is the horseradish; plant the roots 1ft (30cm) apart with the tip 4in (10cm) below the soil level. Instead of sowing seed of chives, established plants may be divided and the offsets replanted 1ft (30cm) apart.

Plant rhubarb Rhubarb is always acceptable and although the succulent sticks should not be pulled during the year of planting, two separate areas alternating with each other ensure a regular supply. Roots planted now will provide the first crop next year and then for two further years before division and replanting is necessary again. Well manured ground is required to sustain the vigorous plant and the root should be planted so that the top of the crown is level with the soil surface.

Preparing an asparagus bed: plant the crowns as quickly as possible.

Prepare asparagus bed Asparagus is really a long-term crop that remains in the ground for very many years. Good soil preparation is therefore necessary by incorporating well rotted farmyard manure or garden compost. Fork out perennial weeds and remove large stones from the site; finally, rake general fertilizer into the surface and firm the soil. One-year-old crowns tend to establish better than older ones and so there is no advantage to be gained in purchasing two- or three-year-old plants sometimes advertised. On no account should the crowns be allowed to dry out and so they will benefit from being covered with damp sacking during planting. Space the plants 18in (45cm) apart each way with the crown 3in (7.5cm) below the soil surface. The planting trench should be large enough to accommodate the roots without buckling and it is as well to spread them out radially from the crown. The plants should really be allowed to establish for at least two years before any crop is taken and then the tips are snapped away just below soil level; traditionally they are cut with a special knife so that 2in (5cm) or so of blanched stem is taken, but that method does in fact reduce the subsequent crop somewhat.

Mulch asparagus beds Established asparagus beds will benefit from mulching with well rotted farmyard manure or garden compost during the early part of the month; the mulch is then usually covered with fertile top soil to a depth of 2 to 3in (5 to 7.5cm) when available. The mulch should suppress any weeds present and encourage sturdy 'tips'. General fertilizer should be applied evenly over the surface and, unless sufficient rain falls, the fertilizer should be washed in within 10 to 14 days.

Plant early potatoes Early potatoes can be planted in favoured areas from the middle of the month. Alkaline soils encourage scab disease although a bed of bulky organic material placed below the tubers will help prevent it. Plant the seed tubers approximately 6in (15cm) deep with the sprouts pointing upwards; the tubers should be spaced 12 to 14in (30 to 35cm) apart with 2ft (60cm) between the rows.

Plant globe artichokes Globe artichoke is another delectable vegetable; set out the plants in well prepared ground: they make large plants and so a generous spacing of up to 4ft (1.2m) should be allowed between them.

Plant onion sets Plant out onion sets towards the end of the month and if sparrows have the habit of pulling at the tuft of withered brown leaf at the top of the set, it is better removed, but take care to avoid damaging the green shoot. Use a trowel to plant the sets otherwise, when pushed into the ground, they invariably push themselves out as roots develop. Onion sets can be planted as close as 3in (7.5cm) apart when only small bulbs are required.

Plant early summer cauliflower Early summer cauliflowers can be planted at 2ft (60cm) spacing each way, provided some protection can be given against cold winds, which cause a check to growth and premature buttoning of the curds.

Feed cabbage Feed early summer cabbage with fast-acting nitrogen: they will soon grow under the more favourable conditions and alternate plants may be harvested.

GREENHOUSE The March bulge always seems to fill up the greenhouse, however large, to bursting point but with forward planning it is surprising how much you can get in the smallest of houses. A thermostatically controlled propagator will be of great help so that those seeds and plants requiring a higher temperature will be satisfied, whilst many subjects will be content with the somewhat lower temperature in the greenhouse. In fact, the sun is now gaining strength and no doubt ventilation will be needed from time to time. This is where automatic vent openers come into their own: they are relatively inexpensive and once set can be left to open and close as necessary.

Shade seedlings Take care to shade seedlings from strong sun, especially when they have recently been pricked out; small plants in the propagator are particularly prone to sun scorch, even when the propagator does have a thermostat.

Pot rooted cuttings Pot off chrysanthemum cuttings when the roots have reached ¾in (19mm) in length; John Innes potting compost No 1 or a peat-based compost and 3in (7.5cm) pots should be used. Gently knock out the root ball from the plants potted off in February to see progress. As soon as the roots can be seen on the outside of the root ball, the plants should be potted on into 5in (12.5cm) pots using John Innes potting compost No 2 or a peat-based compost.

Pot off plants The best time to pot off young cyclamen plants is when they have produced three leaves. By then the small corm should be about the size of a pea and it is important to keep the top half of the corm above the compost level when potting. This will ensure vigorous growth with earlier flowering and less chance of rotting at the leaf base. Use 3in (7.5cm) pots at this stage; smaller pots tend to dry out rapidly and larger ones contain too much compost for the small plant.

Tomatoes, cucumbers, melons and geraniums should all be potted off singly as soon as the seed leaves are large enough to handle. Rooted geranium cuttings can be potted off at the same time and decorative plants like Christmas cactus, fuchsias and *Hibiscus rosa-sinensis* should be potted on into larger pots if necessary.

Sow vegetable seed for planting out of doors later Aubergines, sweet peppers, celery and tomatoes for planting out of doors when the risk of frost is past can be sown in heat during the middle of the month. Melons and cucumbers can be sown at the same time for planting later in the cold greenhouse or frame; they do need a relatively high temperature to germinate properly and sowing is better delayed rather than risk rotting seed or malformed plants.

Sow flower seed Morning glory is an attractive climbing plant for the cold greenhouse; seeds sown now will soon germinate and, looking ahead to next winter, freesia seed sown during the early part of this month will provide most fragrant and colourful flowers for cutting in the cool greenhouse during the winter months. Freesia seed is often erratic to germinate and so it is best mixed with a small quantity of moist sphagnum peat and hung up in a polythene bag in the airing cupboard. As soon as the seed has chitted it must be sown in pots or boxes: 12 chitted seeds would be sufficient for an 8in (20cm) pot using John Innes potting compost No 1 or a peat-based compost.

Other decorative plants which may be sown during this month include abutilon, *Cobaea scandens*, exacum, cacti, coleus, impatiens, kalanchoe, *Mimosa pudica*, *Primula malacoides* and *P. obconica*. Some bedding plants make excellent plants for the greenhouse and pots of trailing lobelia make very good use of the area between the staging and below, a space often wasted.

Summer bedding for planting out of doors later can be sown now including ageratum, alyssum, amaranthus, aster, heliotrope, lobelia, impatiens, kochia, nemesia, petunia, rudbeckia and zinnia. Prick out the seedlings 48 to a standard size seed tray as soon as they can be handled; those plants that grow vigorously like petunia will benefit from pricking out singly into 3in (7.5cm) pots. Do take precautions against slugs – even on the staging in the greenhouse. Damping off diseases can sometimes be a problem and it pays to water the seedlings with a fungicide recommended for that purpose. Unless the rain water is very clean, use only mains water because damping off diseases are often introduced from the rain water butt.

Control greenfly Greenfly often build up quickly in the greenhouse at this time of the year and red spider mites will be emerging from hibernation during the third week of the month: take precautions before they become uncontrollable.

Take cuttings of chrysanthemums and dahlias Early chrysanthemum stools and dahlia tubers should now be producing some healthy young shoots to provide cuttings: snap them from the parent whenever possible to avoid carry over of virus infection on the knife blade. Dip the base of the cutting into hormone rooting powder before inserting in gritty compost, preferably with bottom heat.

Top pelargoniums Pelargoniums rooted last autumn often produce sufficient top growth by this time for the tops to be taken for cuttings. In any case unless the plants have already produced side shoots, it would be as well to pinch out the growing tip to induce bushiness, otherwise some cultivars tend to grow too tall and ungainly.

Sectional drawing showing the composition of a hanging basket.

Make up hanging baskets It is a good idea to make up hanging baskets in time for them to become well established before they are put out of doors when the risk of frost has passed. All sorts of materials can be used for lining the basket including the traditional green sphagnum moss. When moss is used remember to place a plate or shallow dish over the moss at the base of the basket to act as a water reservoir, otherwise the water will simply pass straight through the basket taking most of the plant foods with it. Other lining materials include green polythene sheeting and fibre liners made especially for the purpose.

Most modern baskets have a flat base; any with a rounded base will need to be supported by the rim of a bucket to prevent rolling about while it is being made up. Large baskets can be very heavy when made up and watered and it is a wise precaution to check the supporting chains and bracket where the basket is to be hung. Peat-based compost weighs less than soil and can be used instead.

Place a layer of compost over the base of the container and then push small plants through the side of the basket: lobelia is a good choice. More compost is then added and further plants may be inserted through the side. Finally complete filling with compost until sufficient room is left at the top for plants like ivy-leaved and zonal pelargoniums, nasturtium, petunia, fibrous-rooted begonia and ageratum. A slight hollow in the surface of the compost will facilitate watering otherwise most of the water will run off the sides. Hang the planted basket in the greenhouse and the plants will soon establish.

Pinch fuchsias and schizanthus Fuchsias growing in pots will now be making growth that tends to become rather leggy unless the growing point is pinched out, and the same applies to schizanthus, which makes a nice bushy plant when the leading shoot is pinched out when it has reached a height of 6in (15cm).

Prune plants Prune *Plumbago capensis* by cutting back the shoots to 3 or 4 buds and grape vine shoots should be pinched out 2 leaves beyond the developing bunch of fruit. Grape vine rods in the cold greenhouse should be tied back up to the wires when shoots are 1in (2.5cm) long.

Feed strawberries and pollinate flowers Feed strawberry plants with high potash fertilizer and hand pollinate the flowers with a soft artist's brush. Peach and nectarine flowers should be hand pollinated in the same way.

Plant early tomatoes and cucumbers Tomatoes and cucumbers can now be planted in their final quarters in a heated greenhouse and growing bags are convenient if the border soil has deteriorated by growing similar plants in it for the previous two or three years.

Harden off plants Onions, peas, broad beans and sweet peas can be moved to the cold frame for hardening off before planting out of doors.

Sow ridge cucumbers In mild areas ridge cucumbers can be sown in cold frames towards the end of the month.

April

FLOWERS, TREES AND SHRUBS The ornamental garden becomes more delightful as the season progresses. Evergreen plants and conifers offer interest all the year round and many gardens now open their doors to visitors providing the opportunity to see plants that do well in the locality. April is a good month to plant bare root evergreens, although most plants are available growing in containers these days so that they can be planted at any time provided the soil conditions permit. Evergreen leaves do have a tendency to dry out soon after they are planted and it is a good idea to spray over the plant with S600 which reduces water loss under drying conditions. Some form of protection like hessian or polythene sheeting draped around the plant will do much to aid establishment under windy conditions. Once the soil has warmed up a little, more moisture can be conserved by spreading a layer of bulky organic material over the root zone to act as a mulch.

Select alpines for continuity Alpine plants are so attractive and by selecting a range of different kinds, few weeks will pass without one or another showing colour. They can be planted in sink gardens and other containers so that they are suitable for even the smallest of gardens. This is a good time to plant alpines and to replace those that have not survived the winter for one reason or another: perhaps the soil remains too wet for long periods in which case drainage must be improved for good results; the root zone could be too acid or alkaline for the particular subjects that have not survived and a simple pH soil test will soon show whether or not adjustment is necessary.

Prune shrubs Established evergreen shrubs grown as specimens or hedges can be pruned during the month, the spring-flowering kinds such as camellias should, of course, have completed flowering before the secateurs are taken to them and that applies just as much to deciduous plants like *Ribes* *sanguineum* and forsythia. Plants flowering on the current season's growth can, also be pruned including *Buddleia variabilis, Caryopteris clandonensis, Fuchsia gracilis, F. magellanica, F. riccartonii, Hydrangea paniculata, Leycesteria formosa* and *Romneya coulteri*. Plants grown for their winter bark colour like dogwoods and willows can also be pruned hard back now if that has not already been done. Trim over winter-flowering heathers to keep them neat and tidy; if possible apply a top dressing of sphagnum peat, which will help to suppress weed growth and encourage side shoots to break and furnish next winter's flowers.

Thin out and feed herbaceous plants Dense herbaceous plants like delphiniums, heleniums, lupins and phlox not recently divided will respond to thinning out the shoots to leave 5 or 6 on the plants: the flowers will be much more effective with stronger stems. Fertilizer plays its part here too and a sprinkling of general top dressing will do much to impart healthy vigour in the flower border.

Divide herbaceous perennials Old clumps of herbaceous perennials will benefit from lifting, and being divided and replanted in well cultivated borders; astilbe, alstroemeria, helianthus, helenium, Michaelmas daisies, monarda and rudbeckia all respond to the treatment every three years or so.

Feed bulbs Liquid fertilizer is often more effective with daffodils and other spring-flowering bulbs at this time so that they are able to make use of the food in building up the bulb for next year before their leaves die down. Dead-heading by removing faded flowers so that they do not form seed pods also assists development of the bulb.

Transplant bulbs Transplant bulbs that have been forced when the leaves have died down so that they will establish and eventually flower in the open garden. Chincherinchees make good flowering stems for cutting for indoor decoration and the bulbs can now be planted in a sunny border; space them 3in (7.5cm) apart and 4in (10cm) deep.

Thin hardy annuals Hardy annuals sown earlier will no doubt be ready for their first thinning to approximately 4in (10cm) apart.

Sow biennials *Bellis perennis*, Canterbury bells, forget-me-not and foxgloves can be sown out of doors in well prepared soil after raking in general fertilizer.

Harden off plants before planting out Towards the end of the month later flowering herbaceous plants like kniphofia and schizostylis can be planted out in the open ground; it is most important to harden the plants off properly before planting out and if frost is still expected it may be worthwhile to delay planting for a few days, especially with subjects like early-flowering chrysanthemums. Dormant dahlia tubers can be planted out in favoured areas at the end of the month: space the roots 3ft (1m) apart and the top of the crown should be 4in (10cm) below the soil surface.

Reduce cordon sweet peas Sweet peas are now growing fast and where it is intended to grow cordon plants the stems should be reduced to one. This should be attached to the vertical support and any side shoots and tendrils that appear are best removed at an early stage.

Control weeds Control weeds before they become established, either by hand weeding the beds or by hoeing; the use of a contact herbicide that becomes inactivated once it touches the soil can be advantageous when the ground is too wet to hoe: keep the weedkiller away from the leaves of cultivated plants and read the manufacturer's label carefully.

Watch for rose pests Look out for curling rose leaves which often indicate that the plants have been attacked by rose leaf-rolling sawfly and use a systemic or ordinary insecticide; when just one or two leaves have been attacked they may be picked off and burned.

LAWN Mow the lawn regularly: twice or even three times a week may be necessary during good growing weather. Grass left unmown for any length of time soon looks untidy, the undergrowth turns yellow and gives a most unpleasant appearance when it is finally cut. The cutting height can now be reduced to ¾in (19mm).

Apply fertilizer and weedkiller Towards the end of the month when the grass is dry and the soil moist, a spring fertilizer containing high nitrogen may be applied. Lawn food containing slow release nitrogen will be the most useful to avoid a flush of over lush growth soon after application; fast-acting forms of nitrogen can be lost from the soil by leaching during heavy rain that often occurs at this time of the year. Once the grass is growing actively, any broad-leaved weeds present can be controlled by using a selective weed-killer. This can be used either alone or purchased already mixed with fertilizer so that the two jobs may be done at one and the same time. When hormone type weedkillers are used, it is important to refrain from mowing three days before application to allow sufficient leaf growth to take up the weedkiller and then wait three days after application before mowing again so that the weedkiller will have time to move into all parts of the plant from the leaves.

Control moss Selective hormone weedkillers do not control moss and, where this problem exists, mosskiller should be used. Rake over the lawn two to three weeks later when the moss has died, otherwise it will be spread all over the lawn by small pieces becoming detached as it is being raked out.

Sow grass seed April is a good month for seed sowing because the soil is now warmer and frequent showers often experienced during the month keep the seed moist so that it germinates quickly. If on the other hand, dry weather is experienced, apply sufficient irrigation to moisten the top inch or two of soil; the water must be applied gently with small droplets otherwise the seed will be washed into puddles and produce very uneven germination.

Camellia japonica 'Fascination'.

Any bare or thin patches showing up in the lawn can be sown now and the seed covered with no more than ¼in (6mm) of sifted soil. Lawn seed is usually treated with bird repellent but if not, precautions should be taken by suspending black cotton over the area.

Tidy lawn edges Tidy lawn edges with a 'half moon' and either turn or replace with new turf, any edges that are very ragged.

Scarify lawn Unless already done, scarify the lawn to remove debris and 'thatch' which can build up and restrict water and air movement into the root zone. On any but very small lawn areas, the work is best carried out over several days; on very large lawns a mechanical scarifier will be most useful to prevent fatigue.

Top new lawn New lawns sown earlier will now be making good growth and once the grass is approximately 2in (5cm) long it can be mown with a cylinder or rotary mower set to cut at 1in (2.5cm). A light topping is all that is necessary and the mower blades should be very sharp with a bright cutting edge to avoid ripping the young plants from the soil. A light rolling will benefit the small plants and induce lateral shoot development to thicken up the turf. On no account should the work be carried out when the soil is wet enough to be sticky.

POND Dead plants should be removed before they putrefy the water and they can now be replaced with new ones. This is a good time to plant up water-lilies and old overgrown plants may be taken out and divided. Replant the divided roots with the crown just below soil level in special open-sided water-lily containers so that the roots remain surrounded by moist loamy soil. Water hawthorn (*Aponogeton*) and other overgrown plants can be divided any time now.

Feed water-lilies Established water-lilies will respond to feeding and the most convenient way is to use fertilizer spikes or tablets manufactured for use with houseplants: push the solid fertilizer into the soil surrounding the root and it will slowly dissolve to feed the plant.

Restock fish Restock with fish if necessary, allowing them to acclimatize by immersing their transport container in the pond until the temperature is identical with that in their new home: a sudden change in water temperature can do much harm to fish. Once settled, the fish will look for a daily feed now but no more than can be cleared by them within 10 minutes.

Check equipment Check pumps and other equipment; filters will need cleaning and flushing through and lights may require attention.

FRUIT Growth is well on the move in the fruit garden now and with it

Laburnum x *watereri* 'Vossii'.

comes the tell-tale signs of pest and disease infection: big bud mite attacks black currants causing abnormal swelling of the buds, which become fat and round. Infected buds are best picked off and burned or sprayed with benomyl (normally used as a fungicide) otherwise the mites will migrate to other bushes and infect them with reversion virus which reduces cropping. Gooseberry sawfly often makes an early appearance towards the end of the month and if the pest was a problem last year, no time should be lost in applying an insecticide. Watch out for pests on apple and pear trees too: woolly aphid colonises the rind and bark of twigs and can be detected by its white waxy secretion. These sucking pests remove sap from the plant and by so doing puncture the rind and allow diseases to enter the tree. Greenfly can be particularly troublesome especially with plum leaves.

Control mildew One of the most widespread of diseases in its various forms is mildew. This is liable to attack gooseberries, currants, grapes and apples in particular; try to keep the plants growing without a check and apply a systemic fungicide.

Remove grease bands Grease bands will have fulfilled their purpose by catching insects crawling upwards and may be removed from tree trunk and adjacent stake at the end of the month.

Protect blossom Blossom is still susceptible to frost damage and, where possible, trees and bushes should be protected by draping with muslin or similar material; a lawn sprinkler set up amid the plants and turned on for a short period after a frosty night and before the sun reaches the blossom will help prevent damage. Bare moist soil below the plants is said to raise the temperature of the microclimate slightly, possibly enough to avoid damage to the blossom of low-growing subjects.

Check stakes and ties Check stakes and ties, especially after strong wind.

Check newly planted trees Trees planted during last autumn and through winter and spring may need the soil refirming around their roots, as it is important to prevent drying out during this all important period of establishment. Give the soil a thorough soaking if the weather has been dry and especially after drying winds.

Prune cherries and plums Cherry trees can be pruned now that the sap has begun to rise. Annual pruning is not always necessary but a branch that crosses close to another is best removed to prevent bark damage; some thinning may also be necessary from time to time so that air and light can enter the tree. Young plum trees can also be pruned now (see page 180). Check ties, especially on wall-trained specimens, to ensure they are not cutting into the wood. This can cause much damage by restricting growth and permits entry of disease.

Control pests and diseases The fruit of peach and nectarine trees is delectable but unfortunately both are subject to two persistent problems in the form of peach leaf curl and red spider mite. Interestingly each of the problems occurs under opposing weather conditions: the former when the branches and buds remain wet for long periods during winter and spring, the latter when bright dry weather occurs during late March and April. Pick off any leaves showing the characteristic blistering of peach leaf curl and spray against red spider mite if necessary.

Thin out fruitlets Fan-trained peaches and nectarines growing in favourable areas will have produced fruit the size of marbles and thinning should commence by removing alternate fruits.

De-blossom new plants Generally it is better to pick off any blossom that forms on newly planted trees during the first year after planting. This will encourage satisfactory establishment with the available energy going to form a good framework as a basis for cropping in future years. The same applies to strawberries planted in late autumn and early winter last year or during early spring of the current year.

Ventilate strawberries under cloches Established strawberries growing under cloches should be given ventilation during warm bright weather so that the temperature does not rise too high; ventilation will also be required each day whilst the plants are in flower to enable pollinating insects to gain entry. Slugs can be a problem unless slug pellets are scattered around.

Thin out raspberry canes Summer-fruiting raspberry stools often produce many more suckers than will be needed for the following crop and it is a good idea to begin reducing the excess growth at an early stage: aim to retain 5 or 6 suckers to each plant to grow on into canes for cropping. Suckers arising too far from the original plants should also be removed to keep the garden looking tidy.

Mulch trees and bushes Fruit trees and bushes will benefit from mulching if this has not already been done. Place special mats or straw below strawberries to keep the fruit away from the soil.

VEGETABLES AND HERBS Potatoes planted in favoured localities will already be pushing up above the soil. The growth is very susceptible to frost damage and no time should be lost in covering the protruding leaves with a small ridge of soil. Gardeners who no longer earth up ridges may prefer to protect the growth with a straw covering when frost is forecast, carefully removing it again the next morning. Sturdy growth in full light will result from this treatment. Early potatoes may be planted in colder districts during the second half of the month.

Plant maincrop potatoes Although space is often restricted in modern gardens for such crops, when a maincrop potato harvest is anticipated the 'seed' should go in during this month. Well manured acid soil is ideal but if the soil is alkaline, scab-free tubers may still be enjoyed by setting the 'seed' directly on a layer of bulky organic material, such as sphagnum peat or garden compost, in the bottom of the planting trench.

Plant onion sets Onion sets transplanted from seed trays where they have produced just sufficient root to make good anchorage stand less chance of being unsettled by birds. They like good fertile soil that has been well firmed after the application of garden compost or manure; provided the bulky material was incorporated last autumn, the soil should by now have settled naturally. Salad and pickling onions can now be sown in drills 1ft (30cm) apart.

Sow seed In fact any number of vegetables and herbs are due to be sown during April including Australian-type cauliflower, Brussels sprouts, sprouting broccoli, kale and cabbages for next winter and spring cropping. These can all be sown broadcast in a nursery bed and the ground should be treated with soil insecticide against flea beetle and cabbage root fly. When the soil is infected by club root disease, it is often wiser to sow brassica seed thinly in a container using a peat-based compost and then transplant the resulting seedlings after dipping the roots in fungicide to protect them from the disease.

Sow peas and give early support Wrinkle seeded peas can be sown any time now provided the soil is in a fit state, germination is usually fairly fast now that the ground is warmer and a sowing in the middle of the month will provide the first pickings during early to mid July. Support the young plants at an early stage using pea netting or twigs.

Gather crops when young and tender Kohl-rabi, spinach, lettuce, beetroot and radish are all better for gathering when they are young and tender and should therefore be sown every 10 to 14 days in succession; sow thinly to avoid waste. This applies especially to carrots, which can be sown during the middle of the month as a maincrop for harvesting during winter: they will eventually stand 6in (15cm) apart and there is no point in over sowing to produce too many seedlings that must then be drastically thinned out, attracting carrot root fly in the process. Where germination of carrots already sown is too dense, the seedlings should be thinned out and then dusted or watered with a soil insecticide to prevent attack by carrot fly.

Protect plants from cabbage root flies Another troublesome fly which is persistent from now on, at least from the time when cow parsley and similar weeds flower, is the cabbage root fly: summer cabbage and other brassica plants should always be protected by soil insecticide within three days from planting otherwise eggs will be laid on the soil surface around the plant, they hatch and then the maggots attack the young plant at soil level.

Remove old brassica stumps Any old cabbage and other brassica stumps still remaining should now be dug up, they are hardly likely to produce further worthwhile crops and all the time the stumps linger on they harbour pests like the mealy cabbage aphid, which soon migrate to the new plants coming along.

Harvest asparagus Asparagus is a delectable crop to grow and now that the new tips are pushing up, the long wait seems all worthwhile. Harvesting can begin as soon as the tips are a reasonable size – up to 6in (15cm) long; but no crop should be taken for the first three years after planting so that the crowns have time to establish properly. This is a suitable month to make a new bed, which should be thoroughly prepared as it will crop for many years. One-year-old crowns establish best and nothing is gained by planting older crowns.

Sow rhubarb Rhubarb is another crop which becomes part of the household, roots go on from year to year on condition that they are given a top dressing of general fertilizer during April and a good mulch of garden compost from time to time. Rhubarb plants can be raised from seed sown this month and this is a novel way of growing new plants rather than the more usual lifting and root division after the top growth has died back during winter. The new crop from seed will be ready for harvest in two years time. Established rhubarb often produces flower stems during spring but these should be cut away otherwise they take energy from the plant.

Sow French beans, marrows and sweet corn Where cloches are available, French beans, marrows and sweet corn can be sown after the soil has had a chance to warm up.

Sow herbs Herbs due to be sown this month include dill, fennel, hyssop, marjoram, parsley, rue and thyme. Cut over perennial plants to stimulate growth of side shoots.

Sow broad beans for autumn cropping Living in the age of the freezer, sufficient broad beans are often grown from early sowings to last through the year but a sowing made at the end of the month will provide a welcome fresh crop during autumn.

Prepare trenches for celery When a trench celery crop is planned no time should be lost in preparing the trenches. A trench 18in (45cm) wide to accommodate two rows of plants is normal and where more than one trench is prepared the trenches should be spaced at least 3ft (1m) apart. Remove the top soil and place along the side of the trench as a ridge; liberal quantities of farmyard manure or garden compost are then forked into the subsoil. The top soil is returned to the trench leaving a 3in (7.5cm) gap at the top of the trench for watering. Small ridges left either side of the celery trench can be used for quick maturing crops like lettuce and radish.

GREENHOUSE AND FRAME Cold house tomatoes will be planted in mild districts from the middle of the month although a further two or three weeks will be necessary before it is safe to plant up in less favourable areas. Take care not to overfeed especially during dull weather otherwise much lush growth will be made at the expense of fruit setting; fertilizer containing high potash should be used at this stage. Remove side shoots from tomato plants as soon as they can easily be handled.

Pot on chrysanthemums Mid-season and late-flowering chrysanthemums will now be ready for potting into 5in (12.5cm) pots and the earliest rooted cuttings will be ready for final potting at the end of the month. Good sturdy growth will be achieved by cool growing conditions and the best place for the plants now is in the cold frame. Some cultivars to be flowered on the second crown bud will need their first stop during the second or third week of the month. This is done by pinching out the extreme tip of the main stem.

Harden off bedding plants Bedding plants now established after pricking out into trays should be hardened off in the cold frame to await final planting when the risk of frost has passed. The plants often respond to foliar feeding during the final week or two before planting out.

Control grape vines Grape vines are now making vigorous growth and every opportunity should be taken to keep the plants under control: the tip of each shoot is removed when two leaves have been produced beyond the bunch of grapes; each lateral is then stopped at one leaf and so on as new growth proceeds. The rods need almost daily attention from now on otherwise growth is inclined to get out of hand, which often results in poor air circulation and an onslaught of mildew.

Sow runner beans and sweet corn Runner beans can be sown in boxes or singly in pots or blocks for planting outside later after hardening off. Sweet corn can be treated in the same way except that it dislikes root disturbance and so should always be sown in individual containers or blocks.

Feed strawberries Potted strawberries are now making good growth and will benefit from high potash feeding. Any blossom that is still being produced should continue to be hand pollinated with a soft artist's brush.

Control pests More insects will now be visiting the greenhouse including greenfly, whitefly and red spider mites. Smoke cones deal effectively with the pests but read the label instructions carefully because some plants, especially certain seedlings, may be damaged by their use.

Damp down floor Damping down the floor does much to create good growing conditions during bright weather and the humid atmosphere suppresses red spider mite activity – a pest which soon restricts the growth of many plants including peaches and nectarines.

Thin out fruit Peaches will require their first thinning so that fruit is spaced 4in (10cm) apart along the shoot; do not over-thin because there is a possibility that some fruit will drop of its own accord.

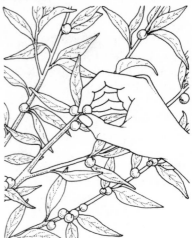

Thinning out peach fruit.

Rest plants after flowering Arum lilies and cyclamen should be gradually dried off after flowering and then rested before they start into growth again later. Young cyclamen plants from seed sown last autumn or winter may need potting on: carefully tap the root ball from the pot and if roots can be seen emerging from the ball, pot on into a larger size pot using John Innes potting compost No 2. The plants will benefit from standing out in the frame for the summer.

Pot on camellias Camellias make attractive plants for the cold greenhouse and after flowering they may require potting on into a larger pot if the existing container is filled with roots. Stand the plants in a shady position out of doors after flowering and on no account must they go short of water otherwise growth and particularly next year's flowers will suffer.

Prick out seedlings Aubergines and sweet peppers should be pricked out into 3 or 4in (7.5 or 10cm) pots when the seed leaves have expanded. Plants sown early and already in pots may be potted on into 5in (12.5cm) pots or planted in growing bags for growing on in the greenhouse or for placing outside when the risk of frost has passed.

Stop fuchsias Fuchsias should now be growing vigorously; lateral shoots may be stopped at 2 pairs of leaves to induce bushiness, although the method does tend to delay the first flush of flowers somewhat. Standards should be potted on into 8in (20cm) pots whereas large bush plants are usually satisfied with 7in (17.5cm) containers.

Sow alpine strawberries Alpine strawberries make attractive little plants, their fruit is ideal for decorating trifles and other dishes. Seed sown now will produce fruiting plants in June to remain in the greenhouse or for planting outside.

Shade plants Temporary shading will be necessary for many plants now. Green polythene is suitable or newspaper can be used to shade seedlings for a day or two after pricking out until they have become established.

Increase watering Plants will be looking for more moisture now that the days are warmer; capillary watering using capillary matting draped over the staging into guttering attached to the side of the bench has much to commend it: the plants then look after their own watering needs provided the gutter is filled each morning.

May

FLOWERS, TREES AND SHRUBS At last we can consider planting out without the risk of severe frost, although there is a possibility that a cold snap may return and tender subjects will need protection in cold districts. Favoured areas, particularly in the south, will see summer bedding planted out in prepared borders that have been allowed to settle. Harden off the plants by giving more air in the cold frame or by placing the plants in a sheltered area before planting out in the garden; so many plants are spoiled each year because they are still too soft prior to planting in the open.

Stagger the planting of gladioli for a long display Gladioli make excellent plants for decoration in the border and for cutting; continuity can be achieved by staggering the planting over a few weeks. The corms should be spaced 6in (15cm) apart, 5in (12.5cm) deep, and if the soil is at all heavy, a sprinkling of sharp sand or grit below the corms will prevent rotting should the weather turn wet. It is a good idea to mark the planting stations with small sticks until growth appears above the ground to avoid planting other subjects too close.

Divide hardy primula and plant out polyanthus Clumps of hardy primula that are beginning to get congested may be divided now: tease the roots apart and replant carefully so that the crown is at the same level as it was before the clump was lifted. Polyanthus grown as houseplants can be planted in the open border once the flowers have faded.

Sow alstroemeria, wallflowers and annuals Alstroemeria is a very showy plant for the summer border and the Ligtu hybrids are particularly good with shades of orange, red, pink and yellow. Seed can be sown now ¾in (19mm) deep in the open border to provide plants to set out in a warm, well drained position later. Germination tends to be rather slow taking from two to three months and so seed is best sown in well marked drills to facilitate weed control. Wallflowers can also be sown now in a nursery bed to be transplanted later for flowering next spring. Annual plants, on the other hand, may be sown thinly direct in the border where they are to flower. Prepare the seedbed well in advance so that the first flush of weed seeds germinate and can be dealt with before the cultivated plant seed is sown.

Layer deciduous azaleas, cytisus and magnolias Deciduous azaleas are not very easy to propagate by cuttings and layering provides a more certain method when extra plants are needed. Low-growing stems near the ground are bent down and secured in the soil (see page 155) when the last flowers have faded. Other plants including cytisus (broom) and magnolias can be propagated in the same way.

Dead-head shrubs and other flowering plants Most decorative plants flower better the following year when old flowers are removed as they fade. This dead-heading is best carried out before seed pods begin to form. Dead-heading can be rather tedious with plants producing many flowers like azaleas and so it is sometimes overlooked but certainly every effort should be made to remove the faded flowers from bulbous plants such as tulips, daffodils and other subjects expected to make a bulb large enough to flower again next year.

Lift bulbs In the case of tulips, when the space is required for bedding plants, the bulbs complete with foliage may, if necessary, be carefully lifted after flowering and then be heeled in elsewhere until the leaves have died down. Then the bulbs are finally lifted, dried off and stored for planting at a later date. Daffodils are inclined to look rather untidy once the flowers have faded but it is important to leave the foliage intact for at least six weeks after flowering, so that the food they contain has a chance to return to the bulb.

Prune perennials and shrubs after flowering Plants like perennial alyssum, arabis, aubrieta and saxifrage respond favourably to being cut hard back with shears after flowering. This helps to maintain compact tidy plants for next spring. Early spring-flowering shrubs produce flowers on wood made during the previous year and they, too, often respond to pruning after flowering. The degree of pruning will depend on the subject (see page 174) but take care to avoid cutting certain plants like cytisus back into hard wood because they are unlikely to grow away again after such treatment.

Clip hedges May is usually a good month to clip privet and other boundary hedges. Once the hedge has started to grow a growth regulator can be sprayed onto the leaves, if wished, so that further clipping during the year should not be necessary.

Make final preparations to the dahlia bed Dahlias like a water-retentive root run and bulky organic material should have already been incorporated in the border, if not take the opportunity to fork in peat or composted bark. Final preparations should be made by broadcasting a general fertilizer and raking over the bed ready for planting young plants at the end of the month, or during the first week or two of next depending on local climatic conditions.

Dormant tubers can be planted now provided they have at least 3in (7.5cm) of soil above the fleshy roots.

Plant early chrysanthemums Early-flowering chrysanthemums can be planted out during mid-May, spacing them 2ft by 2ft (60cm by 60cm) apart.

Plant evergreens and apply mulch Plant bare root evergreens (pot-grown ones can be planted at any time provided the soil is in a fit state) and take precautions so that the soil does not dry out after planting by mulching the surface of moist soil with bulky organic material.

Established shrubs and lilies like *L.henryi, speciosum* and *auratum* also respond to a surface mulch above the root area.

Train sweet peas and support tall herbaceous plants Sweet peas should be watered to prevent the soil drying out, which is one reason for bud drop. They will need a feed now that vigorous growth is being made; remove side shoots and tendrils as they appear so that energy will be diverted into flower stems and the main growing shoot. New growth should be supported as the need arises to keep the main stem of cordon plants growing straight. Other plants will benefit from support and the most unobtrusive for taller growing herbaceous plants is provided by pushing in twiggy sticks amongst them.

Remove excess growth from perennials and roses Many perennial border plants give rise to more stems than necessary and it pays to reduce them by removing the weaker shoots completely. Much the same can be said for rose bushes which sometimes produce weak growth especially when pruning was light.

Set out hanging baskets Towards the end of the month hanging baskets can be set up out of doors; they may need watering daily from now on, evening being a good time, and should be given a liquid feed each week.

Watch for plant pests and diseases Plant pests tend to build up rapidly now that the temperature is rising: be on guard against greenfly, particularly on roses; the rose leaf-rolling sawfly can be a problem too. The garden chafer and cockchafer larvae can do considerable damage to plants by feeding on the roots and should be controlled by using a soil insecticide; adults are now on the wing, they feed on leaves and lay eggs in the soil to hatch later. Slugs can be particularly troublesome to young plants and seedlings.

Continue spraying every two to three weeks to prevent rose black spot and mildew.

LAWN Weekly mowing will be necessary to keep the lawn in trim and the cutting height can be lowered to 1in (2.5cm) for coarse grasses and down to ½in (13mm) for finer grasses provided the soil is not dry, a problem even at this time of the year in some areas with light sandy soil. Seedling grasses can be topped to maintain a height of 1½in (4cm) and irrigation with a lawn sprinkler should be carried out to keep the soil moist but not too wet and to keep the grass growing uniformly.

Control broad-leaved weeds With few exceptions, broad-leaved weeds are easy to control at this time of the year provided they are actively growing. Ideally, fertilizer should be applied a week or two before applying a selective hormone weedkiller although, for convenience, a combined weedkiller and fertilizer can be applied in the form of granules which are broadcast by hand or mechanical spreader. The grass sward should be dry and the soil moist at the time of application. Hormone weedkillers should not be applied to newly sown lawns nor those dry at the root.

Feed the lawn Apply a lawn fertilizer relatively high in nitrogen to keep established grass growing well and irrigation may be necessary during dry spells to water it in. Lawn tonic is available which quickly imparts a lush green colour when the grass is lacking vigour and requires a quick boost.

Control May bugs Watch for May bugs (chafer beetles) which can be particularly troublesome in some areas during the month: they lay eggs on the lawn which hatch into grubs attracting starlings, magpies and other birds.

Apply mosskiller Moss often diminishes naturally during the summer but any still remaining will soon respond to one of the mosskillers available in garden centres or stores.

Prepare new site for sowing in the autumn This is a good month to carry out basic cultivation for a new lawn to be sown in the autumn.

POND Marginal aquatics and pond plants will establish quickly now that the water is warming up.

Divide and replant water-lilies Overgrown plants like water-lilies can be divided and replanted after lowering the water level but take care to avoid disturbing water snail spawn and small fry that may be present.

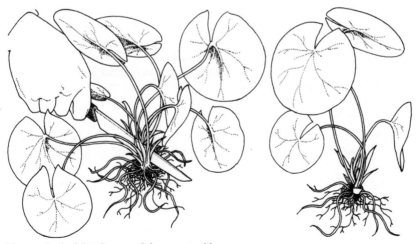

The method of dividing used for a water-lily.

Remove blanket weed Blanket weed is often a problem during bright weather until the water surface is covered by plant leaves; the strands can be removed by carefully twisting a forked stick in the water or by using a rake.

Introduce shade and oxygenating plants The majority of garden centres now stock a wide range of pond plants and a selection of floating aquatics to provide shade, and submerged oxygenating plants will do much to improve the environment of the pond.

FRUIT Strawberries should now be making good progress and any flowers that develop on runners planted since the turn of the year are best removed to enable the plants to establish properly. Cloched strawberries will need ventilation during bright weather to keep temperatures within limits and allow pollinating insects to enter; those growing in the open should be covered with netting before the fruit shows colour to prevent bird damage. Place straw or mats below the developing trusses if that has not already been done and a light scattering of slug pellets will give protection to the fruit.

Thin gooseberry fruit and support low branches Gooseberry bushes invariably produce an ample crop and when large fruit is required, immature fruit can be thinned out as it develops. Certain varieties like 'Leveller' and others growing in shade often produce prostrate branches which should be supported to keep the fruit away from the soil: a simple method of support is to drive four stout canes into the ground, one at each corner of the plant, and attach string from one to another; the lower branches can then be looped over the horizontal strings.

Reduce raspberry suckers Reduce new raspberry suckers as necessary so that no more than 5 or 6 remain on summer-fruiting kinds to develop and fruit next year. This is best done by pulling the growth away rather than hoeing it off as this tends to encourage numerous weak growths to grow from the stub. Any suckers arising too far away from the stool should be treated likewise.

Train wall-grown trees Wall-trained trees need constant attention from now on: remove any shoots from cherries, plums, damsons, peaches and nectarines that grow directly outwards or towards the wall. Peach and nectarine fruit should be thinned by first removing 'doubles'. Once fruit has set it is most important that roots do not dry out at any time. This can happen even during wet weather when the plant is protected by overhanging eaves; water the soil thoroughly if necessary and apply a mulch of bulky organic material.

Mulch fruit trees All fruit trees and bushes will benefit from a mulch provided the soil is moist at the time of application. This will also suppress weed growth which should always be controlled otherwise it will undoubtedly compete with the cultivated plant for nutrients and moisture.

Take frost precautions Blossom will still require protection from frost especially in low-lying areas which tend to be frost pockets where the cold air drains downwards; it often pays to make a hole in a dense hedge at ground level so that frosty air can drain through to lower land.

Tie in cane fruit suckers Vigorous shoots growing up from the rootstocks of cultivated blackberries and loganberries need to be tied in before they grow too long otherwise they are inclined to snap; they can either be bundled together in the centre of the fan-trained growth of the previous year or, preferably, allotted the vacant space to one side where last year's fruiting canes were removed after harvest.

Control pests and diseases Cane midge is usually on the wing during the middle of the month: eggs are laid just below the rind of raspberry and other cane fruit plants. The resulting wound often allows entry of diseases such as cane spot and a combined spray of insecticide and fungicide is worthwhile.

Precautions should also be taken against grey mould disease which attacks strawberries, and mildew on gooseberries, blackcurrants, apples and pears. Apples and pears are also prone to scab disease which can be prevented by applying a suitable fungicide.

Fruit pests to watch out for now include greenfly, especially on plums and apples, sawfly and capsid which mainly attack apples when the blossom is open and the gooseberry sawfly which lays eggs on bushes to give rise to very hungry maggots that soon defoliate the plant. Red spider mite can be a real problem during warm dry weather.

Peach leaf curl may also be a problem unless the trees are protected from damp during the winter as described on page 25.

Read the label It is of course most important to observe label instructions when applying insecticides and fungicides, especially when beneficial insects are visiting the plants. When possible it makes sense to use sprays that do not harm beneficial insects and these are listed in the insecticide and fungicide tables on pages 186 to 197.

Control vigorous growth May is a good month to take steps to control growth in over-vigorous fruit trees. Although root pruning is generally satisfactory, bark ringing is considered to be the most effective method of mechanical control. This is done by removing a ¼in (6mm) strip of bark half way round the main trunk; a similar strip is removed from the opposite side approximately 3in (7.5cm) above the first. The wounds are then immediately covered with adhesive tape to prevent disease spores from gaining entry. Tree growth is also being controlled by an experimental chemical but this is only in the research stage at the time of writing and the method is explained in the section dealing with growth regulators (see page 199).

VEGETABLES AND HERBS There is still a likelihood of frost until the end of the month and it will be necessary to cover up the tender top growth of susceptible plants like potatoes: traditionally, soil was ridged up over the shoots but it is hardly worthwhile excluding light from the leaves that have grown and so it is beneficial, on a small scale, to have flower pots at the ready to cover up the plants when frost is forecast. Straw or bracken can be used to protect the plants on a larger scale and these materials can afterwards be incorporated in the compost heap.

Sow carrots Maincrop carrots require a long growing season to produce the most beneficial crop; good soil preparation by raking to a fine tilth really does pay off so that good germination produces a good stand of plants. In this case seed may be sown thinly to avoid thinning out and then there will be far less chance of the plants being attacked by carrot fly, which causes considerable crop loss. Sow the maincrop carrot seed in shallow drills ½in (13mm) deep and 15in (38cm) apart after the application of general fertilizer at the rate of 4oz per sq yd (136g per m²).

Sow runner beans in well prepared land Runner beans produce the most prolific crop when sufficient moisture is available at the root at all times. The answer here is to incorporate plenty of bulky organic material into the soil well in advance of sowing: autumn is really the best time to carry out the basic cultivation although, should the opportunity have been missed then, do not hesitate to take out a trench 18in (45cm) wide and one spit deep, then fork in the garden compost or other material in the trench and also in the topsoil, return the soil and firm by treading. Insert a double row of bean poles 9 to 12in (23 to 30cm) apart with 15in (38cm) between the rows and sow a seed 3in (7.5cm) deep alongside each pole. It will pay to sow a few spare seeds at the end of the row to fill in any gaps where germination is poor.

Instead of sowing the runner beans in rows, wigwams can be erected by inserting four poles into the ground to form a square and then tying the tops together. This method often produces better crops should the summer turn hot and dry.

Prepare planting sites for cucumbers and pumpkins Planting sites for other crops requiring copious supplies of moisture like marrows, ridge cucumbers and pumpkins should be prepared in good time. Dig out holes 2ft by 2ft (60cm by 60cm), one spit deep, and incorporate a bucketful of rotted manure or garden compost before replacing the top soil. Where space permits, the planting stations should be spaced 3ft (1m) apart to allow the plants sufficient space to develop. Seed will germinate out of doors when sown during the last week of the month and, to ensure success, three seeds may be planted at each station, two of the resulting plants being removed if all germinate.

Prepare for tomatoes Outdoor tomatoes can be grown on sites prepared in much the same way except that they are not so demanding in the amount of bulky organic material required, and they should be planted 18in (45cm) apart allowing 3ft (1m) between the rows. Bush types have much to commend them because they do not require supporting with canes as do cordon plants. Tomatoes can be planted towards the end of the month in favoured areas, especially when cloches are available, otherwise it is prudent to wait until next month before setting them out.

Plant Brussels sprouts Brussels sprouts planted as soon as they are ready will enable the plants to establish before warm dry weather checks their growth. Cabbage root fly can be a problem from now on and it is as well to take precautions by watering the plants in with an insecticide or providing each with a bituminous paper collar at soil level. Club root disease may also be a problem and a fungicide should be used as a preventive measure.

Take care when planting cauliflowers Cauliflower plants set out now will mature during the late summer months; take the usual precautions against root fly and club root and plant out with a trowel if necessary to avoid checking the plants, which often leads to premature curd formation. Firm planting of all brassicas is most important so that they will grow properly.

Sow salads and root crops Successional sowings of lettuce, mustard and cress and radish every 10 to 14 days will provide useful pickings for salads and thinnings of maincrop beetroot sown towards the end of the month will serve the same purpose. The remaining roots can then be allowed to mature and be stored eventually for winter use.

Salsify and scorzonera, on the other hand, are hardy enough to remain in the ground throughout winter and so special storing conditions are not required; sow the seed very thinly 1in (2.5cm) deep in drills 15in (38cm) apart; when the seeds have germinated the young plants are thinned out to stand 8in (20cm) apart. Swedes can also be sown.

Sow French beans and peas Another crop which is much appreciated during the winter, provided a freezer is available, is the French bean. It can, of course, be gathered and eaten fresh during summer and autumn by sowing seed 2in (5cm) deep and 6in (15cm) apart in rows spaced 2ft (60cm) apart. The soil should have warmed up sufficiently by the middle of the month to produce good germination but do avoid soaking the seed before sowing, otherwise disease may be spread from an infected seed to others during the process.

A further sowing of peas will provide continuity and the sugar peas are particularly worthwhile because the pods can also be eaten. Netting or twiggy sticks should be provided to give support.

Raise sweet corn Many dependable sweet corn cultivars are now available to produce a satisfactory crop during cool summers, although it is doubtful whether even these can be guaranteed in very cold localities. Plants raised in containers earlier may be planted out at the end of the month or seed can be sown 1½in (4cm) deep and 1½ft (45cm) apart in a square block rather than in straight rows. This will facilitate fertilization of the cobs by the wind-borne pollen which disperses from the tassels at the top of the plant. As with other seeds which tend to be rather evasive, it is as well to sow three to each station and, if more than one germinates, to remove the surplus at an early stage.

Thin herbs and sow for succession Herbs sown last month will now be large enough to thin out and further sowings can be made of chervil, dill, fennel, hyssop, parsley and sage. Basil tends to be more exacting and seed sowing should be delayed until the end of the month, although seedlings raised indoors can be planted out at any time during the month provided weather and soil condition permit.

Take herb cuttings Some herbs mature faster when they are propagated by 3in (7.5cm) long cuttings taken, with a heel if possible, from the previous year's growth. Pot marjoram, rosemary, sage and thyme root readily when inserted in a well drained compost and placed on a window sill. An alternative method of propagating thyme and other plants which tend to spread vigorously is to simply lift and divide the plant.

Feed established plants Plants that have been growing for any length of time like spring cabbage, early potatoes, onions and rhubarb will benefit from a fertilizer top dressing. Ensure sufficient moisture is at the roots otherwise crops will suffer and carrots are prone to grow coarse whiskers during dry conditions. Rhubarb is inclined to produce flower heads now and these should be removed at an early stage.

Control pests Watch out for blackfly on broad beans and flea beetle on brassica seedlings including turnips. Carrot fly is very difficult to control and many gardeners are using the old-fashioned method of dragging a paraffin rag over the row after thinning the plants to camouflage the smell, which attracts the flies.

GREENHOUSE Temperatures can rise very quickly under glass now and automatic ventilation really is a must when the house is unattended for most of the day. Shading the glass with green polythene, laths or one of the liquid formulations will be necessary to protect tender plants from strong sun. Rapidly growing plants take up substantial amounts of water and it is important to replace that lost the previous day. This is where automatic irrigation equipment comes into its own so that the plants never run short and wilt.

Keep cucumbers growing Cucumbers should be kept growing without check otherwise bitter-tasting fruit will result; much can be done to keep the root system active by top dressing with compost the plants growing in a bed. When rotted manure or garden compost is used for the purpose, a sleeve of sphagnum peat should first be placed around the base of the stem to prevent disease attack; the layer of top dressing is then placed on the bed surface to enable fresh roots to grow from the stem. Fruits developing on the main stem of older varieties like 'Telegraph' and 'Butcher's Disease Resister' should be removed before the flowers fade, otherwise they will check the plant and slow down the growth. Male flowers, those without a small cucumber fruit attached, should be removed whilst still in bud before the flowers open otherwise insects will transfer pollen from them to the female flowers, causing the fruit to develop a bitter flavour. The newer 'all female' cultivars may be allowed to produce some fruit on the main stem and they are less likely to produce male flowers.

Train cucumbers The simplest way to train cucumbers is to twist the growth around a string loosely tied to the base of the stem, the top of the string being attached to a wire stretched above the plant. The growing point of the main stem is then allowed to reach the top of the string and then dangle to extend the growing season. Side shoots will develop from the main stem and these laterals should be removed entirely from the lower 1½ft (45cm) of the main stem. Subsequent side shoots should be stopped by removing their growing tip to leave one leaf beyond one developing fruit on the shoot. A

Training a cucumber by stopping the side shoots.

further shoot (sub lateral) will develop and that in turn is stopped one leaf beyond the fruit and so on as further laterals develop.

Stop melons Although melons are closely related to cucumbers, they need rather different treatment in that both male and female flowers are necessary to produce fruit. Female flowers often only appear on lateral shoots and so as soon as the main stem has produced six leaves, the growing point is pinched out to encourage growth of the laterals. In the case of 'Sweetheart', a much grown cultivar for greenhouse and frame, four fruits may be allowed to develop on each plant and it should be remembered that pollination is necessary for the fruits to grow. The best way of achieving this in case insects do not visit the plants, is to remove a male flower and rub it over the open female flowers, preferably at mid-day when the pollen is likely to be most viable.

Plant tomatoes in cold house Tomatoes will also be looking for more water and they can now be planted up in the cold greenhouse. Many different makes of growing bag are available, removing the necessity of changing or sterilising the border soil and they provide a convenient way of growing a wide range of plants. A level site is important for best results and special plastic trays are available which act as a water reservoir so that the plants can take up just as much moisture as they require. Another method of providing water for the plants is to suspend bags above them to which small bore plastic tubing has been fixed. The bags do, however, hold 2gal (9l) of water and as this is heavy they require substantial support.

Tomato plants will now be producing side shoots and these should be removed as soon as they can be handled without damage being done to the main stem.

Pinch grape vine shoots Grape vines are now making a considerable amount of growth and every effort should be made to keep growth under control. This is best done by first pinching out the growing tip of the shoot one leaf beyond the developing bunch of grapes. Each sub lateral is then stopped at one leaf and so on. Satisfactory growth will be encouraged with sufficient air circulation to help prevent mildew disease developing and, provided the plant is supplied with sufficient water and fertilizer at the root, disease attack should be minimal.

Thin peaches and control red spider mite Peaches should be thinned at an early stage to reduce competition. The ideal stage for final thinning is when the fruit is walnut size; aim to allow 1ft (30cm) between the fruit and a good size will then be achieved. On no account should the plants go short of water at the root otherwise fruit development will be arrested and red spider mite control will be most difficult. This pest is very difficult to control at the best of times, although damping over the floor and plants each day helps.

Feed pot leeks and control disease Pot leek enthusiasts check their plants daily to ensure they are moist without being too wet; the plants will respond to liquid feeding and a spray of Benlate or Dithane will help prevent disease infection.

Harvest early potatoes growing in pots Early potatoes potted up in the greenhouse will soon be ready for cropping; check development by carefully knocking the root system from the pot, remove any tubers ready for harvesting and replace the root ball for further development.

Sow *Campanula pyramidalis* and ripen shoots of *Jasminum polyanthum* *Campanula pyramidalis* is a delectable plant to overwinter in the greenhouse and flower next spring: the 3½ft (1m) tall spikes of bell-shaped blue or white flowers make a sowing of seed this month worthwhile. Another spring-flowering plant, *Jasminum polyanthum*, needs careful attention now to ensure flowers next time: stand the plant out of doors after flowering to ripen the shoots, then flower buds will stand a far better chance of developing properly. The plant can be propagated now if necessary by taking cuttings.

Take herb cuttings Cuttings can be taken now from various herb plants like lavender, rosemary and thyme.

Disbud perpetual-flowering carnations Perpetual-flowering carnations develop very quickly now that the longer days are here and when large flowers are required, it is important to disbud at an early stage by removing the small buds surrounding the central one. The first five side shoots from the top should also be removed from each flowering stem. Rooted cuttings should be potted off and stopped by pinching out the growing tip 10 to 14 days after potting.

Pot on chrysanthemums Mid-season and late-flowering chrysanthemums should now go into their final pots and be stood out of doors in a sheltered but sunny aspect. Use John Innes potting compost No 3 or a peat-based compost and remember to leave sufficient space at the top of the pot for subsequent top dressing with the same sort of compost.

Top dress lilies and stand out arums Lilies growing in pots will respond to top dressing and arum lilies can now be stood out of doors; water and feed them until the foliage dies down and then withhold water.

FLOWERS, TREES AND SHRUBS Chrysanthemums for early flowering outdoors should be stopped during the middle of the month to encourage lateral shoots; only the tip of the main stem should be removed to avoid checking the growth of the plant too much. Exhibitors start to feed their plants at the end of the month by sprinkling general fertilizer over the surface of the soil and watering it in, or liquid fertilizer may be used.

Feed and mulch sweet peas Sweet peas will also respond to feeding; use a fertilizer containing phosphate to encourage further root action which helps to avoid bud drop. The plants use up vast quantities of water during hot weather and should never go short otherwise growth will be checked, which again leads to bud drop. Mulching moist soil with garden compost, peat or composted bark helps to retain soil moisture and control weeds. Really long stems bearing prolific flowers are produced by plants grown as cordons with the tendrils and side shoots being removed at an early stage.

Disbud and dead-head roses Roses come into their own this month and to encourage repeat flowering of the large-flowered kinds, it is advisable to cut flowering stems back to the first strong side shoot on the stem. The same applies when dead-heading faded flowers; this should always be done to prolong flowering unless heps are required. Larger flowers result from disbudding when the cluster of flower buds is immature; this is easily done by simply rubbing out the small flower buds surrounding the larger one in the centre of the group.

Remove suckers and bud roses Suckers arising from the rootstock of roses should be removed when they are still soft: push the soil aside to find the place of origin of the suckers and pull them away from that point. The alternative is to cut them off at ground level but they often grow even more vigorously when part of the sucker is left behind in that way. One way to avoid suckers is to take cuttings from the rose cultivar so that the plant grows on its own roots, but generally the plants are not so long lived as those budded on to special rootstocks. Budding (see page 159) is carried out when the bark lifts from the wood, during this month in most areas.

Spray roses Greenfly can be a real problem now and plants susceptible to blackspot and mildew should receive regular sprays of fungicide.

Control aphids and ants Aphids tend to build up rapidly on many plants during this month and lupins, for example, can be quickly crippled by grey aphids. Another aphid causes pansies and violas to wilt badly but where only one sort of pest like aphid is concerned it is worth using a specific aphicide that will not harm beneficial insects like ladybirds and bees; although this particular insecticide will not control ants, it will help to reduce their activity by removing their food source. Ants can, however, be controlled effectively by using one of the materials suggested on page 186.

Lift tulips and other bulbs Tulips and other bulbs that have died down can now be lifted, cleaned off and stored in the dark. This is of particular importance to deter narcissus flies from laying eggs on the bulbs and also helps to prevent the bulbs shrivelling.

Feed plants before planting out With bulbs out of the way, bedding plants and dahlias can be planted for summer colour, but first remove any weeds present and rake general fertilizer into the soil. Liquid fertilizer applied to the plants a few days before transplanting helps the plants to recover quickly from the check of root disturbance.

Thin out hardy annuals Hardy annuals already sown and growing will need to be thinned out, dwarf kinds to 4in (10cm), the medium ones to 10in (25cm) and vigorous plants to 1½ft (45cm) or more.

Sow biennials Looking forward to next year's spring bedding display, the seeds of many flowers including wallflower, Sweet William, Canterbury bells and pansy can now be sown in a prepared seed bed, although Brompton stock and forget-me-not are best left until the last few days of the month. Sow the seed thinly and in drills if weeds are likely to be a problem, the plants will then be easier to keep clean. Flea beetle can also be a problem with wallflower seedlings and so an application of soil insecticide should be made after sowing the seed to prevent attack.

Plant ornamental gourds Ornamental gourds, with their oddly shaped fruits, make interesting climbers; the plants can be set out in their permanent position during the middle of the month. They will either clamber over raised support or cover the ground but either way should be kept moist at the root.

Keep newly planted shrubs and trees moist Newly planted shrubs and trees should be checked for soil moisture and it is most important that they do not dry out at any stage otherwise the plants will be badly checked and may even die.

Check layered shoots Keep an eye on layered shoots in case they become dislodged. Those already producing roots can be severed from the parent plant but it would be as well to leave them to establish on their own roots before transplanting.

Propagate shrubs This is a good time to propagate shrubs from semi-ripe cuttings: philadelphus, weigela, cotoneaster and honeysuckle are amongst woody plants that can be propagated now. Hydrangea cuttings strike readily from non-flowering shoots. A number of herbaceous plants can also be propagated including arabis, aubrieta, mossy saxifrages, pinks and phlox; *Pulsatilla vulgaris* has fleshy roots that can be used as cuttings. The best way to propagate flag iris and auricula is by division of the rootstock after flowering.

Prune plants after flowering Several plants have now finished flowering and should be pruned to encourage new growth. These include deutzia, weigela, kerria, escallonia, *Clematis montana* and ceanothus; other plants like rhododendron and lilac usually only require dead-heading. Herbaceous plants such as lupins and delphiniums can often be encouraged to flower again on side shoots when the faded main spikes have been removed.

Control weeds in permanently planted areas The more permanent areas of the garden are often encroached upon by difficult weeds over a number of years; the rock garden is a good example and there could be a case for using selective weedkillers in such an area (see page 197).

Stake tall-growing plants Tall-growing plants like chrysanthemums and dahlias should be supported by stakes or canes and twiggy sticks will keep straggly herbaceous perennials up together.

Trim hedges Hedges often receive their first trim of the year during this month and if you find the task something of a chore, consider using a growth regulator to control vigour (see page 199).

LAWN Every effort should be made to keep the grass growing: the lawn is a very important feature of the garden. Mowing needs to be done frequently and during dry spells it is advisable to raise the cutting height so that the sward remaining gives some shade to the grass plants; better root action is also achieved by retaining longer leaves. Removal of the grass box so that clippings are allowed to fly will create a thin mulch to help conserve soil moisture, although clippings should always be removed when plants like annual meadow grass and field woodrush are present.

Irrigate if necessary Irrigation will often be necessary to keep the grass growing during prolonged dry weather and a lawn sprinkler is much more effective than an open-ended hose, but do give a thorough soaking. A well spiked lawn will absorb moisture more readily than one that has a hard surface and so every effort should be made to aerate the lawn with a garden fork, or with a spiking machine on a large lawn, before the dry weather starts.

Control weeds When grass is growing well no doubt weeds are flourishing too and although a few can be dealt with by digging out individually, the method does become a forbidding task when a number are involved. Low-growing weeds, like yellow suckling clover, can often be dealt with by scarifying the lawn immediately before mowing. Selective weedkillers for the lawn are very effective and can be used at any time during good growing weather but should be avoided during drought because they are inclined to damage the grass under such conditions.

Apply fertilizer Use a lawn fertilizer with a high nitrogen content for best results and when a weedkiller is to be used, the fertilizer should be applied a few days before the weedkiller.

Control diseases before they become established A healthy vigorous lawn will usually ward off an attack of disease but it is often necessary to apply a fungicide where diseases gain a foothold.

Trim lawn edges Remember to trim the lawn edges: it really does make all the difference to appearance.

POND Plants establish very quickly in the warm water and those planted last month should be showing signs of healthy growth. Aquatics can still be planted and garden centres have a wide range of plants in stock.

Control pests Watch out for signs of pest attack, particularly on water-lilies which may be infected by midge larvae feeding on the leaves. Water-lily beetle and blackfly can also be a problem and a good way to deal with them is to submerge the leaves for the fish to eat the pests, or they may be sprayed off with clear water.

Top up levels Top up containers with gravel and the water level of the pool can be adjusted by topping up if necessary.

Remove blanket weed Blanket weed is often a problem from now on, particularly in a pool recently constructed or refurbished where dissolved minerals and sunlight, due to the lack of shade from immature plants, abound. The green filaments can be removed to some extent by twisting a stick in the water; alternatively a growth regulating chemical compound (still experimental at the time of writing) shows promise in controlling blanket weed and other encroaching plants including algae.

Keep oxygen levels high Oxygenating plants will help to keep the water well supplied with air provided they have had a chance to establish before fish were reintroduced to the pond; a fountain will do much to keep oxygen levels high enough to prevent the fish from gasping too much.

FRUIT The majority of bush and cane fruits should be netted against birds; do not leave the nets off for too long because fruit is attractive as soon as it begins to turn colour.

Deleaf strawberries Once strawberries have finished cropping cut off all of the leaves and place them, together with the bedding down straw, on the compost heap. When the plants are badly infested by red spider mite it is better to burn straw and leaves on the plant, but take precautions to prevent the fire from getting out of hand. Some cultivars such as 'Red Gauntlet' produce another crop during autumn after this treatment, at least in the south of the country. Where special mats have been used to keep fruit away from the soil, they should be removed before burning off. Strawberry runners should be pegged down to root when new plants are wanted, otherwise they should be removed.

Summer prune gooseberries, red and white currants Gooseberries, red and white currants respond to summer pruning at the end of the month to allow air and light into the plant. Pesticide spraying is more effective and summer pruning also stimulates the plant into producing blossom buds for next spring. Only the side shoots should be pruned now, cutting back to 3 or 5 leaves depending on vigour, the harder pruning being employed when growth is too vigorous.

Tie in new shoots Tie in the new blackberry and loganberry shoots to keep them tidy and free from wind damage; they will make a good deal of new growth from now on and soon become a tangle unless kept under control.

Cut out surplus raspberry canes and control pests Surplus raspberry canes can be removed before they grow too tall so that energy is conserved for those canes to be retained for cropping. Raspberry beetle, and in some years aphids, can be most troublesome and precautions should be taken against them if necessary. Raspberry beetle also gives rise to maggots in the fruit of loganberries and blackberries.

Mulch plants All fruit crops respond favourably to a surface mulch of bulky organic material. This is best applied when the soil is already moist otherwise the mulch is inclined to act more like an umbrella and keeps water away from the surface roots.

Plant alpine strawberries The alpine strawberries raised earlier from seed, or plants purchased from a garden centre, can be planted out now. Spaced 1ft (30cm) apart or planted in a container, these strawberries, although rather small, have a distinctive flavour, are prolific and fruit perpetually over a very long period. Dainty fruits like these make ideal decoration for trifles and other dishes.

Prune outdoor vines Like most fruit plants, the outdoor grape vine responds to summer pruning and there is usually a profusion of buds, many of which will not be required: rub out the surplus and cut back the new shoots that have been made this year to 2ft (60cm). Two shoots growing from the centre of the vine must be left unpruned because these will be trained horizontally in early winter to produce sub laterals to carry next year's crop. Thin out the bunches so that remaining fruit will have a chance to develop properly.

Stop fig trees Fig trees must produce laterals which are given the chance to ripen before autumn and all young laterals on established trees should be pinched back to 5 leaves by the end of the month. Subsequent fruit should then be at the correct stage to overwinter and mature next summer.

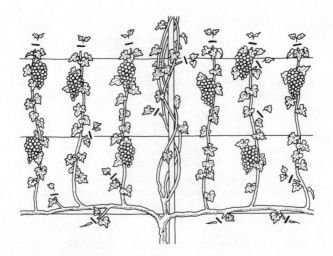

Pruning an outdoor vine: see page 71.

Disbud wall-trained peaches Wall-trained peaches and nectarines should continue to be disbudded and replacement shoots should be tied in. The fruits of peaches in particular should be thinned to approximately 6in (15cm) apart. Any shoots (including those of fan-trained plums and cherries) growing directly towards or outwards from the wall should be removed.

Thin fruit Fruit trees are inclined to set far too much fruit in most years: when excess fruit is allowed to develop on apples, the tree is made susceptible to biennial bearing causing an irregular pattern of too much fruit one year and none the next. This leads to too much vigour and then drastic steps may have to be taken to bring the tree back to a proper cycle. One way to prevent overcropping is to thin out the fruit once it has developed to a certain stage; with apples the stage has been reached with most cultivars towards the end of June. Take care to minimise thinning at that time, however, because there is usually a natural 'June drop' which often takes place in July. It is really only necessary to thin by hand when the crop is very heavy and even then to remove only excess fruits to leave one in each cluster. The same method can be employed for pears; plums are normally thinned first at the beginning of June and then again at the end of the month, if necessary, so that fruit is spaced 2 to 3in (5 to 7.5cm) apart.

Control pests and diseases Continue spraying against pests and diseases and keep weeds and grass under control.

VEGETABLES AND HERBS A critical month for many crops so far as weather is concerned: light soils may dry out severely, particularly those short of humus or with a pan just below the surface. Early potatoes should be checked from time to time and as soon as the tubers are ½in (13mm) in diameter sufficient water should be applied to moisten thoroughly the root run. Runner beans require a moist root run at all times otherwise the flowers tend to drop at the expense of the valuable early crop.

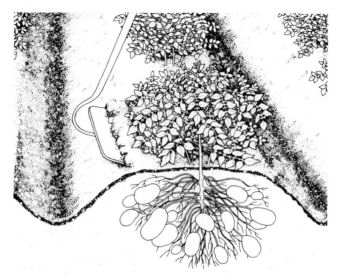

Ridging potatoes: protect potatoes by pulling soil up around the stem.

Ridge potatoes Once the top soil has drained, potatoes may be ridged up after the application of a light fertilizer side dressing. In the case of plants growing without ridging it is only necessary to cover any surface tubers with soil to exclude light which causes them to turn green; any fertilizer applied can be washed in by rain or supplementary irrigation.

Apply fertilizer to established crops The majority of crops, especially those that have been in the ground for any length of time, will benefit from a fertilizer top dressing, watered in if sufficient rain is unlikely to fall within the next day or two. Alternatively, the fertilizer can be hoed into the ground but this needs to be done carefully otherwise surface roots are inclined to be damaged and weed seeds are likely to be brought to the surface to germinate.

Protect cauliflowers Plants benefit from long sunny days but some protection from the sun may be necessary: developing cauliflower curds may be damaged by hot sun and it is worthwhile bending a leaf over the head to provide shade.

Thin seedlings Direct sown crops like salad onions, lettuce and radish should be thinned out at an early stage so that the plants can take up their allocated space without too much competition.

Harvest crops when they are ready Some of the earlier sown crops will now be maturing like kohl-rabi, which should be harvested when it has reached the size of a cricket ball and is still tender. Early sown spinach can be cropped by removing odd leaves from each plant to allow the others to grow on to provide successional crops. Herbs are best gathered on a fine day when they can be more effectively dried and they do appear to freeze better when harvested under such conditions. Peas are at their best when they are young and should be picked over regularly. Japanese onions will now be ready for harvesting and should be used during the summer months because they do not store well for any length of time.

Sow catch crops As vacant ground becomes available no time should be lost in sowing catch crops of quick maturing plants like mustard and cress, turnips, radish and lettuce. A selection of different lettuce cultivars sown thinly in the same drill will tend to mature over a period to stagger cropping.

Sow marrows, swedes and parsley Marrows may be sown in the colder districts using the method suggested in May. There is still time to sow seed of swedes and parsley.

Sow chicory and endive Chicory and endive can be sown out of doors (during the first few days of the month for chicory and at the end for endive) to produce roots for forcing later. Sow the seed in drills ½in (13mm) deep with the rows 1½ft (45cm) apart. The seedlings should be thinned out at an early stage so that the young plants are spaced 6in (15cm) apart. Allowed to mature where they are sown, chicory produces a heart similar to lettuce and will be ready for harvesting in the autumn.

Chicory grown for forcing is produced in much the same way except that it is thinned to 8in (20cm) between plants and the leaves allowed to die down before the roots are lifted in November. Endive is blanched when the plants are fully grown in autumn. The simplest way to blanch is to cover the plants with up-turned flowerpots with the drainage holes covered up – complete darkness is essential for best results. Neither chicory nor endive should ever go short of water during the growing season otherwise they will run up to flower prematurely.

Sow beetroot, carrots and beans Other crops suitable for sowing this month include maincrop carrots and beetroot, French and runner beans.

Plant outdoor tomatoes and other tender plants It is rather unlikely that frost severe enough to damage plants will occur after the middle of the month and so outdoor tomatoes may be planted after hardening off. Bush types are popular and a useful method is to plant through holes made in black polythene layed flat over the prepared soil; the polythene acts as a mulch to retain soil moisture and attracts a considerable degree of warmth. Aubergines, sweet peppers and ridge cucumbers can be grown in the same way. Sweet corn can be planted if this was not done in May.

Plant winter greens Winter greens sown earlier will now be at the stage when they can be planted in their permanent quarters. Should it prove necessary to buy plants, only those raised in peat-based compost should be purchased otherwise there is every chance of importing soil-borne club-root disease. Brassicas require firm soil in good heart with a pH around neutral to do well. A selection of winter greens should include Brussels sprouts, broccoli (including purple sprouting), kale and savoy cabbages. Different cultivars usually need various spacings as recommended on the seed packet.

Plant celery Self-blanching celery planted out on the flat allowing a 9in (23cm) spacing each way should be watered well in and then kept uniformly moist. These plants will mature during late summer and early autumn to be followed by the crop planted in trenches prepared earlier.

Plant leeks The ideal stage for planting leeks is when the stems have reached the thickness of a pencil. Make holes in the ground with a dibber 6in (15cm) apart so that when the plant is dropped in the base of the leaves is at ground level; the root area is then covered by soil which trickles in as the hole is filled with water.

Finish cutting asparagus Finish cropping asparagus during the third week of the month to allow the fern to grow and produce food to pass down to the rootstock for next year's crop. Asparagus beetle usually makes an appearance at this time and precautions should be taken before eggs hatch.

Control pea midge Pea midge adults emerge from the soil at the beginning of the month to lay eggs around the flower buds; the small maggots tunnel into the developing flower and make it sterile with subsequent crop loss.

Stop broad beans Pinch out the tops of broad bean plants to deter an attack by black fly. This also has the added advantage that crops mature sooner.

Control pests and diseases Other pests to look for this month include cabbage white butterflies and leaf miners in celery and parsnips. Leeks are sometimes prone to rust unless precautions are taken by spraying a fungicide before the disease appears.

Water the compost heap When checking soil moisture for growing crops, do not forget the compost heap which has a tendency to dry out.

GREENHOUSE With the warmer weather there is a need for more ventilation but guard against too great a drop in temperature at the beginning of the month when nights can still be cold.

The greenhouse atmosphere will be much improved after damping down the path, which should ideally be done mid-morning and again mid-day. At the same time spray over tomatoes, cucumbers, melons and peaches; orchids and other ornamental plants will also benefit unless they have hairy or otherwise delicate leaves.

Tend freesias Conditions for freesia plants depend very much on whether they have been raised from seed sown during spring or corms saved from plants that have finished flowering. Seedlings should be kept as cool as possible, in fact the best place for them is in a shady spot out of doors; corms, on the other hand, produce better and earlier flowers when they are kept hot and humid. Freesia corms can now be removed from the old potting compost, cleaned and stored in the greenhouse to await planting next month. Seedling plants standing out of doors will be housed during autumn and in the meantime should be kept moist and given a liquid feed once a week.

Pot on plants Carefully knock out the root ball from plants growing in pots and check progress: as soon as the existing pot is full of roots, pot on into a size larger. *Solanum capsicastrum*, ornamental pepper, and cyclamen from seed sown earlier may well need potting on and in any case should be stood out in the frame for the summer until rehousing in autumn. Remember to keep the corm half uncovered when potting on cyclamen otherwise inferior growth will result. Damp the plants over with water occasionally to freshen them up and help set the flowers of those which produce ornamental fruit.

Feed plants Ornamental plants including perpetual-flowering carnations respond to feeding during the summer months with fertilizer containing equal proportions of nitrogen and potash: liquid Growmore is ideal and is also satisfactory for cucumbers and the grape vine. Tomatoes, however, require much more potash than nitrogen and so a tomato fertilizer containing magnesium as well as nitrogen, phosphate and potash should be used.

Trim plants Plants are beginning to grow very quickly now and every effort should be made to keep one step ahead: side shoots on tomato plants are best rubbed out as soon as they can be handled otherwise the crop will suffer; lateral shoots of cucumber should be stopped one leaf beyond the first fruit that develops on the shoot. Fig shoots should be stopped after five leaves and fan-trained peach trees need attention by rubbing out shoots that grow directly outwards from the wall or towards it. Although leading shoots on young peach and nectarine trees may be allowed to grow up to 15in (38cm) long before stopping, side shoots should be pinched at five leaves; the only exception is when a fruiting stem needs to be replaced after harvest when a shoot from the base of that stem is allowed to grow to 15in (38cm).

Stop plants and disbud perpetual-flowering carnations Continue to disbud perpetual-flowering carnations and remove side shoots from the uppermost five leaf joints. This may look drastic at the time but will provide suitable length stems for cutting. Young carnation plants should be given another stop to encourage more lateral growth. Coleus plants grown from cuttings are making good growth and they should be stopped when the main stem has reached 6in (15cm). Mid-season and late-flowering chrysanthemums spending the summer months outside in pots should be given their final stop by the end of the month.

Propagate cinerarias and violas Whilst seeds and cuttings propagated earlier are now ready for potting, a further sowing of cineraria will produce plants to flower next spring. Take viola cuttings 2in (5cm) long.

Plant out forced strawberries Strawberries forced in pots have now finished cropping and may be planted out in the open. This will make room for the alpine strawberries sown earlier and now ready for potting off.

Thin grape bunches and melons Bunches of grapes are swelling rapidly and, although somewhat tedious, it is advisable to thin out the berries with a pair of nail scissors: the fruit is then less prone to disease and is much larger than when left unthinned. Melons are inclined to suffer from overcropping too and it seldom pays to let more than four fruits mature on the same plant.

Control pests Whitefly and red spider mite tend to increase at an alarming rate in the higher temperatures now prevailing. Whitefly is comparatively easy to control but red spider mite has produced strains resistant to many acaricides, in which case it is worth trying biological control.

July

FLOWERS, TREES AND SHRUBS Take every opportunity to visit local gardens to see which plants do well in the area. July is a good month to plan and prepare new flower borders for planting in autumn. Cultivations should be thorough to remove perennial weeds including couch grass which can be a real problem amongst perennial plants. Annual weeds should be forked out or killed off with a contact herbicide which becomes inactive as soon as it touches the soil, otherwise weed growth dug in now will probably grow up again later.

Cut and trim sweet peas Sweet peas need to be cut regularly to stimulate new flower buds: as soon as faded flowers begin to produce pods subsequent flower quality falls off at an alarming rate. The plants should be kept moist at the root too and they will benefit from a mulch of bulky organic material placed on the soil surface if not already done. Continue to remove side shoots and tendrils to conserve energy. Cordon sweet peas have reached the height where they should now be layered. Release the plant from its support and lower to the ground and then train the plant up another support 4ft (1.2m) away; then repeat with the next plant and so on.

Dead-head roses and other plants Roses and other flowers should be dead-headed as the blossom fades, unless, of course, fruit or seed heads are required. Some gardeners leave spent hydrangea heads on the plant to provide frost protection in the winter but it is doubtful whether the habit has much practical value. Herbaceous perennials repeat their flowering over a much longer period when stems are removed as flowers fade.

Cut and dry everlasting flowers Everlasting flowers like helichrysum and statice are at the optimum stage for cutting and drying. Choose a warm dry day for the job and tie the cut stems together loosely. They can then be suspended upside down from the shed roof.

Stake, disbud and rogue dahlias and early chrysanthemums Dahlia and chrysanthemum stems are likely to be snapped off by high winds and rain especially when they are carrying large flowers. Tie the shoots to their supports before they have grown too long to prevent this happening. It is worth checking for abnormal growth at the same time so that virus-infected plants can be removed before sucking insects transmit the disease to other plants. When large flowers are required, disbud at an early stage as soon as the secondary buds can be removed without damaging the central flower bud. Side shoots should be removed at the same time unless sprays are being grown.

Prune early summer-flowering shrubs Prune philadelphus and other early summer-flowering shrubs by cutting out the overcrowded spent wood. This will allow the new shoots plenty of room to develop and ripen to produce blossom next year. Some plants are inclined to produce a second flush of flowers in the same year – wisteria is a good example – and so it is advisable to delay summer pruning until the middle of the month to see which of the current season's growth is going to produce flowers. Shoots that are not going to produce the second flush should then be shortened back to 5 leaves so that bud initiation commences to ensure flowering next year. Summer pruning of roses really consists of cutting the stems long enough – down to the first strong lateral shoot or plump bud.

Keep spring-flowering shrubs moist July is a vital month for plants that flower during early spring and on no account should they lack moisture at the root. Viburnums and camellias are notorious for their shyness in flowering because flower buds are unable to develop properly under drought conditions.

Propagate border carnations and pinks Border carnations and pinks can be propagated by layering this mouth, a method many gardeners find more successful than by taking pipings.

Take soft cuttings of shrubs Soft cuttings can be taken of choisya, hebes, hydrangea, *Hibiscus syriacus*, olearia and osmanthus. Camellias often do better when taken as semi-ripe cuttings with a heel.

Lift and divide bearded irises Bearded irises that have finished flowering can be lifted and divided when they have remained in the same position for three years. Select rhizomes on the outside of the colony for replanting. Cut them away with a sharp knife and replant so that the top half is above soil level. Old leaves may be removed completely and the green leaves should be shortened to avoid wind rock and excessive transpiration. Irises revel in sunshine and well drained soil. The leaves of *Iris unguicularis* should be shortened by cutting back at least half way. This will tidy the clump and help to initiate flowers that will be at their best during next winter and spring.

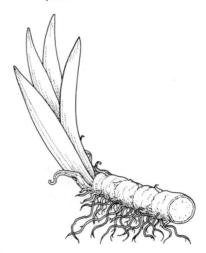

A division of an iris rhizome
ready for replanting.

Transplant biennials Biennial plants like wallflowers and Sweet William sown last month should be transplanted into nursery beds when they are large enough to handle. Plants required for cutting for indoor decoration may be sown in drills where they are to mature during the end of this month and eventually thinned out. Sow polyanthus in a shady cool border for flowering next year.

Plant autumn-flowering bulbs Autumn-flowering bulbs make a fine show and can be planted now. *Amaryllis belladonna* and the various autumn crocus are particularly good; favoured gardens in a sheltered spot should not be without *Nerine bowdenii*, which makes a most attractive plant. Planting depth is critical and the tip of the bulb should be just below the soil surface.

Feed established plants Plants in full growth often need a helping hand at this time of the year and it is a good plan to sprinkle rose fertilizer around the bushes. The same fertilizer can be used for other ornamental plants and, unless the weather is showery, the fertilizer should be hoed or watered into the soil.

Control pests and diseases Watch out for pests and diseases attacking plants, especially mildew on Michaelmas daisy, spiraea and other plants, black spot and mildew on roses, rust on antirrhinum, thrips on gladioli and aphids and earwigs on most soft growth. Ants can be a particular pest during the warm weather.

LAWN Turf can dry out surprisingly fast during this month, which is usually the hottest of the year. Irrigation with the lawn sprinkler may be necessary and a quick-acting lawn tonic type of fertilizer will help to keep the grass looking attractive.

Control weeds Do not cut the grass too short and avoid scalping, otherwise weeds and moss will be given the opportunity to establish. Certain weeds like clover, plantain, yarrow and chickweed often present themselves now and no time should be lost in applying a selective weedkiller, provided the turf is not suffering from drought. New lawns should by now have been cleared of annual weeds through continuous mowing and where establishment has been good, perennial weeds can be controlled by selective weed-killer. The lawn may, however, still be sensitive to some formulations and so the manufacturer's label instructions should, of course, be followed carefully.

Prepare for new lawn Preparations can now be made for the establishment of a new lawn in autumn: dig over the site to remove debris. This is of particular importance so far as a new building site is concerned. Deep-rooted weeds should be removed and where weed growth is significant, it is a good idea to treat the area with a fast-acting contact weedkiller before an attempt is made to cultivate. Finally rake over the area and allow it to settle for a few weeks. This will give residual weed seeds time to germinate and be dealt with.

POND Substantial water loss can occur this month and although it has the effect of cooling the pond somewhat, the water level should be brought back to normal at every opportunity: a hose fitted with a rose spray is ideal because the water droplets pick up oxygen as they pass through the air.

Thin out oxygenating plants Fish graze on oxygenating plants but if the foliage has become overgrown, it would be as well to thin out some of the growth carefully so that water snails, fish spawn and small fry are not removed at the same time. Blanket weed can be a problem, especially where cultivated plants have not established properly, and should be dealt with as suggested last month.

Remove excess water-lily leaves Water-lily pads of the more vigorous cultivars which are overlapping flowers can be cut away but do not remove too many of the leaves at one time.

Control pests Plant pests can often be dealt with by submerging the leaves and allowing the fish to deal with them but the larger beetles are more effectively removed by netting.

FRUIT July is the month when most of the soft fruit is harvested. Strawberries grown in the open will finish by the end of the month and beds that have been established for three years and those infected by virus should first be flamed over and then dug up. It is then advisable to plant a different crop on the site rather than replant with strawberries, so that diseases such as red core may be avoided; certain eelworms can also become a problem when strawberries are grown continuously for a number of years in the same area.

Young beds of strawberries should also be flamed over or defoliated by

Above: Strawberry 'Cambridge Favourite'. *Below*: A vegetable garden in full production.

cutting off the leaves unless the plants are being used to produce runners, when an application of general insecticide is all that is required if red spider mites or greenfly are present.

Prune black currants Black currant bushes may be pruned immediately after the fruit has been harvested by cutting out some of the fruited wood. Some cultivars produce abundant new shoots from ground level so that complete spent stems may be removed, otherwise cut back the fruited wood to where a strong lateral shoot emerges low down. Aim to remove at least one-third of the wood each year so that the plant is encouraged to produce sufficient new growth to fruit the following season. Where space permits and to facilitate picking, the bushes can be divided up so that half of the plants produce fruit one year and the other set of plants produce fruit the following year. This is achieved by cutting away all growth at harvesting time and new shoots will be made next year to fruit the following year. Few gardens are large enough for this system, however, and it is more usual to crop each plant every year.

Prune cane fruits after harvesting Cultivated blackberries, loganberries and summer-fruiting raspberries should all be pruned as soon as the crop is harvested. This is a simple procedure in that all of the old fruiting canes are cut out completely to soil level and the new growths are tied in to replace the old. These new growths will then crop next year.

Propagate blackberries and loganberries Blackberries growing in less favourable areas will not be ripe until later and should be sprayed to control raspberry beetle. When new plants are required, tips of blackberry and loganberry shoots can be buried 6in (15cm) below the soil towards the end of the month. The layered tips will eventually produce roots and a shoot and they may then be severed from the parent plant and transplanted.

Thin out apples Top fruit will not yet be fit for harvesting except very early apple and plum cultivars, although final thinning of apples should be completed by the end of the month and heavily laden branches should be supported by tying strong string from the branch to a higher position on the tree stake or main stem. Young plum and damson trees may be supported in the same way although older ones will need to be propped up with poles. Damaged branches are often difficult to repair and silver leaf disease may gain entry through any wounds that are made.

Check tree ties Now that considerable growth has been made during the year, it is as well to check tree ties and loosen them if necessary to avoid cutting into the stem: severe constriction can eventually lead to the death of the tree.

Summer prune Summer pruning of apples and pears can begin when the current season's shoots have become firm at the base. This operation should

The plants in this well filled conservatory include calceolaria, impatiens, primula, cineraria and pelargoniums.

be delayed if the base of the shoots is still green and soft, otherwise it will be necessary to carry out further pruning when the shoots regrow later. Restricted forms of apples and pears are summer pruned by reducing the current season's wood by one-half; any shoots less than 9in (23cm) long are left unpruned. So far as cordons are concerned, the shoots growing out from the main stem are cut back to 3 leaves beyond the basal cluster, and those from existing side shoots to one leaf. Any subsequent growth during the year is cut back to one leaf.

Tie in new fig shoots Fig tree shoots that have grown since pruning before the end of last month should be tied in to avoid damage and no further pruning should be carried out until the tree is dormant and then not until March.

Prune fan-trained trees Prune fan-trained plums and sweet cherries by shortening the current season's wood by one-third but do not touch the leaders. Continue to pinch out the tips of fan-trained peach and cherry side shoots at 5 leaves and remove those growing directly outwards or in towards the wall; regrowth from those shoots stopped earlier should be pinched back to one leaf. Leave the leaders unpruned unless they grow beyond 15in (38cm); one shoot at the base of the fruiting lateral should also be left unpruned.

Protect fruits from birds Netting protecting soft fruit as it ripened should now be used for the tree fruits: cherries and peaches are particularly prone to bird damage.

Watch out for pests Codling moth is still likely to be a problem on apples and so a further preventive spray should be given, although mildew and scab sprays may be discontinued after the middle of the month. Woolly aphid can be severe in some seasons, sucking sap and causing nodules to form on the current season's wood. Check plum trees for silver leaf disease and remove any infected branches.

Thin out grape bunches Grape vines should be making good progress and provided growth has been regular, no sign of mildew should be apparent. Continue pruning; keep the soil moist without being too wet and apply a mulch if that has not already been done. Fruit will be at a stage where thinning is beneficial. Remove every other berry with a pair of pointed scissors.

VEGETABLES AND HERBS Several of the crops we grow in the vegetable garden originate from warmer climates and they appreciate the higher temperatures encountered this month.

Stop and water tomatoes Tomatoes, for example, make a good deal of growth and as soon as they have produced three or four flower trusses the plants should be stopped by pinching out the growing tip one leaf beyond the highest flower truss. Tie the plant to its support and damp over with clear water each day to help set the fruit. Continue to remove side shoots except from bush cultivars. Tomatoes, especially those growing in containers (including growing bags), can take up a considerable amount of water during warm sunny weather and they should never be allowed to go dry at the root.

Mulch bush tomatoes Bush-growing tomatoes do not require stopping due to their habit of growth. Plants growing directly in the soil will benefit from mulching with straw to keep the fruit away from the ground; straw also acts as surface drainage in case of prolonged wet weather when fruit and leaves of bush tomatoes are liable to rot.

Mulch runner beans Runner beans are thirsty plants too and although roots will by now have established well down into the humus incorporated in the trench, extra moisture may be required in dry seasons particularly when the soil is light and free draining. A mulch of black polythene or bulky organic material placed over damp soil after irrigating will do much to conserve moisture and encourage a good crop. When the growth reaches the top of its support, pinch out the growing tips so that the crop develops in good time.

Dry off shallots and Japanese onions Shallots have now made sufficient growth and should be lifted carefully with a garden fork to dry off and ripen. Onions grown from sets planted last autumn and Japanese seed-grown crops are also ready for lifting and, provided they are ripened well, should keep until Christmas. Onions being grown for winter storage should be given their last fertilizer top dressing as excessive nitrogen given beyond the end of the month will encourage them to develop thick necks and have poor keeping quality.

Water and feed marrows Gather courgettes when they are young and before they have developed into marrows; they are so prolific when grown that way that it may be necessary to chop them up for the freezer. Alternatively, they can be grown on into marrows and a visit to the local horticultural society's summer show this month will demonstrate how large marrows can grow. Keep them well watered, feed them every seven to ten days. It is hardly necessary to hand pollinate at this time of the year due to the number of insects visiting the garden, but should the weather turn cold and wet, it would be as well to hand pollinate by brushing male flowers over the female flowers to be sure of fruit development.

Plant winter greens The planting of winter greens should be completed by the middle of the month otherwise there will not be time for them to establish to make worthwhile crops.

Sow spinach beet Spinach beet can still be sown up to the middle of the month; make the drills 1in (2.5cm) deep and space them 1½ft (45cm) apart. Thin the seedlings to 6in (15cm) apart as soon as they can be handled. The leaves will be ready for harvesting during late autumn and through the winter.

Sow winter spinach Winter spinach can be sown at the end of this month or the beginning of next; hoe off any weeds present and then rake in general fertilizer. The drills should be 1in (2.5cm) deep and spaced 1ft (30cm) apart.

Thin out seedlings to 3in (7.5cm) and then remove alternate plants three or four weeks later for use in the kitchen.

Sow turnips An early cultivar of turnip for pulling young can be sown during the first week of the month but after that time it is better to sow the late cultivars suitable for winter storage. Ground manured for the previous crop is ideal with the addition of general fertilizer lightly forked or raked into the surface. Sow the seed thinly in drills ¾in (19mm) deep spaced 15in (38cm) apart.

Sow endive Endive sown during the month will mature for autumn salads. Sow the seed in drills ½in (13mm) deep spaced 1ft (30cm) apart and thin the young plants to 1ft (30cm) apart when they have made one or two true leaves.

Earth up celery Maincrop celery growing in trenches and kept well watered will now be ready for earthing up. First remove any side shoots that are growing and then loosely tie the stalks just below the leaves. Newspaper or brown paper wrapped around the plant will keep soil away from the heart. Next scatter slug pellets around the soil and gradually fill in the trench up to one-third of the height of the stalks. Further earthing up can take place every three weeks until the stalks are covered completely up to the leaves.

Sow peas Round seeded peas sown this month will just have time to mature this season and it pays to sow the seed in single drills 2 to 3in (5 to 7.5cm) deep and spacing the seeds 3in (7.5cm) apart along the drill.

Sow spring cabbage in northern areas Spring cabbage is due to be sown at the middle of the month in northern areas and towards the end of this month or the beginning of next in the south. The seed may be sown thinly in rows 6in (15cm) apart for transplanting later.

Sow herbs Further sowings of parsley, chervil and dill can be made this month.

Sow carrots It is not too late to sow carrots to provide succulent roots for the autumn. Areas badly infested by carrot fly rely on this late crop because the pest is less likely to be so troublesome at this late stage.

Control pests and diseases Cabbage root fly can, however, still be a problem, not so much attacking the root system as the top of the plant, especially in Brussels sprouts and cauliflower. The insecticides used against cabbage cater-pillar will also control cabbage root fly at this time.

Celery fly also attacks parsnips and this crop should be inspected for the tell-tale white spots and blotches in the leaf.

Celery leaf spot and potato blight can be most destructive in some years and it pays to apply a preventive fungicide spray now.

GREENHOUSE Copious amounts of water will be necessary to keep large plants happy – mature tomato plants, for example, will be looking for ½gal (2.25l) of water each on a long bright day. Plants in pots dry out quickly as well and this is where some form of automatic watering system comes into its own. Do not forget to feed the plants in the greenhouse, or those spending the summer months out of doors: chrysanthemums in pots outside on the standing ground should be fed and given a further shallow top dressing with potting compost.

Take cuttings of fuchsias Fuchsias make ideal plants for growing in the greenhouse and outside. Soft tip cuttings 2in (5cm) long taken during this month and inserted into well drained compost will soon root and the stems will be sufficiently firm to overwinter in the greenhouse. These early cuttings make good sized plants to train as standards and for use in hanging baskets.

Take coleus cuttings and remove flower buds from mature plants Coleus plants can also be grown as standards and cuttings may be taken now for that purpose. Mature plants are producing flower buds and these should always be removed before they develop too far: the flowers are insignificant and tend to make the plants woody so that they become leggy without producing as many side shoots.

Sow calceolaria, mignonette and cacti seed Calceolaria seed sown during the month will produce plants to flower next spring when the brightly coloured flowers will be much appreciated. Mignonette seed can also be sown for winter-flowering pot plants. Other seed which may be sown this month include the various types of cacti.

Start poinsettias Poinsettias should now be revived from their rest by watering the compost and then giving a weak liquid feed. Placed on the bench they will soon begin active growth and the resulting shoots may be taken as soft tip cuttings.

Pot up late struck chrysanthemum cuttings Rooted cuttings of spray-type late-flowering chrysanthemums are available from some nurseries now and, potted up three to a 9in (23cm) pot, will make useful cut flowers for late autumn and winter. Cuttings taken in late winter or early spring need to be grown without check to make the best long-term plant, and this late struck cutting method overcomes many of the problems encountered.

Thin grapes and stop shoots Grapes should be given a final thinning and sub-lateral shoots continue to be stopped at one new leaf.

Train tomatoes Tomato plants carrying a heavy crop of fruit may possibly be going thin in the top, especially when the weather is bright and hot. This is an indication that nitrogen is deficient and the fertilizer should be changed to one containing extra nitrogen for two or three weeks. Side shoots will then again develop more quickly and should be removed at an early stage. Remove leaves from the plant by snapping upwards from the base of the stalk but do not remove leaves higher than the truss that is beginning to ripen.

Harvest cucumbers Continue to stop cucumber lateral shoots and cut fruit when it is moderately young: very mature fruit tends to impede further crop production and it is better to harvest regardless of whether fruit is required for immediate use or not.

Support melon fruits Early sown melons in the greenhouse are developing well and the fruits should be supported by being suspended in nets. Melons in the frame should be hand pollinated by rubbing a male flower over the female (a flower with small round fruit attached is the female) and it is advisable to restrict the crop to 3 or 4 similar sized fruits on each plant.

Damp down stone fruit plants after fruit is picked Growth of stone fruit trees will slow down as the fruit ripens and then when the crop is harvested daily spraying overhead with clear water may be restarted. Continue to damp down paths and borders, at least once each day and more frequently if possible on bright sunny days.

Watch for pests and diseases Whitefly can be a problem and should be dealt with before it gets out of hand. If grey mould puts in an appearance it suggests that ventilation is not as good as it should be, because the air is stagnant and too humid. Lack of ventilation together with dry roots causes mildew to attack plants, particularly grapes which are rather prone to the disease under such conditions. Fungicides can be used but prevention by cultural control is the best method of solving the problem.

Move on plants before they spoil Young seedlings should be pricked out or potted off before they get too large and plants requiring potting on will be far more healthy when the work is carried out at the correct stage of growth.

Disbud perpetual-flowering carnations Perpetual-flowering carnation flower buds develop very quickly during these long days and need disbudding at an early stage, unless they are being grown as sprays. No more stopping of shoots should take place otherwise plants will not have time to initiate and develop sufficient flowers for the winter period. Young plants may be given their first stop if that has not already been done.

Night ventilation Leave the ventilators open a chink at night to allow some air movement.

August

FLOWERS, TREES AND SHRUBS Daytime temperature can still be high during this month and yet the longer nights often bring cool freshness or even cold air, especially in the north. Chrysanthemum enthusiasts have a long held belief that these conditions promote rapid bud development and so disbudding should be kept up to date for the largest blooms. The same conditions can, however, cause flowers to damp off, especially when thunderstorms occur as they often do now. Incurves and some decorative-type early chrysanthemum blooms are liable to hold a good deal of water and it is prudent to cut the flowers before they are fully open when they are grown as cut flowers.

Trap earwigs Large-flowered dahlias are also prone to rain damage and earwigs are particularly active at this time: traps made from rolled up newspaper or upturned flowerpots filled with straw are attractive to them and since the pests tend to fly into the plant, any insecticide is inclined to be ineffective unless a residual spray is used.

Disbud dahlias and chrysanthemums and tie in stems Continue to disbud dahlias and chrysanthemums and keep them watered during dry periods. Dahlias should still receive fertilizer until the end of the month because they will continue to flower until the frosts cut them down. Keep stems tied in to prevent damage by the wind which can be very strong particularly towards the end of the month. Now is a good time to label plants to be kept for stock and take the opportunity to remove any showing symptoms of virus disease.

Tend to roses Roses will be happy enough to draw on residual fertilizer in the soil applied earlier in the year: any further application would only lead to soft growth that may not mature and stand up to winter conditions. Extra plants can be raised by taking cuttings during this month and inserting them in well drained soil: they will soon take root provided the soil is kept moist without being too wet. Greenfly, black spot and mildew can still be a problem and the routine spraying should be maintained. Continue dead-heading unless heps are required and remove any late suckers that have appeared.

Prune ramblers Ramblers can be pruned when they have finished flowering: lay all of the shoots on the ground and cut out all of those that have flowered. Stems produced this year will flower next year. Some cultivars are rather shy to produce new stems and so some of the old wood should be saved.

Cut back herbaceous plants Remove dead flower heads from herbaceous plants, and any plants that are not showing basal growth by the end of the month should be cut back. Those plants that have finished flowering can be tidied up by removing the twiggy supports and shortening weak straggly stems.

Renovate borders August is a good month for renovating herbaceous borders. Fork them over to remove weeds and lift and divide any congested plants that have been established for three years or more. Later-flowering bearded irises can be lifted and divided by using the outer rhizomes. Spaces may be left for any new plants and it is as well to order them early so that they may be planted in good time before heavy soil becomes unworkable due to autumn rain. Remember that three plants of a kind planted in a group make an effective display more quickly than a single plant.

Plant lilies Lilies are amongst the most fragrant and colourful flowers. Bulbs do need to be planted as soon as they are available and no time should be lost in planting the Madonna lily (*Lilium candidum*). Some lily plants produce little bulbils between stem and leaf; these bulbils should now come away at the touch of a finger and they may be boxed up in John Innes potting compost No 1. Home-saved seed can also be sown now in seed trays to germinate next spring. The young plants will take up to three years to flower but it is a very good way of building up a collection.

When planting lily bulbs place them on a thin layer of sand to help prevent rotting.

Sever layered carnations Border carnations layered earlier may by now have produced new roots and if so the layered plant may be severed from the parent. Leave the new plant undisturbed for a further month before transplanting in well drained soil.

Plant bulbs Plant spring-flowering bulbs by the end of the month if possible; those giving a long display include snowdrop, snowflake, winter aconite, crocus, chionodoxa, daffodils, hyacinths, tulips and fritillaria. Bulbous irises are well worth growing and can be planted now. Autumn-flowering bulbs which should be planted without delay include *Nerine bowdenii*, colchicum, *Sternbergia lutea* and *Zephyranthes candida*. Established and congested beds of the autumn crocus will benefit from dividing during the month.

Reprune wisteria, clip lavender and box Wisteria shoots that have regrown since summer pruning can be shortened to one leaf and shrubs that have finished flowering may be pruned as the flowers fade by shortening the spent wood and thinning out old unproductive wood. Clip over lavender but take care not to cut into old wood; some of the prunings may be used as cuttings if new plants are required. Lavender makes a very attractive edging plant. Box is also attractive when grown in the same way and can be clipped now to produce propagating material: cuttings with a heel tend to root more readily.

Dead-head hydrangeas The majority of hydrangeas will have finished flowering now and can be dead-headed back to the first fat bud.

Propagate shrubs Shrubs that can be propagated from cuttings taken this month include aucuba, buddleia, berberis, ceanothus, cotoneaster, escallonia, deutzia, garrya, hibiscus, hypericum, lonicera, ilex, kalmia, olearia, ribes, rubus, philadelphus and *Viburnum tinus*. Rhododendrons and azaleas can also be propagated but the success rate is inclined to be low by the cutting method and so layering should be carried out using low-growing shoots.

Take cuttings of pelargoniums Extra and replacement plants can be produced by taking cuttings of pelargoniums to overwinter in frost-free conditions, although now that the zonal kinds can be raised so easily from seed it may be more convenient to avoid the overwintering routine by sowing seed early next year in heat. On the other hand, cuttings taken now should provide plants large enough to 'top' in the spring to produce yet more plants. Watch out for rust and black leg disease and avoid propagating from any plants that are infected.

Plant biennials and perennials Polyanthus sown earlier should be transplanted in a shady moist border when the young plants are large enough to handle. Biennials and other perennial plants can also be planted in their permanent position, or in nursery beds for planting when the border is vacant during late autumn or next spring.

Sow hardy annuals for an early show A really early show next spring can be achieved by sowing some hardy annuals now; cloches will need to be used in all but mild districts and even then the plants are unlikely to survive a hard winter. Try sowing subjects like alyssum, agrostemma, calendula, candytuft, clarkia, cornflower, echium, eschscholzia, godetia, larkspur, nigella and sweet sultan.

Harvest gourds Ornamental gourds will now be firm to the touch and may be harvested during fine dry weather for use as an ornamental winter decoration in the home.

LAWN Grass growth tends to slow down somewhat as the nights lengthen, a time when, unfortunately, moss begins to gain a foothold, especially when feeding has been neglected, and drought or some other factor has reduced turf vigour. This is really the last chance to apply a nitrogen top dressing and a useful way to achieve rapid uptake is to use one of the lawn tonics based on soluble quick-acting nitrogen. Apart from moss, corticium red thread disease is likely to be a significant problem where nitrogen is deficient. Areas below trees are particularly prone to low nitrogen level and the shade cast by trees and other objects can lead to lack of vigour. Consider using one of the dwarf rye grass mixtures for re-seeding such areas: they appear to tolerate shade better than other species.

Sow new lawns The dwarf rye grasses, although reasonably fine and attractive, are ideal for sowing in areas that are likely to be well worn and should be considered when sowing a new lawn towards the end of the month. A rate of 1oz per sq yd (34g per m^2) should be sufficient for a new lawn with half that quantity for oversowing bare or worn areas in an existing lawn. Fertilizer should be applied 7 to 10 days before sowing and the new site can be cleared of annual weeds by applying a contact herbicide which becomes inactive as it touches the soil. Turves can also be laid during this month and the same thorough site preparation should be given for them as for seed.

Remove worm casts Worm casts can lead to problems at this time of the year, particularly when the soil is alkaline. Casts are best removed when they are dry using a garden cane or brush. Left on the surface, worm casts tend to make the lawn very uneven, causing problems with mowing, and they bring up weed seeds to germinate on the bare patch which is often smeared as the cast is trodden on. Insecticides could be used to control worms but that does seem rather destructive for a creature that otherwise helps a good deal with soil drainage.

Control weeds There is still time to control broad-leaved weeds with a selective herbicide provided the grass is not under stress due to drought.

Spike and top dress August is a good month to spike and top dress the lawn with compost brushed or luted into the surface; use only enough compost to leave a bare ¼in (6mm) depth on the lawn.

Mow or use a growth retardant Do not forget to cut the lawn reasonably short before going away on holiday and if arrangements can be made to have it cut whilst away, so much the better; alternatively one of the growth retardants may be used to keep the lawn short (see page 199).

POND Blanket weed and the lack of oxygen are likely to be the problems, if any, encountered this month. The remedies for both were given last month. Some thinning of aquatic plants may still be necessary or, on the other hand, plants may not be giving sufficient shade for the fish. In that case polystyrene tiles make very efficient sun shades when they are floated on the surface of the water, not only to provide shade but to give temporary hiding for the fish.

Continue to feed fish Fish should continue to be fed and they appreciate the occasional feed of ant eggs – there is usually the odd nest to be found in the garden. Although regular feeding is important the fish should clear all that is given within ten minutes.

Remove leaves and other debris Remove dead evergreen shrub leaves that tend to fall at this time of the year and other debris from the water before it has a chance to sink to the bottom.

FRUIT Harvesting fruit will be the main occupation this month; depending on cultivar and garden location cane fruit like raspberries, loganberries and blackberries will be ready. As soon as the crop has been picked, prune out old fruited wood and tie in the current season's growth to fruit next year; choose the evening after a hot day if possible when the shoots are not so brittle and less inclined to snap at the end. When strawberries have finished cropping, remove the leaves unless young plants are being produced by runners; straw or mats should also be removed.

Gooseberries, black, red and white currants should be picked when ready and not left on the plants too long so that they spoil. Black currants may be pruned as suggested last month.

Harvest top fruit Some top fruit will also be ready to harvest depending on cultivar grown: apples, pears, cherries, nectarines, peaches, damsons, figs and plums should all be checked for maturity. Apples are ready to pick when the fruit comes away from the tree without difficulty: lift the apple gently and if the stalk snaps away without effort, the fruit is ripe enough for harvesting. Do not be too impatient because fruit picked before it is at the correct stage will never reach its full potential off the tree; conversely, fruit left too long on the tree, particularly early cultivars, may become woolly and keeping quality may be impaired. This is not so important with very late cultivars which may be left on the tree until after leaf fall in sheltered gardens.

Stagger picking Not all of the fruit on a tree will mature at the same time: on large old trees the harvesting may be spread over three weeks. The fruit at the top of the tree is usually ready first of all and every care should be taken when using ladders or steps to ensure that they are positioned properly to avoid accidental damage to oneself and the tree. Take care to handle the fruit gently and place it carefully in a basket or bucket. The same principles apply to pears, except that early cultivars are better for picking green and hard otherwise if left on the tree for too long they tend to ripen unevenly. Again, very late cultivars should be left on the tree as long as possible.

Cut cherry stems with scissors Cherries may remain on the tree until they are fully ripe; unfortunately they do not keep well once picked. Cut the stems away with scissors otherwise damage caused to the tree may introduce infection.

Harvest figs, peaches and nectarines Figs must be left on the tree until they are perfectly ripe otherwise they are not worth eating. Peaches and nectarines need to be well on the way to ripeness too: the best way to test them is to lightly press the flesh near the stalk, if it feels soft then the fruit is ready to pick: place one finger either side of the fruit to steady the stem and carefully pull away the fruit with the other hand. This will avoid stripping the rind from the stem. It is unlikely that all of the fruit will be ready at the same time but if more has to be harvested than can be consumed at the time, find a cool place to store the excess for a few days.

Leave plums for as long as possible When eaten raw, plums are best left on the tree for as long as possible, otherwise they are better picked just before they are fully ripe. This can work well because seldom, if ever, does the whole crop ripen at the same time.

Protect fruit from birds and wasps Birds and wasps find ripe fruit most attractive and whilst birds can be deterred by growing crops under netting, wasps are rather more difficult to keep at bay: jars of water containing a spoonful or two of honey suspended in the trees make good traps and it is often surprising how many wasps can be caught in this way.

Remove diseased fruit Whilst harvesting, it is a good plan to pick off any diseased fruit at the same time: apples and plums infected by brown rot become mummified and often persist on the trees overwinter to reinfect next year's crop. This is also a very good opportunity to cut away any diseased wood and where bacterial canker of plums is concerned the tree should be treated with a copper fungicide spray after removing the infected parts.

Prune plums after harvesting After removing any diseased or damaged wood, plums can be pruned when harvesting is complete. Thin out over-crowded branches and with fan-trained plums, shoots that have already been pinched may be further shortened by half. Tie in position shoots for fruiting next year.

Prune peaches and nectarines Fan-trained peaches and nectarines should also be pruned immediately after harvesting by removing fruited wood and then replacement shoots may be tied in to take over.

Continue to summer prune and remove suckers Continue to summer prune restricted forms of apples, pears and plums. Suckers arising from the root-stock and vigorous vertical water shoots from branches should also be removed.

Plant strawberries August is a good month to plant out strawberries. The plants are likely to be in position for three years and so thorough preparation of the soil by forking out perennial weeds and incorporating bulky organic material is worthwhile. Ideally, the basic cultivations should be carried out in time for the ground to settle, otherwise the soil should be made firm by treading. Potash and phosphate are most important and to ensure levels are satisfactory a base dressing of ½oz per sq yd (17g per m²) sulphate of potash and 2oz per sq yd (68g per m²) superphosphate should be applied and raked into the surface before planting. Other things being equal, the crop harvested usually relates to the planting distance and so liberal space should be given when possible: 1½ft (45cm) between plants, with the rows spaced 2½ft (75cm) apart is ideal for most cultivars.

The plants should be set out with a trowel and planted firmly with the crown level with the soil surface.

Control pests and diseases Even though crops have been or are about to be harvested, pest and disease control should not be forgotten: apples to be picked later and stored will benefit from fungicidal spraying during the middle of the month against storage rots. Spray also against leaf spot and mildew on gooseberry and black currant bushes but do read the precautions printed on the label. Grease bands should also be applied to the trunk and stakes of trees and woolly aphid may be a problem with apple trees.

VEGETABLES AND HERBS Gardening seasons come and go so quickly that it is already time to sow spring cabbage. Seed may be sown thinly broadcast or in drills ½in (13mm) deep spaced 6in (15cm) apart in ground that was manured for the previous crop. Make sure that a cultivar is chosen which will succeed from early autumn sowing such as 'Flower of Spring' or 'Wheeler's Imperial'.

Sow lettuce seed Lettuce seed may be sown direct until the middle of the month and 'All Year Round' has been consistently good for cutting in late autumn and early winter; plants do not grow as large compared with summer crops and may be thinned out to stand 8in (20cm) apart. Some lettuce cultivars will stand the winter without protection but they do need a long period of growth and so seed of 'Arctic King' or 'Valdor' may be sown in less favourable districts towards the end of the month; milder areas should wait until next month before sowing the seed shallowly in a nursery seedbed for transplanting in October.

Sow spring and Japanese onions Sow spring onions for pulling during the early months of next year, 'White Lisbon' is excellent for the purpose and should be sown thinly in drills ½in (13mm) deep and 9in (23cm) apart. Spring onions are not normally grown on to produce bulbs and for that purpose to mature next summer, one of the Japanese cultivars is ideal for sowing in northern gardens towards the end of the month. Sow the seed 1in (2.5cm) apart and thin the resulting seedlings to 2in (5cm) apart after the turn of the year. The idea is to have seedlings well established but not so large that they do not overwinter satisfactorily and so southern gardeners should delay sowing until the first week of next month. Onion sets are also now available for planting during autumn.

Make successional sowings Successional sowings can still be made of radish, stump-rooted carrots and mustard and cress. Turnips can be sown to produce a crop of greens by harvesting the leaves and a sowing of winter spinach can also be made now. Before freezers became so popular, it was the custom to sow Brussels sprouts this month to transplant later for harvesting next summer: a method that is still worthwhile.

Thin seedlings Continue to thin out seedlings before they develop too much and some young plants like lettuce may be lifted carefully to be transplanted under cloches or in a garden frame.

Blanch endive The earliest sowing of endive should now be ready for blanching; it is most important to exclude all light and perhaps an obvious choice might be to use black polythene but even with a short burst of sun, the temperature underneath rises to prohibitive levels. The easiest way to blanch is to cover the plant with an upturned flowerpot with the drainage holes blanked off. Allow approximately three weeks for blanching to take place and cover plants accordingly.

Stop outdoor tomatoes Since it takes approximately two months according to weather conditions for tomatoes to develop and mature, outdoor plants should be stopped this month by pinching out the growing point one leaf beyond the third or fourth truss. Continue to remove side shoots at an early stage and it may be necessary to protect the ripening fruit from bird damage. Old leaves now beginning to curl may be removed from the plants by snapping upwards; it is better not to cut the leaves from the plant otherwise a stub is usually left behind which is inclined to rot back into the stem. Plants will still require feeding until the end of the month.

Ripen onions Onions grown from sets and those sown under glass early in the year will soon be mature enough to ripen off. Traditionally, tops are bent over towards the end of the month but it is doubtful whether that really aids ripening although the bed does look more tidy than when the top growth is straggly. Fully grown mature onions ripen best of all when they are spread out on raised frames made from wire netting, the bulbs are well away from the ground and will not be encouraged to produce roots.

Earth up celery Trench celery will require further earthing up as outlined for last month and particular attention should be paid to slug control.

Support sprouts Brussels sprouts should be given support by inserting a stake alongside if there is any chance of the plant being blown over. This causes the buttons to 'blow' and be open rather than in the more acceptable tight ball.

Crop celery Remove suckers from self-blanching celery; well grown plants will be ready for harvesting during the month and it is essential that they do not go short of water at any time otherwise they are inclined to grow tough and stringy and run up to produce flower heads.

Gather crops whilst they are young The majority of crops are better for gathering when they are young and in this way they are likely to be more prolific: runner beans, cucumbers, courgettes and marrows certainly respond in that way. Main crop carrots and beetroot will be ready for lifting at the end of the month and early potatoes should still be dug.

Test sweet corn cobs when they feel firm: the seed should exude creamy liquid when it is pressed with the thumb nail to indicate that it is ready for harvesting.

Green manure vacant ground Any land not required for immediate use will benefit from green manuring, which is simply a case of broadcasting rape seed or some other quick maturing crop to dig in whilst it is still green.

Gather herbs for drying Continue to gather herbs for drying during warm dry weather. Certain kinds like hyssop, lavender, rosemary, rue and sage can be propagated by taking cuttings to insert in pots containing well drained compost or directly into the border or the garden frame or under a cloche.

Control pests and diseases Take precautions against mealy cabbage aphid, cabbage root fly and cabbage moth caterpillars, they can build up at an alarming rate especially during an absence due to holiday.

Water and mulch plants Make sure that the soil is moist and it is still not too late to apply a mulch around plants.

GREENHOUSE Forced strawberries must surely be one of the easiest yet most rewarding crops to grow: pot up rooted runners so that the crowns are level with the top of the compost in 5 or 6in (12.5 or 15cm) pots filled with John Innes potting compost No 2, and water well. The pots are best stood outside until the turn of the year; in this way the plants will be subjected to low and even freezing temperatures to initiate the flower buds. Very little, if any, heat will be required once they are moved into the greenhouse and yet they will crop far in advance of the outdoor plants.

Pot off rooted cuttings Fuchsia and other cuttings taken last month should be ready for potting off singly into 3in (7.5cm) pots using John Innes potting compost No 1 or a peat-based medium. Water well and keep them shaded for a day or two to help establishment.

Start nerines Start nerines into growth by placing the pots on the staging and watering the compost.

Plant freesia corms Freesia corms that were cleaned off earlier and kept in the greenhouse may now be planted up in pots or fish boxes. Space them approximately 2in (5cm) apart with the top of the corm 1in (2.5cm) below the level of the compost in John Innes potting compost No 1 and place the containers outside in a shady spot. They can remain outside if necessary until the tomatoes and other crops are cleared in September.

Pot up bulbs Lachenalia and other bulbs including daffodils can be planted up in containers as soon as they are available. Bulbs for forcing in spring should be plunged outside in the cool so that a good root system will establish before bringing them indoors. Arum lilies make particularly fine specimens and should be started into growth now by removing them from their pots, shaking away old compost and repotting one crown in a 6in

(15cm) pot of John Innes potting compost No 2. Stand the pots outside until growth begins.

Rest Christmas cactus and hippeastrums Christmas cactus and hippeastrums, on the other hand, need resting now by withholding water and although the former may be allowed to dry out in the container, the compost should never be allowed to go completely dry around hippeastrum bulbs.

Feed and disbud chrysanthemums Continue feeding mid-season and late-flowering chrysanthemums that are standing in pots out of doors. A further shallow top dressing of potting compost may be given to encourage new roots and a number of plants will begin to show flower buds during the month. Large single blooms will develop when the buds are reduced at an early stage: remove all but the central bud on each stem together with any side shoots. Spray chrysanthemums should also be disbudded but in this case only the central bud is removed to allow the axillary buds to grow on and flower. By disbudding in this way, a far more attractive spray will result rather than by allowing the terminal bud to develop, as this would tend to dominate the remainder.

Take pelargonium and coleus cuttings Root zonal pelargonium cuttings and establish the plants before winter but avoid any plants showing signs of rust or black leg disease. Coleus cuttings from plants producing the best leaf colour and form can also be taken now.

Sow cyclamen seed Cyclamen seed sown this month will make very large plants for flowering next autumn. Seed soaked for 24 hours before sowing is easier to handle and germinates faster. Spot sow the seed so that it is spaced 1in (2.5cm) apart each way in the container filled with John Innes potting compost No 1 or peat-based medium. The containers should be kept in a temperature of 60°F (16°C).

Sow annuals for potting Various plants that are normally grown as annuals out of doors make very attractive plants for flowering in the greenhouse next spring. These include calendula, godetia, mesembryanthemum and salpiglossis; schizanthus, often called the poor man's orchid, is particularly good when sown now or during the early part of next month. Exacum is a greenhouse plant with most fragrant mauve flowers and seed sown now in a temperature of 65 to 70°F (18 to 21°C) will flower next spring.

House pot plants Plants like *Solanum capsicastrum*, ornamental pepper, and cyclamen that have stood outside for the summer should now be brought into the greenhouse. Cyclamen plants grown from seed often produce one or two premature flowers and these are best removed whilst still in bud. Make sure the plants are free from pests like greenfly and whitefly before

The water-lily *Nymphaea* x *marliacea* 'Carnea'.

they are brought inside, otherwise they will soon infect the plants already in the house.

Feed, stop and deleaf tomatoes Tomatoes should continue to be fed until one month before they finish cropping; it takes approximately six weeks for a set flower to produce mature fruit under glass and so plants should be stopped in good time by removing the growing point to avoid wasted immature fruit. Continue to deleaf the plants up to the truss that is ripening. Grey mould disease can be a problem from now on and any damping of paths should be done first thing in the morning so that the atmosphere has time to dry a little before late afternoon. Any fruit showing ghost spotting (greyish-white circles) should be removed, together with infected leaves and stem lesions. Fungicide smokes can be useful in preventing an occurrence but check the label for sensitive plants and the interval required between application and the harvesting of the crop. Greater care is now needed with ventilation to control humidity and night time temperature.

Prune peach and nectarine plants Peach and nectarine plants should be pruned when the last fruit is picked: cut out any dead shoots and those that have borne fruit and tie in the new shoots to fruit next year.

Sow then plant lettuce Lettuce to harvest during winter should be sown now. Select a cultivar suitable for growing under glass in the winter and sow thinly in a seed tray at a temperature below 60°F (16°C) if possible. Cover the seed with a thin layer of compost and spread a sheet of newspaper over the surface; the paper may be damped over if necessary to keep the compost moist. The resulting seedlings may be planted out in the greenhouse border at an 8 by 8in (20 by 20cm) spacing, or planted up in a growing bag that was used to crop tomatoes previously. In that case it would be as well first to flood the bag to remove excess fertilizer that may damage the tender young lettuce plants.

Control pests and diseases Watch for whitefly, mealy bug, scale insects, leaf miner and grey mould on plants in general.

Remove shading Any greenhouse shading that still persists should be removed at the end of the month.

A decorative display of petunia, lobelia and pelargoniums in hanging baskets and troughs.

September

FLOWERS, TREES AND SHRUBS Bedding plants with so much to offer during the summer months are now beyond their best and can be removed and added to the compost heap once they have faded. This will make way for spring-flowering bulbs which should be planted as soon as possible. Fork over the beds to remove any perennial weeds and to incorporate the mulch that was applied earlier; further garden compost or other bulky organic material may also be dug in. Rake over the bed and firm by treading unless the soil is wet enough to stick to footwear, which is unlikely unless it has been an abnormally wet summer. Bulbs growing in straight rows look formal and unattractive and so the best way to distribute the bulbs for planting is to scatter them over the surface of the soil so that daffodils, hyacinths and tulips are approximately 6in (15cm) apart; provided they are uniformly spaced they may be planted where they land. Planting depth is important because when the bulbs are too deep much energy is lost in growing leaves through the soil to reach the light. Generally, bulbs should be planted at a depth equal to twice their height, for example if a bulb is 1in (2.5cm) high then it should be planted with 2in (5cm) of soil over the top.

Plant bulbs amongst spring bedding Bulbs look very attractive when planted amongst other spring-flowering plants like wallflowers, *Bellis perennis* and polyanthus. Plant up the bedding plants first, working from a timber board if possible so that the soil does not become too compacted. Once the plants are set out, the bulbs can be planted in between. This combination, whilst looking very attractive during spring, also helps to camouflage the rather unsightly bulb foliage as it ripens in late spring before the bulbs are lifted after flowering.

Plant crocus and hardy cyclamen around the base of trees Crocus and hardy cyclamen in particular look most attractive when planted around the base of trees, whether the area is cultivated or not; they make ideal specimens for planting in the lawn too, as do snowdrops and winter aconites. Make holes with a dibber or crowbar for small bulbs and corms and drop the bulb or corm in. Should the soil be on the heavy side and rather poorly drained, it will pay to trickle some coarse sand into the hole first of all. Having inserted the bulb, fill the hole up with garden soil. Should mowing be necessary before the leaves die down next spring it may be a case of replanting again next autumn but the effort will certainly be worthwhile. Hardy cyclamen will grow on for many years provided the leaves are allowed to die back naturally and they are not disturbed.

Plant lilies Congested groups of basal-rooted lilies can be lifted and transplanted as soon as the foliage withers; stem rooters are best planted during spring. Replant at the same depth as they were growing before; in the case of new bulbs just purchased plant them 2½ times as deep as their height, the Madonna lily (*Lilium candidum*) is the exception which should be planted with no more than 1in (2.5cm) of soil above the bulb and in any case this particular species should have been planted during summertime.

Different kinds of iris prolong flowering Bulbous iris provide flowers over a long period and by selecting Dutch, Spanish and English kinds, colour will be available from May until July. Irises should be given a sunny border for best results and, although the soil should be well drained, the addition of bulky organic material (other than animal manure) will enhance the growing conditions. The bulbs are planted 6in (15cm) apart and 3in (7.5cm) deep and may be left to naturalise until they become overcrowded. Again, staggered planting is better for garden display. *Iris unguicularis* is the earliest to flower and again should be planted in a sheltered position where it will receive as much sun as possible, especially during winter. Drainage is important and although a fertile soil is not necessary, on the contrary the plant is less leafy and produces better flowers in a poor soil, lime should be added if the soil is very acid.

Plant biennials Biennial plants like Sweet Williams and hollyhock should be planted out during the month; lift the young plants carefully and if the soil is at all dry, give it a thorough watering a day or two before lifting.

Divide and replant alpines Alpine plants that have outgrown their allotted space may be lifted and replanted at the end of the month, dividing up the rootstock as required. Alpines thrive best in well drained soil.

Prepare planting site for evergreens Bare root evergreen plants ordered during the growing season will be delivered any time now and it would be as well if the planting stations are ready for them: fork over the area to remove perennial weeds and other plants in the way. Check that supplies of peat, composted bark or other bulky materials are sufficient and that tree stakes and ties are available. Plants that arrive and which cannot be set out straight away may be heeled in for a few days to await planting.

Clip hedges Hedges that were not treated with growth regulator during late spring should be given their final clip to tidy them until growth begins next year. The only exception is for a spring-flowering hedge which produces its flowers on growth made this year, and in this case clipping should be done immediately after the flowers fade.

This is a very good time to trim conifers for which only one clip a year is usually necessary.

Retain gladiolus leaves until they die back naturally Continue to dead-head plants as flowers fade and cut off flowered stems from gladioli; the leaves should remain until they die back and the corms can then be carefully lifted and dried off. Small cormels will be found attached to the parent. These may be removed for sowing next spring if more plants are required. When the corms have dried, the old shrivelled corm can be removed and discarded.

Rogue dahlia and chrysanthemum plants Check labels on early outdoor chrysanthemums and dahlias and mark those to be saved as stock plants whilst they are still in bloom. Any plants showing signs of virus infection should be lifted and destroyed without delay.

Check stakes and ties Stakes and ties supporting trees and standard roses may need adjusting and refirming after summer growth. This is important now before autumn gales cause damage. New growth made by climbing roses can be damaged by high wind unless it is tied in now; make the ties secure but allow sufficient room for the stem to thicken as it grows.

Rose climbers and ramblers Non-repeat flowering climbers and ramblers can now be pruned by removing old spent wood which flowered this summer. The old wood can be cut back to a strong side shoot low down, or if numerous new sucker growths have been produced, take out the old wood to ground level.

Use rose prunings as cuttings Rose prunings make ideal cuttings which should be approximately 10in (25cm) long and cut below a leaf joint and just above a leaf at the top. Remove the thorns and all leaves except the two uppermost on the stem. The cuttings are then inserted in well drained soil spaced 6in (15cm) apart in a shady part of the garden.

Take half-ripe cuttings of shrubs Shrub cuttings in general can be taken during this month and subjects that do well as half-ripe cuttings include aucuba, berberis, griselinia, juniper, laurel, lavender, *Lonicera nitida*, phlomis, potentilla and privet. Take the cuttings approximately 8in (20cm) long and with a heel and insert them in well drained soil in a shady part of the garden or garden frame; those in the open will need cloche protection during hard winter weather.

Lift layered border carnations Border carnations layered earlier should now be well rooted and ready for lifting to plant in their permanent position. Cut the stem joining the young plant to the parent a few days before transplanting so that the offset will depend upon its own roots.

Change the plants in hanging baskets Unless hanging baskets can be taken under cover to continue growing during the autumn, it is a good plan to make use of them through the winter by replanting them now with hardy plants like winter-flowering heather and decorative ivy.

Sow hardy annuals Sweet pea enthusiasts will be sowing sweet peas at the end of this month although many wait until next month. Hardy annuals can be sown out of doors now in milder areas for an early display next year and amongst those worth trying are calendula, candytuft, echium, eschscholzia, godetia, larkspur, limnanthes and nigella.

Lift tender plants It would be prudent to lift susceptible plants like pelargoniums, tuberous begonias and fuchsias from borders subject to early frosts; pot them up and be ready to take them under cover should frost threaten.

LAWN Although the turf requires less attention so far as mowing is concerned, the blades may now be lifted to cut at 1¼in (30mm) with coarse grasses and ¾in (19mm) for fine. There is plenty to do in other respects: autumn fertilizer containing high phosphate and potash should be applied to strengthen the grass for winter. This is the last chance to apply selective weedkillers where weeds are a problem and even then this late treatment is really only worthwhile in mild districts.

Control diseases and moles Moss is unlikely to be a problem although one or two disease patches may be showing and treatment with a fungicide is necessary at an early stage. Moles are often active now and so traps or mole smokes should be used to control them; these pests are usually more active where the worm population is high and it may be necessary to deal with the worms as described last month. In any case worm casts should be brushed off daily if possible.

Scarify, spike and top dress Scarification will remove vast quantities of dead plant material, particularly if it is not carried out on a regular basis; the thatch makes ideal material for the compost heap provided couch grass and other difficult weeds are not present. The turf should then be spiked and a top dressing may be applied if that was not done last month.

Repair damaged areas Repair worn areas and edges by inserting a new turf or, in the case of a damaged edge, the turf may be lifted and turned round so that the damaged area can be filled with soil and sown with grass seed. Any hollows should first have the turf removed, and then be made level with soil which is firmed and the turf replaced. Humps are dealt with by first removing the turf, then shaving off the offending surplus soil before finally replacing the turf. If the depth of soil removed has brought poor soil to the surface it would be as well to remove a further 6in (15cm) and fill in the dip with top soil before replacing the turf. Tamp the new turf down with the back of a spade but do not firm with a roller.

Seed thin areas Thin and worn areas of turf may be overseeded by first pricking over the area with a garden fork then raking off the debris. Seed is then sown at the rate of ½oz per sq yd (17g per m^2) and covered very lightly with sifted soil. Most seed is treated against birds but protection may be necessary to deter cats.

Sow and cut new lawn Seed may be sown to make a new lawn this month. The soil is still warm and germination is usually fast. Seed sown at the beginning of last month should be showing good growth and a light rolling will stimulate shoots as well as firming the roots. On no account should a roller be used if the soil is wet otherwise damage will result from the soil sticking to the roller. Top the grass when it reaches 2in (5cm) in length using sharp garden shears or a really sharp mower. Subsequent cuts may be necessary during the autumn to keep the sward no more than 1½in (4cm) long.

Lay turves Turf can be established at almost any time of the year but this month and next usually provide the best conditions provided the ground is not too wet. Try to inspect the field from which the turf will be lifted as some weeds are very difficult to eradicate once imported. Full details of the best way to lay turf are given on page 166.

POND An early frost will bring down leaves and, combined with strong winds that usually occur this month, most of the debris will end up in the water unless precautions are taken. Netting draped over the pond makes a very useful collector and the leaves may then easily be removed to the compost heap.

Collect winter buds When frogbit and bladderwort are grown it is prudent to collect the winter buds before they sink to the bottom; the best way to overwinter the buds is to keep them in a jar of pond water. Dead leaves, flower buds and other debris should be removed at the same time.

Feed fish Although fish are not very active during the winter months, they do need a certain amount of energy and so feeding should continue all the time they can clear offerings within ten minutes.

Insulate or remove equipment A sudden cold snap can do considerable damage to pumps and other equipment and, unless they are properly insulated, it would be as well to drain and disconnect. Take the opportunity to clean out equipment thoroughly before it is put away for the winter. Needless to say any electrical equipment must be disconnected before work proceeds.

FRUIT Autumn-fruiting raspberries are now beginning to crop on current season's canes and second crop 'Red Gauntlet' strawberries will be producing fruit in favoured areas; fruit yet to mature on this cultivar may be protected by covering with cloches. Perpetual-fruiting strawberries will also be cropping. Otherwise, harvesting will follow much the same pattern as last month.

Complete summer pruning Summer pruning of apples and pears should be completed as soon as possible with any secondary growth being pinched back to one leaf. Plums and damsons should be pruned by removing any diseased or damaged wood and then thinning out as necessary. On no account should these plants be pruned during the winter for fear of silver leaf infection.

Prune fan-trained cherries Fan-trained cherries already summer pruned should now be further shortened unless the shoots were dealt with last month. Any strong-growing vertical shoots should be either cut out completely or tied down. Growth that has reached the top of the supports is best tied down horizontally rather than cut out as this would only encourage vigorous growth requiring further attention.

Check stakes Check stakes for firmness and tree ties may need adjusting after the season's growth.

Propagate new soft fruit plants Any replacement or additional plants should be ordered in good time but several can be propagated at home. Black currants, for example, root readily from cuttings taken this month. The best type of cutting is one taken from the current season's wood with the soft immature tip removed. The base should also be cut away just below a bud to leave approximately 8in (20cm) of firm stem. Leave all the buds intact so that the lower ones will develop as suckers. The cuttings are inserted in well drained soil so that only the top two buds are protruding from the soil.

Gooseberry cuttings are prepared in the same way except that they should be 1ft (30cm) long and although they will be grown on a 'leg' all of the buds are retained because the cutting appears to root more effectively by that method. But all buds, except the top 4, could be removed in the traditional way. Insert the cutting so that half of its length is below soil level. Prepare red and white currant cuttings from current season's shoots, cutting off the soft top and thick base to leave approximately 1ft (30cm) for the cutting; remove all of the buds except 4 at the top and then insert the cutting in well drained soil to half its length.

Hardwood cuttings of soft fruit.

All of the bush fruit cuttings should be spaced 6in (15cm) apart and should have rooted sufficiently to be planted in their final position this time next year.

Prepare new planting site Cultivate ground to remove weeds and incorporate bulky organic material in sites to be planted with new bushes and fruit trees. Check for a pan below the soil surface and dig sufficiently deep to remove the barrier which would otherwise impede drainage and the upward movement of subsoil moisture reserve. Planting holes need not yet be dug as these are best taken out at planting time.

Take precautions against damage and disease Apples picked for keeping should be free from bruising or other blemish and a special preserving dip is available to give them some protection whilst in store. A further fungicide spray may be applied to late cultivars not yet ready for harvesting. This will help to prevent storage rots and protect from a late infection of scab. Watch for apple and pear canker and remove infected wood. Plum trees and other stone fruits will benefit from a further spray against bacterial canker. Once leaves have fallen from peach, nectarine and apricot trees, a fungicide to control peach leaf curl may be applied.

Apply grease bands Grease bands attached to apple and other trees and adjacent stakes will prevent winter moths from crawling into the trees to lay eggs. These bands also trap various other pests which would otherwise cause damage.

VEGETABLES AND HERBS Maincrop carrots may be lifted when the leaves die down; shrivelled tops should be removed and any split and otherwise damaged roots should be used up first, the remainder being put in store. Beetroot should also be lifted and onions ripened as described last month.

Support marrows and pumpkin Marrows and pumpkins grown on for storage should be left to mature properly and a support, such as upturned seed trays, which lifts them away from the ground, will do much to assist the ripening process.

Blanch chicory and endive Lift chicory roots and cut the tops back to within 1in (2.5cm). The roots may then be potted or boxed up in garden soil and placed in the dark. Alternatively, they may be left in the ground outside when the tops are cut back and soil ridged up 9in (23cm) above the roots. When growth appears above the ridge, the chicons may be harvested.

Another batch of endive can be blanched as outlined last month but precautions should be taken against slugs which are usually particularly active at this time.

Lift potatoes Whilst lifting potatoes, check for wireworm and if tubers are infected it would be as well to dig the remainder to try to avoid further attack; infected tubers should not be bagged up or clamped. Potato haulm is best removed now whether the crop is to be dug or left in the ground for a while.

Pick outdoor tomatoes The remaining outdoor tomatoes can now be picked and taken indoors to ripen; alternatively, plants may be lowered to the ground and covered by cloches.

Cut self-blanching celery Self-blanching celery should be used as soon as possible otherwise damp weather and frost will soon cause the sticks to deteriorate. Trench celery will still make growth and supplementary irrigation should be given to keep the soil moist if the weather is at all dry. Continue to earth up as suggested last month.

Cloche parsley and make another sowing Parsley can be kept growing for a considerable time by removing the tough outer leaves and placing a cloche over the plants. A further sowing of parsley and chervil can be made now for use in the spring.

Lift and divide rhubarb Now that most of the leaves have died down, rhubarb crowns that have remained in the same position for three years may be lifted and divided for replanting on a different site. The best way to do this is to slice the crowns with a garden spade. Surplus crowns may be left on the surface to be frosted, when they can then be potted or boxed up later for forcing.

Protect cauliflower curds Developing cauliflower curds will need protection from the elements by snapping a leaf over the head.

Plant out spring cabbage Spring cabbages sown earlier should be planted out in northern areas towards the end of the month and the last week in the south. This is a good crop to follow potatoes and after a dusting of lime, if necessary, raked into the surface the plants should be set out 1ft (30cm) apart with the rows spaced 1½ft (45cm) apart. Take precautions against club root and remember to plant firmly.

Turn in green manure crop Rape or other green manure crops should be dug in before they become woody and any vacant ground should be culti-vated for the following crop. Autumn is a good time to apply a dressing of lime when required but a simple pH test should always be carried out first to assess the amount, if any, that may be needed. Lime should not be applied at the same time as animal manure or fertilizer, otherwise nitrogen will be released to the atmosphere and wasted.

Control weeds Weeds often take root and regrow when they are hoed at this time of the year and it is often better to apply a contact weedkiller that becomes inactivated once it touches the soil.

Sow Japanese onions in the South Japanese onions will already have been sown in the North as suggested last month. Timing is rather critical for best results but the majority of southern areas will find that a sowing made during the first week of this month will produce young plants to overwinter at the correct stage of growth.

Sow winter lettuce Some seed may already have been sown to produce winter lettuce, but again in the South, a sowing made now may well produce the ideal plant should the season be abnormally good, or poor, for growth. Seed should be sown thinly whether broadcast or in drills ¼in (6mm) deep spaced 6in (15cm) apart.

Sow cauliflower Cauliflower seed may be sown thinly and covered with ½in (13mm) of sifted soil.

Thin out seedlings Winter spinach, endive and lettuce sown earlier will need thinning as soon as the plants can be handled: spinach should first be thinned to approximately 4in (10cm), the endive 1ft (30cm) apart and the lettuce 8in (20cm) apart. Surplus lettuce plants may be planted in the garden frame to harvest before the outdoor crop is ready.

Tidy globe artichokes Although globe artichokes are most decorative and the flower buds good for eating, the plants do become rather unattractive during the autumn: cut away old stems and any withered leaves to tidy the plants.

Control pests Celery plants may need spraying against rust and slugs can now be particularly destructive, as can pigeons and rabbits.

GREENHOUSE September is the change-over month in the greenhouse: tomatoes, cucumbers, melons and other crops come to an end to be replaced by plants that have stood outside for the summer.

Stop feeding and pinch out the tip of tomatoes When tomatoes are fed regularly throughout the season, residual fertilizer builds up in the compost and so plants can feed on that for the last four weeks of their existence. This will reduce salt levels for the other crops to follow like lettuce, radish and carrots that do not require such high levels of fertility. Pinch out the growing tip of tomato plants one leaf beyond the truss in flower six weeks before the tomato plants are to be removed from the house: it is hardly worth carrying the plants on after mid-October because the days are getting short and no doubt grey mould will be a problem due to the damp atmosphere, unless the heater is used.

Clear out the house Ideally, the plants occupying the greenhouse for the summer months should be removed a few days before housing the next ones. This will give sufficient time to give the house a thorough clean. Winter light transmission into the greenhouse is nearly always deficient and everything should be done to ensure that as much light as possible gains entry.

Start the change over by first picking any fruit still remaining, then by controlling any pests and diseases lurking on the plants. Red spider mite in particular should be dealt with before it goes into hibernation for the winter months. When all of the plants occupying the greenhouse are to be taken out to the compost heap, it is a good idea to burn a sulphur candle in the greenhouse whilst the plants are still growing, but do remove any plants you wish to keep because burning sulphur will kill all living plants as well as most of the pests and diseases. Do make sure that the ventilators are closed properly and that broken glass is replaced before going ahead with the fumigation. Sulphur fumes seep through cracks and gaps and so it should not be used where plants are growing in an adjacent compartment or close to a dwelling house.

Open the door and ventilators the next day, then once the fumes have dispersed, work may proceed to remove the plants. Roots should always be dug up from the border so that as much root as possible is removed; simply pulling up the roots will leave much behind and soil sickness will develop sooner than it should. Cut the stems up so that they are easier to carry out and if they are to be placed on the compost heap, it would be as well to remove any polypropylene string that has been used in supporting the plants.

Plants growing in containers may be cut off close to the base of the stem;

the container compost can then be used as a mulch or for digging in the border outside. Growing bags can usually be brought into service again for the winter crop: remove the existing plants and any thick roots, then flood the bag with clear water to remove excess residual fertilizer, allow to drain and the bag will be ready to plant up with lettuce or another crop to harvest during wintertime.

Wash down the structure Wash down the structure using a tar oil formulation (the same one as used for fruit tree winter wash will do) and then hose off with clear water. Algae and mould growth between glass overlaps can be difficult to remove and the best way is to use a seed label to slide between the glass. Finally wash the outside of the greenhouse using detergent and water, but do rinse off with clear water afterwards otherwise a deposit may be left on the glass.

Fix insulation for heat retention Whilst the house is empty, it is a good opportunity to fix insulating material like clear or bubble polythene to reduce heat loss in winter. The ventilators should not on any account be covered otherwise air exchange will be impeded.

Spray plants before housing All should now be ready to bring the outdoor plants inside. It would be a pity to introduce pests and diseases into the clean greenhouse and so the plants should be sprayed with a fungicide and insecticide before housing, first removing any damaged or diseased leaves. So far as chrysanthemums are concerned, they should be defoliated up to the first break where laterals emerge from the single stem. This will allow better air circulation around the plants inside the greenhouse.

When carrying large plants like chrysanthemums and fuchsias into the greenhouse, take them in pot first otherwise top growth may be damaged if it strikes the door frame.

Acclimatise plants gradually Keep the ventilators and door open, weather permitting, so that the plants gradually acclimatise to their new environment. Extra care should be taken to avoid splashing water about and, when possible, the chrysanthemum and fuchsia pots should be plunged into the border soil so that any excess water draining from the pots will not evaporate to raise the humidity of the atmosphere. A relatively dry atmosphere is important to help control fungal diseases that can destroy flowers and leaves quickly during the autumn and winter months.

Feed plants Continue to feed chrysanthemums, cyclamen, *Solanum capsicastrum*, cineraria and freesia now that they are inside the greenhouse but take particular care with cineraria as they can so easily be overwatered. Chrysanthemums should be disbudded as necessary and the odd premature flower bud may be removed from cyclamen plants before it develops too far. Freesia growth should be supported with twiggy sticks if that has not already been done.

House pot-grown potatoes Potato foliage is very tender and the plants growing in pots for a late crop should now be brought into the greenhouse.

Feed and divide arum lilies Arum lilies that have become congested in their containers can be divided and planted up singly, one crown to each 6in (15cm) pot using John Innes potting compost No 2. Arum lilies remaining in their existing pot should be given a liquid feed.

Pot on plants Pot on schizanthus and other plants that are ready and continue to grow during autumn and winter. Zonal pelargonium cuttings struck earlier should now be ready for potting off into John Innes potting compost No 1 or a peat-based medium. When the latter is used, extra care should be taken with watering during the winter months otherwise plants may remain too wet or, conversely, the compost may dry out to such an extent that it is difficult to wet again. Pot up a few bushy wallflower plants to give an early display. Sow a further batch of schizanthus to follow on.

Prick out lettuce Prick out lettuce sown earlier into pots or boxes; kept growing on steadily they will be suitable for planting later in the border.

Take cuttings Penstemon, viola and pansy cuttings can be taken now from non-flowering side shoots for planting out next spring.

Pot bulbs Pot up spring-flowering bulbs and corms. Early-flowering gladioli are excellent for the greenhouse, particularly *Gladiolus byzantinus*, *G.colvillei* and *G.nanus*. Like similar plants they need to be kept plunged in a cold frame until well rooted.

Poinsettia flower bracts are initiated by providing short days Poinsettia plants are now making good growth and should be in a temperature of 60°F (16°C) to avoid root rotting diseases gaining a foothold. The plants may be given short days of no more than ten hours of light by covering them with a black polythene hood. This will encourage them to develop flower buds and the bracts should be fully coloured by Christmas. It is important, however, to give short days every day until the bracts begin to show colour.

Reduce humidity for grapes Humidity should now be reduced in houses where grape vines are ripening fruit. This will help to avoid disease infection.

Stop feeding peaches and nectarines Peach and nectarine trees should have their last feed of the season no later than the end of the first week in the month.

Control pests and diseases Watch for pests and diseases, particularly greenfly which suck sap causing small wounds that allow diseases such as petal blight to gain entry into chrysanthemum flowers. Grey mould can also be a problem. These problems may be controlled by ventilation and the use of pesticide smokes as necessary.

Check equipment Check heating equipment and have the appliances serviced in good time.

House delicate containers Some patio containers are made from materials (including clay) which do not weather very well. If in doubt it is prudent to bring them under cover for the winter; they look most attractive when planted up with ivy or other decorative plants.

October

FLOWERS, TREES AND SHRUBS There is every chance that we shall have a stiff frost some time during this month and so tender plants should be protected by a covering of straw or bracken.

Lift dahlias, begonias, gladioli and cut back early chrysanthemums Even if frost has not blackened dahlia foliage it would be as well to lift any tubers that are to be saved for stock: cut back the stems to 6in (15cm), lift the tubers carefully with a fork and remove as much soil as possible then hang them upside down under cover to dry off. When dry the tubers may be dusted with fungicide and boxed up in a dry peat-based compost or John Innes potting compost No 1 ready for next spring. They should be overwintered in a dry, frost-free place. Chrysanthemum stools should be cut back in a similar way, lifted and boxed up for the winter. Tuberous begonias lifted and placed in trays will eventually die back when the foliage can be removed cleanly from the tuber; gladioli can be treated similarly and, in this case, the old shrivelled corm and cormels should also be removed.

Continue to plant bulbs Continue to plant bulbs for flowering next spring. Crown imperials are particularly effective although somewhat difficult to keep if the soil is heavy. In this case, plant the bulbs on their side on a base of sand. The bulbs should be planted 6in (15cm) deep. These plants are said to deter rabbits because they have a smell similar to that of a fox but it is doubtful whether they would be effective for that purpose unless planted on a large scale.

Plant peonies, Canterbury bells, forget-me-nots, polyanthus, Sweet William and wallflowers Spring-flowering subjects often go well interplanted with bulbs as suggested last month.

Lift and divide herbaceous perennials Herbaceous perennials may still be lifted and divided provided the soil is in a fit state. Plants ordered earlier will now be arriving and there is usually a good selection available from garden centres.

Prepare soil for evergreen shrubs and roses Prepare the soil in good time for evergreen shrubs, which are best planted this month whilst the soil is comparatively warm and it should not be too wet. If the leaves are sprayed over with S.600 solution, it will help to prevent them from drying out after planting before they have had a chance to establish. Plants budded on to special rootstocks usually need to be planted with the union just above soil level but in the case of large-flowered hybrid tea roses, they should be planted with the union just below soil level. Any additional plants required should be ordered without delay.

Plant heathers Heathers are excellent for ground cover when they are massed in a group and whilst generally these are lime-hating, a liberal dressing of acid sphagnum peat will enable plants like the lime-tolerant *Erica carnea*, *E.darleyensis* and *E.mediterranea* and their varieties to do even better than they would anyway.

Make a new rock garden October is a good month to construct or renovate a rock garden. An open site overlying well drained soil is essential for success. Before attempting the work it would be worthwhile obtaining quotations for delivery of suitable rock. First dig over the site incorporating coarse stones or rubble and top off with a thin layer of shingle to prevent soil passing through. Limestone, in particular, is very heavy and it may be worthwhile obtaining tufa which is light but usually much more expensive. Alternatively, false tufa can easily be made at home by mixing together 1 part cement, 2 parts sand and 2 parts sphagnum peat by volume; make a stiff mix by adding water and then shovel the mixture into cardboard boxes. When set after a few days, the cardboard can be torn away and the sides of the block shaped and rippled with an old wood chisel.

Constructing a rock garden: make sure the rocks are tilted slightly inwards.

A variety of different sizes of rock makes for a pleasing appearance and they should be placed to imitate a natural outcrop. Settle the rocks firmly and ram soil between with a sawn-off broom handle. One heavy rock set upon another may be supported by small stones. Slope the rocks slightly so that rain drains back into the soil. Finally allow time for the soil to settle before planting the alpines.

Protect alpines Alpine plants with hairy leaves and those about to flower should be protected with a sheet of glass or PVC as suggested on page 21. Remove fallen leaves and other debris from the rock garden.

Sow alpine seed Alpine seed may be sown now in pans or seed trays in moist well drained compost. Cover the containers with a sheet of glass or place them in a cold frame. Various shrub and tree seeds may also be sown and kept outside during winter to vernalise.

Take conifer and shrub cuttings Cuttings can be taken now of *Cupressocyparis leylandii*, *Chamaecyparis lawsoniana* and other conifers. This is also an ideal time to take hardwood cuttings of aucuba, buddleia, cornus, salix, deutzia, escallonia, kerria, philadelphus, spiraea and weigela. Firm young shoots approximately 1ft (30cm) long with the soft tip removed may be inserted in well drained soil outside or in a cold frame.

Check trees for wind damage Check trees for damage caused by autumn gales as the leaves begin to fall and carry out any tree surgery that is necessary. Stakes and tree ties should be checked at the same time.

Pot up a young Christmas tree Most people like to have a Christmas tree for the festive season but unfortunately the plants do not establish well when they are potted up during mid-winter, especially when the roots are somewhat lacking in fibre. Choose a small plant to pot up now in John Innes potting compost No 2. It will be interesting to keep from season to season and will take several years to outgrow its situation.

Complete basic cultivations before the weather restricts progress Any basic cultivations still to be done should be carried out as weather permits before the ground gets too wet or frosted. This is particularly important on heavy soil that soon gets sticky during late autumn as heavy rain has less chance to drain away or evaporate.

Prepare for sweet peas Prepare the sweet pea trench by incorporating a liberal amount of bulky organic matter into the second spit. Sweet peas may be sown in the open ground in mild districts this month allowing 1in (2.5cm) between each seed in the row, otherwise they should be sown in small pots and be placed in a sheltered area or in the cold frame.

LAWN Turf growing on light soil often shows spectacular recovery from a summer drought and will probably require cutting once or twice during the month. Heavier soil also maintains growth and care should be taken not to mow the grass when the soil is too wet otherwise skidding may occur. In all cases, moisture should be flicked from the grass leaf before mowing using a long bamboo cane or besom broom. Raise the mower cutting height so that the remaining portion of leaf will give protection should frost occur after cutting. New lawns from seed may be topped at 2in (5cm) provided the ground is not too wet. A final trim should be made to the lawn edges to tidy the area for the remainder of the year.

Continue to renovate Continue to renovate worn areas and seed may still be sown in milder areas for that purpose. Spiking and top dressing may be carried out if not already completed.

Rake up leaves and control moss The main occupation for the next few weeks will be to collect up leaves. This should be done regularly otherwise worms may make the job more difficult by pulling them partially into the soil. Fallen leaves remaining on the surface tend to encourage moss growth and aggravate disease problems. Do not be tempted to rake out moss unless a mosskiller has been used, otherwise the particles will be spread all over to make the problem even worse. Fungicide should be applied where diseases persist.

Complete laying turves October is usually the ideal month for laying turves and every opportunity should be taken to complete the job before severe frost or wet weather hinders progress.

POND Remove submersible pumps and lights from the water if not already taken out for the winter. A pond heater is most useful to keep a breathing hole open during very cold weather. This is hardly likely to occur for a few weeks but once the heater is installed it will be ready for use at any time. The power supply must, of course, be turned off before working with electrical equipment.

Consider enlarging the pool or, for that matter, constructing a new one.

Replenish gravel Fish often disturb and remove gravel topping from containers and now is a good time to replenish any that has been disturbed.

Remove dying leaves Withering leaves may be removed from plants at the same time before they have a chance to rot or fall to the bottom of the pond. This is particularly important so far as large leaves are concerned. Net off any leaves that have blown into the water from surrounding trees and drape netting over the surface of the water as suggested last month.

Thin out plants and replenish murky water Thin out congested oxygenating plants as necessary and replenish part of the water with fresh if it has become murky. Avoid clearing out the pond entirely, however, because the over-wintering parts of some plants will be hidden amongst the material in the base of the pond.

Lift and divide plants Plants growing in the moist soil alongside the water's edge can now be lifted, divided and replanted as required. Remove faded leaves from the remaining plants together with any weeds that are present.

Continue to feed fish The fish are still reasonably active and will take feed to help build them up for the winter months. Do not give more than can be taken within ten minutes however.

FRUIT Prepare the site in good time for new plants: it can be most frustrating when the plants arrive and then must be heeled in because the ground is not ready for them. They are likely to be in their final position for a number of years and so thorough preparation is necessary.

Sample a fruit variety before ordering Local fruit farms in some areas have fruit tasting days. This is an ideal opportunity to see and taste different kinds before ordering new trees. It is also a good opportunity to see the stock a grower has for sale.

Continue to harvest fruit Continue to harvest fruit as it is ready; any remaining apples on the tree at the end of the month would be better picked. When storing, each cultivar should be kept separate because they tend to mature at different times and one or two ripe fruits may cause adjacent ones to mature prematurely. It pays to wrap individual apples in greaseproof or newspaper, or polythene bags may be used to contain a number of fruits provided the top is left open and of course only fruit of one cultivar should be stored together in the bag.

Remove damaged and fallen fruit Remove any fallen fruit from the ground and damaged fruit should be taken from the tree as soon as possible.

Root prune plums and damsons Plum and damson trees that are not cropping properly because they are too vigorous may be root pruned (see page 172).

Prune soft fruit Blackberries and loganberries that have not yet been pruned should be attended to without delay together with any other bush and cane fruit except autumn-fruiting raspberries.

Take hardwood cuttings Take hardwood cuttings of bush fruits if required, see page 156.

Control weeds around plants Weed growth reduces extension growth and fruiting considerably and it is a good time to apply a herbicide around trees and bushes. Use a contact weedkiller which becomes inactivated as soon as it touches the soil, or a residual herbicide may be used but do read the label instructions carefully before application.

Control pests and diseases Continue to spray for late pests and diseases, especially apple canker, before leaf fall. Trees that cropped much better than usual and yet suffered premature leaf fall should be inspected at ground and root level. There is just a chance that boot lace (honey fungus) has attacked the tree: lift a small portion of bark from the trunk at ground level and if a sweet honey smell and white cotton-like threads can be seen there is every possibility that the disease is present. Unfortunately there is no effective practical cure for this disease and the tree plus its roots should be grubbed out without delay because the disease can spread rapidly to other plants. Before taking such drastic action however, it would be prudent to seek expert advice and some county Agricultural Colleges have staff available for that purpose.

VEGETABLES AND HERBS October is very much a clearing up month in the vegetable garden. Cut off asparagus fern close to the soil now that it has died back; leaving the bower on any longer will only cause the wind to rock the stems and create holes with glazed sides that will allow water to lay above the crowns.

Remove artichoke tops Jerusalem artichoke tops should also be cut down to within 6in (15cm) of the ground although the tubers can remain in the soil because they are completely hardy. Remove foliage and old flower stems from globe artichokes and, so far as heavy soil is concerned, a liberal sprinkling of grit around the crown will help. Some protection from frost may also be required and it is prudent to cover the crowns with leaves or bracken, preferably secured by netting so that they do not blow away.

Soften large stems before adding them to the compost heap All of the old vegetation removed from the plants makes excellent material for the compost heap; rough thick stems should be chopped and smashed before being added to the heap.

Store plant support stakes and canes Plant support stakes and canes no longer required should be taken up, cleaned and dipped into preservative. Once dried off, they should be tied in bundles and stored under cover for the winter to prolong their life.

Earth up trench celery Trench celery should now be ready for its final earthing up and no doubt soil will need to be taken from well into the first spit either side of the plants but away from them to form what has now become a ridge to the leaves. Pat the soil firm with the back of the spade so that it looks tidy and there is then less chance of heavy rain eroding it away.

Thin out small lettuce plants Thin lettuce seedlings sown for the overwintering crop. They should be spaced at least 8in (20cm) apart and any weeds present should be removed at the same time.

Blanch endive and gather winter greens A further batch of endive may now be blanched as suggested on page 94, harvesting those already blanched as required. Sprouts will be ready for harvesting now and the task is made easier by removing the lower leaves from the plant. Remove blown sprouts as picking proceeds because they are the ones that often harbour mealy cabbage aphid. This pest should be controlled by using an insecticide before it has a chance to spoil the crop. Spring cabbage to follow on after sprouts and other winter greens, can be planted in southern gardens but do set them out by the middle of the month otherwise they will not establish properly.

Protect cauliflower curds Snap a leaf or two over developing cauliflower curds to protect them from rain and frost.

Store root crops Turnips and beetroot are now ready for lifting to store; twist the tops from the roots and store them as described on page 183. Some of the turnips may be left in the ground if the site is not required immediately. Potatoes should now be lifted and spread out to dry off thoroughly before bagging up. Do not bag damaged tubers or those that have been attacked by pests otherwise they will rot and the infection will soon spread to other tubers in store. Any remaining outdoor tomatoes should be picked and taken indoors to ripen off: place the ones showing colour in a light position; those still green can be placed in boxes covered by newspaper.

Cultivate and add lime only if required Once crops have been cleared, take the opportunity to dig and apply bulky organic material as necessary. This is particularly important where heavy ground is concerned so that winter weather will break the soil down to a fine tilth for the spring sowing and planting. Left much later and such soils will be unworkable. Lime may be required and a simple pH soil test will indicate the need, but consider the crops to follow before adding the lime: potatoes, for example, grow far better without lime in the soil. (See crop rotation, page 148.)

Sow broad beans and peas for an early crop The earliest broad bean seed may now be sown on a sheltered well drained site to germinate and stand the winter. Soak the seed overnight to assist germination and then sow the seed. 'Aquadulce' is a well proven cultivar for sowing during autumn. It is also worth trying an early sowing of round seeded peas such as 'Meteor'.

Control weeds Hoe through winter greens to loosen the top inch of soil and any weeds present should be raked up and disposed of because they often take root again in the soil. Alternatively, a herbicide may be used but read the label carefully before application to ensure that the selected weedkiller may be used amongst vegetables.

Control pests Fortunately, pests are not a problem in all gardens every year but those to look out for now include mealy cabbage aphids mentioned earlier, pigeons, rabbits, rats and mice.

GREENHOUSE Take the first opportunity to clean out and wash down the greenhouse if that has not already been done (see September); the work becomes rather unpleasant as the weather gets very cold or wet.

Reduce watering but continue to feed those plants still in active growth Reduce watering still further for those plants that rest during winter. These include fuchsias and zonal pelargoniums; regal pelargoniums will still produce some growth and flowers but these will have a smaller water requirement now that the days are short and often dull. Actively growing plants like cyclamen, primulas and cineraria should continue to be fed every 10 to 14 days. Mid-season and late-flowering chrysanthemums should be fed until colour shows in the flower bud and it is then better to give clear water otherwise overfeeding often leads to rotting within the bloom. Enthusiasts who grow for exhibition, however, continue to feed to a much later stage to increase the size of the bloom. This needs to be done with care or the whole of the year's work may be ruined.

Continue to water and feed nerines Continue to water and feed nerines growing in pots but as soon as the foliage begins to turn yellow on the earlier plants, supplementary feeding should cease.

Pot lilies Pot up lilies as soon as they become available because they soon spoil when allowed to dry out; 6in (15cm) pots are usually satisfactory unless the bulbs are very large when a 7in (17.5cm) pot size would be better. Stem-rooting types like *L.auratum, formosanum, nepalense, philippinense, primulinum, speciosum* and *sulphureum,* should be planted in the lower half of the pot just covered with ½in (13mm) of compost. This will allow room for top dressing with further compost at a later stage as the stems grow. Those types that do not root at the stem should be planted close to the surface in a pot with 3in (7.5cm) covering of John Innes potting compost No 1. The pots are then left in an unheated greenhouse or frame until shoots appear when they may be taken into gentle heat.

Pot on hippeastrums Pot on hippeastrums requiring a slightly larger size of pot so that there is not more than the width of a finger between the bulb and side of the pot. The top half of the bulb should remain above the surface of the compost. Keep the compost moist without being too wet; plants that have not been repotted now should be given a liquid feed.

House tender plants Several somewhat tender plants make ideal subjects for the greenhouse including the bottle brush (*Callistemon linearis*), camellia, *Daphne odora, Fatsia japonica* and *Nerium oleander.* They may all be potted up now and kept in the greenhouse until next year when the risk of frost has passed and then be stood outside for the summer to make room for other plants in the greenhouse.

Sow *Celsia arcturus* This is a greenhouse perennial plant well worth growing for its long stems of yellow flowers with prominent purple anthers. Seed sown now in John Innes seed compost or a peat-based medium will produce plants 1½ to 2ft (45 to 60cm) tall to flower in 5in (12.5cm) pots next year in late spring or early summer.

Stop schizanthus Pinch out the growing tips of schizanthus so that they will make attractive bushy plants.

Box up mint roots for out-of-season crop Lift some mint roots and place them in boxes of garden soil with added peat, for forcing in the greenhouse. The roots will produce shoots in comparatively low temperatures and will be most acceptable to use with the potatoes growing in pots which should be brought in during the first few days of the month if not housed last month.

Prepare soil for lettuce Prepare the greenhouse or frame border for lettuce plants due to be set out next month. Any farmyard manure available may be dug in but it is important to ensure that none remains on the surface otherwise the plants will be subject to rotting at soil level. Flood the soil after cultivating so that the plants will grow without a check; fertilizer can then be raked in a few days before setting out the plants.

Sow sweet pea seeds Sow sweet pea seeds singly in tube pots, if possible, because they do not take kindly to root disturbance; seed trays may be used as a last resort when the seeds are spaced 2in (5cm) apart. Fill the containers with John Innes potting compost No 1 or a peat-based medium. The seeds should be sown ½in (13mm) deep and well watered so that the compost is uniformly moist throughout. After sowing, the containers should be placed in the cold frame since it is most important to keep temperature at a minimum to encourage sturdy growth. Seed and young plants are attractive to mice and birds and so precautions, in the form of mouse bait or traps and bird netting, should be applied in good time. Take care to avoid overwatering otherwise seed rot may occur and the plants will be more susceptible to frost damage.

Reduce watering carnations and continue to disbud Perpetual-flowering carnations will be slower growing now and so less water will be required. Buds will still develop although slowly and should be removed when large single blooms are required.

Keep atmosphere as dry as possible and check thermostat The greenhouse atmosphere should be kept as dry as possible from now on, all overhead damping should cease and it may even be necessary to turn the heat on from time to time to provide a congenial atmosphere. The vast majority of plants will tolerate a temperature of between 45 to 50°F (7 to 10°C) and so the thermostat can be set to that regime unless plants are being grown that require a higher temperature. Check the thermostat setting with an accurate thermometer because most equipment loses calibration once it has been re-set a few times. It is worth noting that for every extra 5°F (3°C) the fuel consumption is virtually doubled.

Tie back leaves to avoid shading fruit Figs and grapes almost ripe can be hastened to maturity by removing or tying back leaves to avoid shading the fruit; here again a slight raising of the temperature if necessary will help.

Arum lilies for Christmas Although often considered to be a flower for Easter, arum lilies may be encouraged to flower for Christmas by placing the pots in a light position in the greenhouse. The night temperature should be set to maintain 55°F (13°C) with a day time temperature of 10°F (6°C) higher. Ensure regular growth by keeping the compost moist and feed every 14 days.

Stagger the housing of lachenalias and freesias Lachenalias planted in containers earlier in the year can be brought in one by one over a period to stagger flowering and the same applies to freesias, although both of these subjects should be housed before severe frost threatens. Plant up the final batch of freesia corms before the middle of the month if continuity of flowers is required when existing plants finish flowering.

Sow cauliflower seed Sow cauliflower seed thinly in a seed tray to prick off singly in 3in (7.5cm) pots to overwinter in a cold greenhouse or frame. These plants will eventually be planted in the open garden next spring. Seed sown earlier, however, should by now have produced sturdy young plants to transplant in a well prepared frame at a spacing of 3 by 3in (7.5 by 7.5cm).

Pot off annuals Flower seeds sown earlier are now ready for potting off. Use John Innes potting compost No 1 for preference: peat-based mediums tend to grow a rather leafy plant during winter unless watering and feeding is carefully monitored.

Pot up some lily of the valley Pot up some lily of the valley crowns; those with one or two plump buds should be used, and just lightly cover the crowns with compost. The pots should be kept just moist and placed in good light in a cool atmosphere to promote sturdy growth.

Plant a fig tree Figs are very easy to grow in the greenhouse and where space permits a plant may be planted now. 'Brown Turkey' is a good cultivator to grow. The main advantage in greenhouse growing is that once established the tree will produce two or three crops each year; the third crop is only guaranteed, however, when a night temperature of 60°F (16°C) is maintained with a day temperature of 75°F (24°C) for the dormant tree to start growing in early December. The first crop should then be ready for harvest in May.

Fig trees make very vigorous growth and so the plant may either be grown in a container or the roots restricted in some way, otherwise much wood and little, if any, fruit will develop. The plant should, however, never lack moisture at the root even when it appears dormant during the winter, otherwise the small pin-head fruits present at that time will not develop when active growth begins. As the fruit is ripening, watering may be reduced otherwise fruit cracking and subsequent disease may occur before the fruit is ready to harvest.

Figs already established in containers may be potted on if necessary as soon as the leaves begin to show autumn colour.

Plant a grape vine Another delectable fruit which may be grown in the greenhouse is the grape. This plant requires an unheated greenhouse during at least part of the winter; it can be grown in a house without artificial heat at all, and it is not satisfactory to grow a grape vine with other plants requiring a high winter temperature.

Good drainage is essential and so the proposed root zone should be deeply dug and brick rubble or other aggregate should be added to the subsoil if necessary. Plant the vine 2ft (60cm) from the wall and at a depth approximately 1in (2.5cm) deeper than it was growing when purchased. When more than one vine is planted a spacing of 4ft (1.2m) should be provided between the plants. Cut back the cane to 1½ft (45cm) in January. 'Black Hamburgh' is a good cultivar for the greenhouse.

November

FLOWERS, TREES AND SHRUBS November can be a fickle month and it is very much a case of working in the garden at every opportunity the weather provides. Bare root trees and shrubs, including roses that have been recently purchased, may have to be heeled in a shallow trench so that their roots are covered with soil to avoid drying out before they can be permanently planted.

Half-prune tall shrubs Winds can be very blustery and so vigorous shrubs that flower on the current season's shoots like *Buddleia davidii* and large-flowered hybrid tea roses should be half pruned by cutting back the shoots half way to reduce wind rock. Check stakes and ties for firmness to prevent storm damage.

Protect plants that are about to flower Alpines and other plants likely to flower during the next few weeks will benefit from covering with a sheet of glass, pvc or a cloche. *Helleborus niger* may be induced to flower earlier and the blooms will be protected by taking prudent action now and providing protection in the form of cloches. Tender plants which have died down to ground level should be protected by covering the rootstock with bracken, straw or even fallen leaves held down with twiggy sticks. Newly planted evergreens and conifers may be sprayed with S600 to reduce transpiration and wind scorch. They can be shielded from the wind by erecting a hessian or polythene screen secured to upright posts. This may also prevent rabbits from grazing on the bark and leaves which causes considerable damage to the plants.

Autumn-sown hardy annuals will also benefit from the protection of cloches during severe weather.

Pick up fallen leaves Remove fallen leaves from beds and borders. An area worthy of particular attention in this respect is the rose bed: fallen leaves may harbour black spot disease and these are best removed as soon as possible and disposed of, preferably on the bonfire.

Plant bulbs and corms Complete bulb planting by the end of the month working from a board if necessary to avoid trampling on wet ground. De Caen and St Brigid anemone corms can be planted in well drained soil and it is often necessary to soak the corms in water for a few hours before planting if they are excessively dry.

Cultivate soil for next year's cut flowers Dig over the early outdoor chrysanthemum and dahlia beds when the soil is not too wet or frosted. Digging when the soil is frozen causes the subsoil to cool off rapidly and the soil then often takes longer to warm up in spring. Work in farmyard manure or garden compost to encourage soil moisture retention and good growth next year.

Shrub borders should also be lightly forked over to remove any surface pan and the residue of any mulch applied during the year should be worked in.

Prepare sweet pea trench No time should be lost in preparing the sweet pea trench by digging bulky organic material into the second spit and leaving the top soil rough for frost to work the soil into a fine tilth.

Control weeds and clean up hard surfaces Certain weeds such as chickweed and groundsel continue to grow during the winter months and so a suitable herbicide that controls them should be applied without delay.

Clean up hard surfaces like patio slabs and steps with a tar oil formulation, first checking that it does not stain light-coloured materials. These areas, paths and drives can be dangerously slippery due to the growth of slime moulds and algae during wet weather.

Check plants lifted for the winter Check dahlia tubers and other plants in store and if necessary remove any infection. Dahlia tubers are inclined to shrivel in a dry atmosphere and if that has happened, soak them in water overnight. A further dusting with fungicide would be worthwhile.

Stratify tree and shrub seeds Tree and shrub seeds often require to be stratified during winter before they will germinate. The best way to do this is to mix larger seeds with sand in a container placed outside, protected from mice and birds. Smaller seeds may be sown in pans or seed trays and then be placed in the cold frame or an area where they can be frozen.

Control slugs and birds Slugs can be particularly active in the garden during mild spells and early winter flowers are often attacked by birds. They can be deterred to a certain extent by spraying a bird repellent but this often needs to be re-applied after rain; black cotton can be draped over plants but looks rather unsightly. Some flowers like *Iris unguicularis* may be picked before the flower buds show colour and they can then at least be appreciated as decoration for indoors.

Berried shrub stems required for indoor decoration next month can be protected from birds by covering them with a polythene bag. Certain flowering shrubs like *Ribes sanguineum* can be encouraged to flower during the winter by cutting an odd branch towards the end of the month and then bringing it into a cool room.

Visit gardens open to the public November is usually a good month for autumn colour, provided frost and high wind has not been too severe; try to visit gardens open to the public to enjoy the colour and perhaps note plants worth growing.

Induce early flowering Some small plants in containers like Japanese azaleas may be kept indoors to induce early flowering and then be planted in their final quarters outside later.

LAWN Mowing may still be necessary provided the ground is not too wet.

Remove worm casts Brush away worm casts before they get trampled and smeared.

Lay turves November is a good month to lay turves provided the ground is free from frost and excessive moisture. Preparation can be made for a new lawn to be grown from seed next spring.

Sweep up leaves but not if the grass is frosty Leaves may still be falling unless a severe frost has brought them all down. Sweep them up as soon as possible but avoid walking on the grass when it is frosted otherwise damage will be done to the sward.

Run machinery and have it serviced Machinery should be started up and run for a few minutes to keep it in good working order and it is a good plan to have it serviced during the off peak period so that any replacement parts can be ordered and installed in good time for next season.

POND Remove tender plants from the pond and cut back any dead foliage. The plants can remain potted up in their containers and be kept moist throughout winter in a frost-free greenhouse or other suitable area.

Remove leaves Leaves will be gradually dying back and should be cut from plants before they have a chance to contaminate the water; leaves that have fallen from the trees should also be removed for the same reason. The leaves on marginal plants like rushes should be left for as long as possible because they do afford some protection against frost.

Empty shallow concrete pools Shallow concrete lined pools are best emptied during the month because they are rather susceptible to cracking during hard weather.

FRUIT This is the ideal month for planting bare root fruit trees and bushes provided the leaves have fallen naturally before the plants are lifted from the nursery. Remember to dig a hole large enough to accommodate the roots without buckling and to drive the stake into the hole before inserting the tree roots (see page 142). Use a tree tie to secure the tree to the stake; the special tie may then be loosened easily as the tree girth increases in due course.

Grape vines prefer a sunny spot Grape vines can be planted out of doors now selecting a sheltered and sunny spot for them: a south-facing wall is ideal, or they may be trained on post and wire framework. Plants growing in containers often establish better when the roots are carefully disentangled from the root ball, but do not attempt to free them if there is any chance of damage.

Cut back black currants after planting Black currants once planted firmly should be cut back to two buds from the ground and the prunings may then be used as hardwood cuttings.

Plant layered tips Blackberry and loganberry tips earthed over earlier should now be well rooted and the layers may be cut from the parent and planted separately. These plants need sufficient room to do well and a minimum space of 10ft (3m) should be allowed between plants.

Check tree supports Check stakes for firmness and ties for tightness supporting free-standing trees, posts and wires supporting fan-trained and cordon plants.

Rake up leaves Rake up leaves and deposit them in polythene bags to rot down or put them on the compost heap.

Prune fruit trees and bushes Winter pruning of fruit trees and bushes should be started once the majority of leaves has fallen. First cut out any diseased wood, looking in particular for canker lesions and the white shoot tips caused by mildew; crossing branches are dealt with next and then make cuts according to the training method adopted for that particular plant. Secondary shoots arising from summer pruning should be cut back to firm wood. Root prune over-vigorous trees if necessary.

Check fruit in store Check fruit in store and remove any showing signs of disease. Ventilation may be required if any amount of fruit is being stored.

Renew tree guards and fruit cage netting Rabbits will cause a great deal of damage to the bark of trees and chew the stems of bush fruits in some districts. See that the fruit cage netting is in good order and apply tree guards or wire netting columns to protect plants not enclosed by a fruit cage.

Apply winter wash Although not necessary every year, dormant trees may be sprayed with tar oil winter wash to control over-wintering pests and diseases. Spray peaches and nectarines against peach leaf curl or erect a rainproof cover over the tree if possible: trees kept dry during winter are unlikely to become infected next year.

Tidy strawberries Clean up the strawberry bed by removing runners, dead leaves and weeds.

VEGETABLES AND HERBS Take every opportunity to dig vacant ground before it becomes too wet or frosted. The runner bean and celery trenches are top priority jobs because deep cultivation is required to fork bulky organic material into the second spit.

Test soil for lime requirement Check the pH of the soil and apply lime if necessary so that the winter rains will wash the material into the soil. Free-draining sandy soils are better limed in the spring otherwise much of the application will be lost in leaching.

Lift root crops Jerusalem artichokes, parsnips and swedes may be lifted as they are required for the kitchen otherwise they may be left in the ground since they are quite hardy; it is worthwhile harvesting a week or two's supply in case the ground becomes too frozen to dig. This is unlikely to happen in most areas until after the turn of the year.

Give celery its final earthing up Celery may still need a final earthing up but do not cover the leaves with soil otherwise they will be inclined to rot off and the sticks will be spoiled.

Mulch asparagus The asparagus bed should now be mulched with garden compost; well rotted farmyard manure may be used instead but it does often introduce a high population of weed seeds.

Mulch globe artichokes Globe artichokes benefit from mulching not only to benefit the soil but to help protect the crowns from frost damage.

Protect herbs Parsley and other herbs sown earlier will benefit from covering with cloches and mature herbs should now be harvested.

Sow broad beans and peas Make a sowing of broad beans and round seeded peas as suggested last month. They will germinate and stand the winter to provide an early crop for next year. 'The Sutton' broad bean can be sown under cloches this month for an early crop; remember to put a mouse trap under the cloches.

Store beetroot and turnips Beetroot and turnips should now be lifted and stored in peat or sand as suggested on page 183.

Force chicory Lift a batch of chicory roots for forcing in pots or boxes filled with garden soil. Complete darkness is required and a temperature of 60°F (16°C) will produce chicons in two or three weeks.

Pest and disease control Remove diseased and yellowing leaves from brassicas and apply slug pellets to susceptible crops. Mice are likely to be a problem especially where vegetables are stored.

Protect brassicas Bend a leaf or two over developing cauliflower heads to protect them from frost. Winter greens should be secure otherwise wind rock will cause a hole close to the stem for water to accumulate: provide plants with a short stake if necessary but take care when bending over to harvest the crop; alternatively soil may be ridged up around the stem.

GREENHOUSE Mid-season chrysanthemums are in bloom now and it is worth taking note of the date when they are at their peak so that if it is intended to enter for autumn shows next year, stopping dates which have a bearing on flowering time can be amended accordingly; other things being equal, a chrysanthemum cultivar usually flowers within a few days of a specific date each year although weather conditions play a significant role in the actual date. Stems should be cut down to within 9in (23cm) of the root after flowering and, after removing the canes, the pots may be stood close together in a frost-free frame. The stools can withstand relatively low temperatures provided the compost is on the dry side.

Water and feed plants in active growth Continue to feed and carefully water plants like freesias and poinsettia in active growth.

Ventilate when possible The greenhouse atmosphere should be kept on the dry side by providing ventilation at every opportunity and using pesticide smokes to fumigate as necessary, rather than using wet sprays.

Pot up lily of the valley and lilies A further batch of lily of the valley crowns may be potted up as described last month and there is still time to pot lilies like *L.henryi, regale* and *rubellum.*

Plant lettuce Plant lettuce in the greenhouse or frame – an 8in (20cm) spacing each way is sufficient – and remember to protect the plants by dusting fungicide and scattering slug pellets immediately after planting.

Force rhubarb Rhubarb can be forced once the roots have been subjected to frost for a few days. Simply box or pot the roots up in garden soil and place them under the bench in the greenhouse. Drape them with black polythene to keep them dark; alternatively they may simply be packed together in the dark without actually planting should they not be required for planting out of doors later.

Pinch sweet peas Autumn-sown sweet peas that have made good growth should now be stopped by pinching out the growing tip of the plant. This will encourage sturdy growth to arise as lateral shoots.

Inspect plunged bulbs Check plunged bulbs in the cold frame for growth and to make sure that they are not lacking water. Slug pellets may need to be replenished. Mice and woodlice may also be a problem. Some of the earlier bulbs may be ready to bring in provided the pots are full of roots and the shoots are well developed.

Take root cuttings Root cuttings can be taken from a number of plants now including anchusa, gaillardia, hollyhock, oriental poppy, perennial phlox, *Primula denticulata* and *Romneya coulteri.*

Pot up fruit trees Fruit trees grown in a restricted form in pots in the greenhouse add much interest during the winter and early spring; they produce their crop that much earlier than those planted in the open garden and they can be moved outside for the summer to make room for other plants in the greenhouse. Apples make ideal subjects because family trees may be purchased containing three or four different cultivars budded onto the same tree. This ensures adequate pollen to cross pollinate for a worthwhile crop; alternatively, two or three individual plants of different cultivars should be chosen which are compatible and flower at the same time. The trees may be potted up now in 10in (25cm) pots using John Innes potting compost No 2.

Clean the greenhouse exterior Take the opportunity provided by a foggy morning to remove any algae and grime still adhering to the glass, it is usually more easily removed under those conditions, especially when it has already been subjected to frost.

Keep plants as dry as possible Generally, plants should be kept as dry as possible in keeping with their requirements to harden growth for the winter, especially in a cold greenhouse. One type of plant that revels in an airy cold greenhouse is the alpine. Many kinds are available and they will add much interest to the house.

Tidy plants Dead-head plants and pick off any yellowing leaves, especially from overwintering pelargoniums. Leaves from grape vines and other fruit should also be removed from the house as soon as possible otherwise they will encourage grey mould and woodlice.

Ripen fruit wood Greenhouses containing only fruit plants like peaches and grapes may be given continuous ventilation, weather permitting. Late grapes still to ripen should be given a temperature of 50°F (10°C) otherwise fruit splitting will occur, especially when the atmospheric humidity is high. Any bunches remaining at the end of the month should be cut off with a handle of rod sufficiently long to be immersed in a bottle of water. The container should be placed in a wine bottle rack or be supported horizontally so that the grapes do not touch the sides.

Prune early grapes Grape vines to be started into growth early with heat should be pruned at the end of the month. This is a simple procedure by cutting away all of the fruited rods back to two fat buds at their base near the main rods. Should both buds develop into shoots, one will be rubbed out at an early stage. The rods should then be untied and lowered so that they are parallel with the floor; then all of the shoots will develop uniformly along the rods. It is often recommended that the loose rind should be removed at this stage although it is really only necessary when the rods are infected by scale insects or other pests so that an insecticide may be applied more effectively.

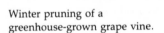

Winter pruning of a
greenhouse-grown grape vine.

December

FLOWERS, TREES AND SHRUBS The end of the calendar year but not the end of the gardening year for that is a continuous cycle: the end of the year for one plant is midway for another and yet the beginning for others.

Cut shoots to bring indoors A good example of the way in which plant seasons can be mixed is when shoots of spring-flowering shrubs like flowering currant, forsythia, *Jasminum nudiflorum* and mahonia when cut now and brought indoors will produce their flowers that much sooner. Placed in a container of water in a warm room during the first few days of the month, they may even be in flower for Christmas.

Protect buds from birds Buds developing on shrubs outside in the border may require protection from birds.

Snow can cause damage Shake snow from branches to avoid damage that can soon spoil the look of a plant and allow diseases to enter the wood. Bulb shoots will not be harmed by a layer of snow but fallen leaves should certainly be removed to prevent slug damage.

Refirm soil loosened by frost Soil around newly planted trees and shrubs and particularly alongside hardwood cuttings is often loosened by frost: tread the soil back firmly with the feet.

Plant trees and shrubs when conditions permit Deciduous shrubs and trees including roses may still be planted provided the soil is not frozen or too wet. Plants delivered from the nursery will, no doubt, be wrapped in straw. This may remain around the plants for up to one week but after that time has elapsed, and if the soil is still not fit for planting, the plants should be unwrapped and heeled in until they can be planted. Take precautions against rabbits if they are likely to be a problem. Should the soil be unfit for even heeling in, then the plants must still be unwrapped and the roots covered with moist sacking and kept in a frost-free place. On no account should the roots dry out otherwise irreversible damage may result.

Collect up leaves Continue to collect up fallen leaves from the borders, particularly from the rose bed where overwintering black spot spores will linger. Hand weed the beds or apply a contact herbicide.

Inspect tubers and corms Inspect tubers and corms in store and remove any that show rotting. Large rootstocks like dahlia tubers may still be saved by cutting away the infection and dusting with fungicide. Tubers may be dehydrated and shrivelled in which case they should be soaked in water overnight and then be boxed up in peat the following day.

Check supports and prune climbers Check wall supports for climbers and prune back ivy and Virginia creeper; *Clematis jackmanii* may also be pruned by cutting the shoots back to within 1ft (30cm) of the ground; alternatively build up a main framework by cutting the side growths to one leaf joint from the old wood. Wisteria growth may also be pruned back to two buds.

LAWN Avoid walking on frosted grass but, whenever possible, brush away worm casts if they still appear and collect up leaves which have a habit of blowing in from outside the garden.

Run machinery Start up and run machinery for a few minutes to keep points etc. in good order. Have machinery serviced if not already attended to.

Cultivate areas to be seeded in spring Areas to be seeded in the spring should be dug over provided the soil is not too wet or frozen. Previously cultivated areas for that purpose may be raked to remove stones and other bits of debris that are working to the surface.

Control leatherjackets Leatherjackets can be a problem on established lawns during mild weather and precautions should be taken against them.

POND Check the surface to ensure the pond heater is working or float a rubber ball in the water to prevent damage to the container sides. An area free from ice is necessary to allow the escape of toxic gases but do not crack the ice with a hammer otherwise shock waves will damage the fish.

FRUIT Complete winter pruning but not in freezing winds otherwise the wood is likely to be damaged. Stone fruits should not be pruned during winter due to the susceptibility of silver leaf disease. Root pruning, when necessary, should be completed as soon as possible.

Plant trees and bushes Plant fruit trees and bushes unless the soil is too wet or frozen, when the plants should be stored as suggested for trees and shrubs on page 140.

Protect from frost In colder districts blackberry, loganberry and fig shoots should be loosely tied together. The latter will benefit from being protected by a covering of bracken or straw.

Apply winter wash Spray trees and bushes with tar oil wash unless the weather is frosty or the dormant season spray has already been applied.

Remove mummified fruit Inspect the trees for mummified fruit to avoid carry over of the brown rot disease. The diseased fruit should be burned.

VEGETABLES Japanese onions or onion sets set out last autumn should be kept weed free by hand weeding or the application of a contact weedkiller that becomes inactive as it touches the soil; take care not to splash the onion leaves.

Lift root crops a week or two before use Jerusalem artichokes, parsnips and other root crops should be lifted a week or so in advance of use as the opportunity arises in case the ground becomes too frozen.

Heel in winter cauliflower away from the wind Winter cauliflower plants may be lifted carefully, faced away from cold winds and then be heeled firmly into the soil; they will remain in better condition than when growing upright.

Refirm brassicas Refirm brassica plants after frosts have loosened the soil.

Inspect celery Remove damaged and diseased leaves from celery. Straw may be placed over the plants for protection in severe weather.

Wheel compost into position When the ground is frozen, it is a good plan to barrow compost or farmyard manure into position for digging in when conditions improve but do not attempt to dig until the soil has thawed out.

Protect compost heap Cover over the compost heap with old sacking or other material to help retain heat and keep out excess water.

Lift and store turnips and swedes Turnips and swedes still left in the ground are better lifted and stored; in mild districts, however, it should be sufficient to ridge up soil over the roots leaving the tops unearthed.

GREENHOUSE Prune grape vines and lower the rods as suggested last month if that has not already been done. If peach and nectarines have not already been pruned, the job should be done as soon as possible by cutting out spent fruited wood and then tying in the replacement shoots.

Water figs if necessary Check that fig roots are not dry and water the border if necessary. All watering should be carried out during the early morning to allow the plants and air to dry off before night time. An open day is ideal for the job but when plants are dry they should be attended to rather than wait for the perfect day.

Check pelargoniums, fuchsias and chrysanthemum stools for dryness The stools should not be allowed to dry out completely.

The lovely climbing rose 'Mme Grégoire Staechelin'.

Take cuttings of large exhibition chrysanthemums Chrysanthemum cuttings of the large exhibition cultivars may be taken as soon as they are ready; the stools of other types should be kept cool so that they vernalize to avoid rosetting. This is a condition where shoots do not elongate.

Select carnation cuttings Perpetual-flowering carnation cuttings may be taken from shoots with less than five leaves, those with more have probably initiated a flower bud. Only take vigorous shoots otherwise it would be better to wait until later because spindly cuttings seldom make good plants.

House potted strawberries The first batch of pot strawberries may now be placed on the staging in the greenhouse. They may require watering, particularly if the weather has been frosty outside. Once the roots have become active, the plants may be given a liquid feed containing high potash.

Cut freesia stems Freesias are now developing flower buds and as soon as the first bud on the stem is showing colour, the stem may be cut but do not cut down too low or the lateral stem arising from the existing main shoot may be wasted.

House bulbs when they are ready Bulbs plunged in the frame outside will in some cases be ready for housing; wait until the shoots appear above the compost in the container. The ideal time to bring in hyacinths is when the flower bud can be felt at the base of the stem.

Sow onion seed for big bulbs Enthusiasts sow exhibition onion seed during the month. A temperature of at least 50°F (10°C) should be provided and once the seedlings have germinated they are pricked out at the 'crook' stage. This is when the first leaf is still bent before it has straightened. Plants may be pricked out singly in small pots or 48 to a standard sized seed tray. Leeks may also be sown, and treated in the same way will make some large roots at harvest time.

Sow radish and carrots Carrot seed may be sown after the shortest day selecting an early cultivar. Radish seed can also be sown.

Force chicory Another batch of chicory can now be brought in for forcing as described on page 123.

Protect plants in cold frames Plants in cold frames can be protected in severe weather by laying sacking over the lights at night time but it is best removed the following morning so that plants in leaf receive maximum light.

Wash pots and trays This is a good opportunity to wash any pots and seed trays still requiring attention. Broken and cracked pots may be repaired with one of the resin kits often used to repair damaged metal.

Control pests Watch out for pests such as slugs, greenfly and mice.

A blaze of summer-flowering annuals which includes petunias, tagetes and alyssum with the perennial *Mimulus moschatus*.

GARDENING TECHNIQUES

BASIC CULTIVATION

Many plants growing well in natural surroundings thrive and appear happy enough, so why should gardeners bother to take the trouble to dig and otherwise prepare the ground for cultivated plants? Well, there are many reasons for this, not least of which are the beneficial effects of gentle exercise and the satisfaction of achieving a job well done. Many weeds that would otherwise compete with crop plants for light, air, plant foods and moisture can be eliminated by digging them into the ground where they will decompose and add to the general fertility of the soil. Bulky organic material is incorporated to a depth where it will help to retain moisture and plant foods so that it will encourage the roots of crop plants to develop and search at lower levels and consequently withstand drought conditions better.

Soil cultivation enables air to percolate through the particles to provide oxygen for the micro-organisms and roots, also organisms and decomposing organic material can more easily move upwards and be released from the soil. Hard surface and subsoil layers known as 'pans' can be broken up to facilitate drainage by the downward movement of surface water and an important factor, often overlooked, is the fact that during spells of dry weather, subsoil moisture is more readily available to plants when its upward movement is not restricted by a subsoil pan.

In addition to controlling weed growth as mentioned earlier, digging the soil also helps to control pests by disturbing them: the flock of birds following a tractor and plough in the farmer's field is more often than not seen on a much smaller scale in the garden by a robin and other birds observing the soil as it is turned over.

Although not important for gardens with light sandy soil, the heavier soils and especially those with a clay content benefit considerably from being cultivated during autumn and then left rough for the winter. The subsequent effects from alternate wetting and drying by rain, wind and frost improves the crumb structure and results in a fine tilth for sowing and planting during the following spring.

The most fertile part of undisturbed soil is that which is near the surface because air and sunlight are utilized by micro-organisms. By inverting this portion of the soil through digging, the depth of fertile soil may be increased and at the same time a larger proportion of soil particles will be exposed to the elements. Whilst the beneficial surface layer is being distributed lower down, nitrogen, which has previously been leached downwards, is brought to the surface so that it is more readily available for uptake by plants.

Over cultivation is detrimental Although most experienced gardeners consider that cultivations improve the soil in various ways, too much of a good thing can lead to problems with structure and tilth so that the natural adhesive materials that hold the soil particles together become unstable and the crumbs are reduced to dust, which can easily be blown away by wind. This is hardly likely to happen in a garden where bulky organic material like farmyard manure or compost is incorporated during annual digging and where subsequent digging in the 12 months following is restricted to lightly forking the ground between crops.

Trampling over wet ground, particularly if it is heavy, will do considerable harm to the soil structure, as will digging the ground when it is too wet. In fact, the heavier types of soil need careful handling to build up and preserve good tilth and structure: the best time of year to cultivate such soils is during autumn when they are moist without being too wet. On no account should the main cultivation be left until late spring otherwise the sticky clods will pack together and bake like bricks to make working a fine surface practically impossible.

Very light sandy soils, on the other hand, are generally best left until spring for the main cultivations: turned over during autumn and left to be pounded by winter rains may cause them to become rather too compacted for early sown seed and transplants to flourish well; alternatively a dry spell with severe frost will destroy the structure of newly dug sandy soil because the pockets of soil between ice films are too dry.

On no account should ground be dug when it is frozen or covered with snow because the soil structure and organisms will be harmed.

The no-digging method Whilst it may appear attractive to be able to grow plants without first cultivating the ground, in practical terms it is just not feasable. This method requires that vast quantities of bulky organic material – certainly far more than can be generated from the average garden – should be placed on the soil surface each year. In theory, worms then do all the cultivating that is necessary by pulling some of the organic material into the ground. Unfortunately the system seldom works properly due to the lack of sufficient bulky organic material.

CULTIVATING A SEQUENCE The usual order of events leading up to planting or sowing starts with digging the ground. This can be a fairly shallow cultivation – one spit deep – using a spade, or maybe deeper for a special purpose. A digging fork is then used at a later date to knock down the lumps. This is followed by raking to give a level surface, the fineness of the tilth obtained depending on the size of seeds or type of plants to be set out.

Single digging In most cases, especially when the ground has previously been cropped, single digging is all that will be necessary. This means turning the soil over one spit deep, that is to the full depth of the spade. Clearly all weed growth and bulky organic material like farmyard manure or garden compost will need to be buried completely and to do that properly a space should be provided for the turned soil to be moved into. The best way to

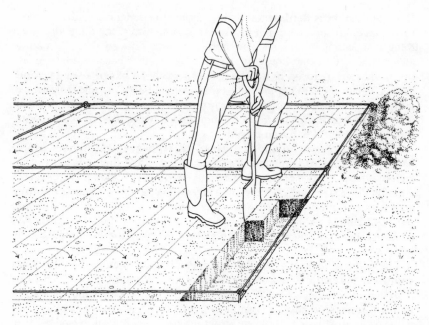

Single digging on a plot which has been divided into two strips.

accomplish this is to take out a trench two spade widths wide and one spit deep at one end of the plot and deposit the soil removed at the other end of the plot. Remove the crumbs and loose soil particles at the bottom of the trench: it is surprising how much space is needed by the soil as digging proceeds. When everything has gone according to plan, the soil taken from the first trench and deposited at the end of the plot will be just sufficient to fill in the similar trench made when digging is completed.

A considerable amount of soil will need to be taken from one end to the other if the plot is very wide and to avoid unnecessary effort and time, it is a good idea to divide the plot longitudinally down the centre with a taut garden line; a trench is then taken out as before but only on one half of the plot. Instead of piling the soil at the opposite end it is moved over to the other side but at the same end. Deposit the soil outside of the area to be dug otherwise it will mean moving it again. The idea is to dig down one side of the divided plot, turn at the bottom and fill in the trench at that end by opening up a similar trench on the adjacent half of the plot. Work backwards down the second half and finally fill in the last trench with the soil taken from the first.

Digging really can be most relaxing and enjoyable provided it is not hurried. Take time to work up a rhythm and do not try to lift more soil than can be moved without strain. Try to keep the digging edge straight across the plot and push the spade into the soil so that it is vertical: digging will be found to be much easier and a greater depth of soil will be effectively cultivated. Before lifting the spadeful of soil cut a nick in the surface of the ground at right angles to the trench so that the block of soil will come away cleanly as the spade is lifted. Having thrust the spade into the ground and removed the spadeful, turn the spade so that the soil falls upside down in the trench to cover any manure or compost that has been deposited at the bottom. When a large amount of manure or compost is used, it is better to either fork it into the bottom of the trench or to place it onto the sloping side of the previous spit turned over. This will avoid a wad of uncongenial material persisting should conditions become unfavourable.

DIG IN WEEDS. Annual weeds may be dug in provided they are covered completely with soil, otherwise if any leaf is showing above ground the weed may recover and grow on. Perennial weeds like couch grass, ground elder and bindweed should be removed completely or they will soon regenerate to become more of a problem.

Grass-covered ground is best tackled by removing a thin layer of grass as if lifting turves, turning each turf upside down at the bottom of the trench and then chopping it up into small pieces with the spade; unless that is done there is just a possibility that an impermeable layer may be formed by the anaerobic decomposition of the grass.

Continue digging to the side of the plot and then place the manure or upturned grass in position before starting the next trench, and so on. There is a tendency to try to take a larger spadeful as work proceeds but it is seldom worthwhile because in the end the total time taken will be much the same, and an aching back takes much pleasure from the activity.

Double digging This is sometimes called bastard or mock trenching and is particularly useful for new gardens so that sunken debris can be removed. It is also beneficial for heavier soils when done every three years to loosen and aerate the subsoil; the other reason for double digging is to remove and break up a subsoil mineral or cultivation pan: the latter is unlikely to occur when soil is cultivated by hand although it may result from over-use of a mechanical cultivator.

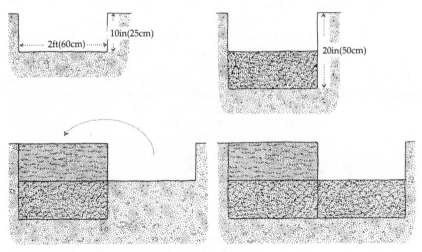

Diagrams to show the procedure for double digging.

When double digging, the ground is dug two spits deep but the two spits are always kept at their original level so that the less fertile subsoil is never brought to the surface.

The plot is divided, if necessary, as for single digging and a first trench taken out. In this case the trench will need to be three spade widths, approximately 2ft (60cm) wide, to enable you to get into the trench to dig the second spit. Make sure the sides of the trench are vertical and that the loose crumbs have been removed from the base. Having taken out the trench, the second spit can be dug over using a garden fork; remove any debris that may be present and then shake out manure or garden compost over the bottom of the trench. This is now worked into the second spit although when the ground has previously been double dug on other occasions to remove debris, the manure may simply be spread over the bottom of the trench.

Cut a measuring stick for each side of the trench so that subsequent trench widths remain the same. The next trench width to be dug is three individual spade widths when facing at right angles to the open trench and the measuring sticks can be used to mark the exact place to insert a garden line. Cut a small groove along the line to make the straight edge of the second trench and then remove the string to avoid cutting it as digging proceeds.

You will now find that it is easier to start digging facing the side of the plot rather than facing the open trench. Insert the spade to its full depth down through the marker groove, then make a similar slit in the soil parallel to the first but a spade width away. Remove the spade and then dig up the spadeful of soil. Place the clod upside down in the trench alongside the nearest 'wall' of the open trench. Next remove a spadeful of soil from the next width and place upside down next to the first. Finally remove the third spadeful and place upside down in the remaining gap. Now go back to the groove and work towards the open trench as before. This method ensures that trenches remain open with parallel sides and prevents soil from falling into the trench as work proceeds.

Continue working in this way until the second trench is complete. Then fork over the second spit and incorporate manure as before. Mark off the next trench with the measuring sticks and garden line and so on.

Ridging Since the elements have a beneficial effect on heavy soils, it would seem sensible to expose as much surface area as possible to winter weather. Ridging provides such a method and given a hard winter can be most successful; unfortunately if the winter months remain mild it can be rather less effective to leave ridges of sticky clay to be worked down in the spring. However, the method has stood the test of time and is now described for what it is worth. Divide the plot to be dug into 3ft (90cm) wide strips. Start, at one end of the first strip, by making a 12in (30cm) wide trench across the width of the strip, one spit deep. Now work backwards down this strip as for single/double digging. Turn each spadeful of soil forward and over; but turn the spadeful towards the centre of the trench, as shown in the diagram. By doing this a continuous ridge is created down the length of the strip. Make the ridges as steep as possible.

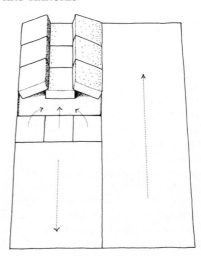

A diagrammatic illustration of ridging.

Forking Although the spade is a most useful tool for basic cultivation its use is somewhat limited when the ground is very stony. In that case a digging fork must be used to loosen the top soil which may then be removed with a spade to form a trench.

Producing a tilth Once basic cultivations have been completed, the next stage is to knock down the soil with a fork or the back of a rake. This is best done when the soil is moist but not too wet so that it does not stick to footwear.

RAKING Finally the soil is levelled by raking but care should be taken to avoid bringing up lumps from below; fertilizers may then be applied.

Applying fertilizers Usually two or more applications of fertilizers are given to a crop. The first normally consists of a general fertilizer in granular or powdered form scattered over the soil surface and lightly forked or raked in a few days before sowing or planting. This is the base dressing. The second is known as a top dressing or a side dressing and is applied as a booster once the crop is established. Top dressings may be general fertilizers or contain only one or two elements according to the needs of the crop.

Mechanical cultivations Various machines are available to till the ground and rotary cultivators provide a fairly quick way of turning the soil. They tend to cultivate less deeply than by hand digging and in certain heavy soils may cause a pan to form just below the surface. Care should be taken to avoid their use too frequently otherwise soil structure may be impaired.

FERTILIZERS AND MANURES

Plants need a balanced diet to grow properly and whilst they are to a certain extent selective in the different kinds of nutrient they take in, deficiencies can occur if one of the elements is lacking. Plant food is derived from various sources including farmyard manure and garden compost. They are known as bulky organic manures because they have considerable bulk and contain comparatively small amounts of actual plant food, although they are excellent for conditioning the soil and encouraging earthworms and beneficial bacteria. Other organic fertilizers include dried blood which contains between 10 and 14 per cent nitrogen; it is very soluble and fast acting compared with other forms of organic nitrogen and was once used extensively for liquid feeding. Fish manure contains nitrogen, so essential for healthy growth of leaves and shoots; fish manure also contains phosphoric acid (phosphate) necessary for good root development. Hoof and horn fertilizer tends to vary in texture from fine dust particles that become available as plant food much faster than the larger grist, which may take weeks or even months to benefit plants; different samples of hoof and horn range from 12 to 14.5 per cent nitrogen. Soot also provides up to approximately 6 per cent nitrogen and it is usually weathered before use around tender plants to avoid scorch.

Wool shoddy is available in some areas and is valued more for the fibre content than food value, which varies considerably according to source. Shoddy consists of waste from wool mills where fleeces are processed; another source is the reclamation of wool rags and carpets. A good sample should contain up to 14 per cent nitrogen although 3 per cent is not uncommon. Poultry manure is an organic material that is available in certain districts, it contains a good deal of nitrogen in the form of ammonia but this is inclined to scorch the roots and leaves of plants unless used with care: a good sample will have approximately 6 times as much nitrogen as an average sample of farmyard manure. Sewage sludge is being processed by some local authorities and may be used as a mulch or for digging into the ground. Dried sludge is much easier to handle and contains up to 1.4 per cent nitrogen plus a rather lower quantity of phosphoric acid and a trace of potash. Spent hops provide a valuable source of organic matter and contain around 0.6 per cent nitrogen with 0.2 per cent phosphoric acid but considering the amount that can be dug into the soil or used as a mulch, the plant food value is reasonably good. Spent mushroom compost is ideal for digging into the soil especially if the soil has a low pH that needs to be raised: mushroom compost often contains a considerable amount of chalk and so its use with lime-hating plants should be avoided. The nitrogen level is comparatively high for a bulky organic at around 0.75 per cent; phosphates and potash are also present.

Seaweed contains 0.5 per cent nitrogen, some phosphate and potash together with a fairly high level of common salt at 1.3 per cent; many trace elements so essential for healthy plant growth are also present. Fresh seaweed is better added to the compost heap before digging into the ground, although gardeners by the coast where supplies are plentiful often spread it over the garden and turn it from time to time before digging it in.

Many gardeners use organic fertilizers because it seems more natural. Certainly bulky organics like farmyard manure and garden compost are excellent for soil conditioning, but so far as the plant is concerned, concentrated inorganic fertilizers like ammonium nitrate might just as well be used as concentrated organics like hoof and horn: soil bacteria convert the nitrogen – regardless of source – into nitrates which can be taken up by plants.

Inorganic fertilizers are produced in a factory and whilst their use may appear to be artificial, the food content is usually higher than organic fertilizers and the cost lower. Synthetic urea, for example, contains 46 per cent nitrogen, sulphate of ammonia 21 per cent and nitrate of ammonia 36 per cent. Inorganic fertilizers are usually very quick acting and may be used to correct nitrogen deficiency in plants and to boost growth as in the case of spring cabbage at the turn of the year.

Some inorganic fertilizers are slower acting and give up their nitrogen over a long period: urea formaldehyde with 38 per cent nitrogen and EN-Mag containing 5.5 per cent nitrogen, 20.7 per cent phosphoric acid, 10.5 per cent potassium and 8.5 per cent magnesium are good examples. Slower-acting fertilizers are often better to use during wet seasons because their nitrogen content is less likely to be washed out of the soil by rain.

Like nitrogen, phosphorus is also available in both organic and inorganic forms. Phosphate is important for proper root growth which has an overall effect on the general development of the plant. Bone meal contains 22 per cent phosphoric acid and is often recommended as a base dressing for plants because of its slow-release action. Steamed bone flour contains 28 per cent phosphorus, is very fine and therefore more readily available to plants. Meat and bone meal, a variable product, contains approximately 16 per cent phosphorus and around 7 per cent nitrogen. It is most important to use only sterilized bone products to avoid the transmission of certain diseases.

Superphosphate is a form of inorganic phosphate and one source is processed from ground rock imported from Morocco.

Potassium is one of the major plant foods necessary for balanced healthy growth and good flower and fruit development. The main source of organic potash is bonfire ash which contains up to 15 per cent; seaweed contains a small amount as does farmyard manure and garden compost. Inorganic forms of potash are sulphate of potash with 48.6 per cent potassium and muriate of potash containing 50.4 per cent.

All of the major plant foods, nitrogen, phosphate and potash, may be purchased as single items known as 'straights' and then applied singly or mixed at home before application. Alternatively they may be purchased already mixed when they are known as 'compound' fertilizers.

Another element, magnesium, is required to a somewhat lesser degree and is an important constituent in the green colouring of leaves to enable them to trap sunlight. Magnesium is supplied by Epsom salts, which are very soluble and fast acting, Kieserite, a slower-acting form and magnesian limestone which is particularly useful when lime is also required.

Various other elements are also required by plants in minute quantities. These trace elements are usually available in garden soil and they include boron, zinc, molybdenum, iron, sulphur and manganese.

Whilst the majority of plant food is taken up as liquid through the root system, foliar feeding by applying very dilute liquid to the leaves is beneficial under certain conditions: ailing plants through lack of moisture at the root, those attacked by root diseases and plants growing in exceptionally acid or alkaline soils often respond to foliar feeds. Young plants about to be planted out tend to establish faster following a foliar feed. Although foliar feeding is an extra benefit it really only supplements plant foods taken up by the roots since only comparatively small amounts can be taken in by the leaves.

SOIL TESTING Base fertilizer and lime application is often done in a hap-hazard way with no real indication of the amounts, if any, of the various elements that might be necessary. Soil testing to determine the pH level for lime requirement is very simple and various kits are available for use in the garden. Soil fertility is rather more difficult to determine but here again various kits are available to test for phosphate and potash; nitrogen is far more difficult to ascertain because the levels are changing all the time according to temperature and subsequent bacterial activity. Interpretation of the results for various crops will soon come with experience so that full use of the kit can be made.

COMPOST MAKING A regular supply of well made garden compost is valuable for mulching and digging into the soil. Unfortunately there never seems to be quite enough but certainly significant amounts can be achieved by saving every scrap of garden waste, provided it is not infected by club root or other serious disease: lawn clippings, soft hedge clippings, leaves and stalks and anything else that comes to hand; carpet sweepings and wood ash from the bonfire are all most acceptable. Tough woody material is best avoided although twigs, mature flower stems and those from cabbage and other brassica plants can be smashed up or ground with a special grinder available from garden centres.

Site the compost heap in a sheltered position, shaded from strong sun and wind that tends to dry out the heap and reduces the activity of bacteria and beneficial fungi. An old carpet, sacking or sheet of polythene draped over the top will keep out heavy rain which would chill and waterlog the compost. Special compost bins may be purchased or a simple compost container can be made by driving four posts into the ground and attaching wire, or poly-propylene, netting. Corrugated iron is sometimes used but is not ideal because gaps around the sides are needed to allow sufficient air to enter. A large box made of spaced wooden slats provides an excellent container. Whatever the material used, the container should have a removeable front so that the compost can easily be taken out when required.

In addition to the bulky compost ingredients, two other supplements will be necessary: a form of quick-acting nitrogen to feed the bacteria that help to decompose and generate heat within the heap, and lime. This is necessary to neutralize the acidity created as fermentation proceeds. Unless corrected, the acidity would inhibit further bacterial activity and the compost may not be satisfactory for general use in the garden.

The best way to incorporate the nitrogen and lime is to use a proprietory compost accelerator which is sprinkled over each 6 to 9in (15 to 23cm) layer of material and then watered in. Alternatively, sprinkle sulphate of ammonia at the rate of ½oz per sq yd (17g per m²) to supply nitrogen over the first layer, then ground limestone over the next and so on. Avoid applying lime together with sulphate of ammonia or a chemical reaction will result in the nitrogen being lost to the atmosphere.

Continue building up the layers within the heap until the container is filled. The material will start heating up quickly during warm weather but will take rather longer during cold spells. The compost should be ready to use in approximately six months.

PLANTING

When you consider that a shrub or tree is likely to be growing in the spot where it is planted for decades, it really is worthwhile giving the plant a good start in life by preparing the ground thoroughly as explained in the section dealing with basic cultivation.

Plant selection is important too: there is hardly any point in preparing the soil well and then planting a spindly, sickly subject which takes too long to establish, if it ever does, even though it appears to be cheap at the time of purchase. Paying a fair price is a good investment in the long run. Avoid tall spindly trees that are cramped for space and growing in containers much too small for them; the chances are that they were left over from last year and have become starved and pot bound. Such plants seldom develop a spreading root system to make a good specimen. Plants with damaged branches are usually best avoided, because there is a chance that diseases have already entered the wound and, although the tree may otherwise look healthy, infection may have spread well beyond the wound to cause the remainder of that branch to die later and spoil the overall shape.

SOIL CONDITION AND WHEN TO PLANT Try to avoid planting when the soil is wet. This is particularly important when the soil is on the heavy side because the roots need air to work properly and much damage is likely to be done to the roots as they are firmed in; an additional reason is that the soil loosens considerably as it thaws. Very dry soil is difficult to wet properly unless sufficient irrigation can be given and it is surprising just how much water is necessary to penetrate the subsoil in times of drought – roots are unlikely to grow into dust-dry soil. When the moisture content is ideal a handful of soil should hold together in the palm of the hand when squeezed but shatter when dropped to the ground.

So far as established container-grown plants are concerned, the actual time of planting is of less importance than the soil conditions, because the plants are happy to remain in their pots until satisfactory soil conditions permit planting. During the active growth stage, plants growing in containers should, of course, be kept moist at the root and an occasional liquid feed will be appreciated. Because such plants do not endure a root check as the roots remain undistrubed, they may be planted at any time of the year, weather permitting.

On the other hand, the planting time of bare-root plants (plants dug up from the soil to be transplanted) depends on whether they are deciduous or evergreen: most deciduous subjects can be transplanted at any time after natural leaf fall in the autumn and before new growth commences in the spring. Given the choice, however, the start of the dormant period is to be preferred so that the roots have a better chance to become established before the sap begins to rise in the spring.

Bare-root evergreen plants tend to establish better when there is some warmth in the soil so that the roots are able to take up the limited amount of moisture necessary to prevent wilting leaves. Again, a time when they are not making active growth should be chosen and in most years the optimum for these plants would be late September or October or late spring; try to avoid planting before the strong winds that often occur in March and April. In favoured areas there is no reason why evergreens should not be planted during mid-winter provided a mild spell is chosen for the work.

Planting in grass Some subjects appear more attractive when they are established in a lawn. But it is most important to remove the turf from the planting area before the specimen is set out and then to keep the area free from grass and weeds for two or three years until the plant is well established; otherwise the grass will compete for soil moisture and plant foods to the detriment of growth, which can easily be suppressed by 75 per cent. The area of bare soil surface will depend upon the size of subject but normally a diameter of 4ft (1.2m) will be sufficient for larger plants and 3ft (1m) for smaller trees and shrubs.

Heeling in When bare-root plants are delivered at an inconvenient time and planting cannot be done for more than 10 days, the roots should be removed from the packing material and then heeled in. The best way to do this is to open up a shallow trench in a sheltered spot in the garden, lay the plants at an angle of 45 degrees with the roots in the trench and then cover the roots over with soil which is made firm by treading. In frost or windy weather, the tops of evergreen plants should be protected by straw or sacking to avoid drying out. Do take precautions against rabbits if they visit the garden: such pests find twigs and bark most attractive. When plants need to be kept for up to 10 days before planting, store them in a frost-free building, remove the transit packing material and cover them with sacking or moist peat so that they do not dry out.

Making the hole There is no point in removing the soil from the actual planting hole before the specimen is to hand: open holes will become either waterlogged during heavy rain or dry out too much. There should, therefore, be as little time as possible between digging the hole and planting. Roots should not be allowed to dry out completely at any time: when any number of bare-root plants are to be set out, cover those awaiting planting with damp sacking. If roots are dry when they are unwrapped from the transit material, soak them in water for up to one hour but no longer otherwise the fibrous roots will rot. The size of the hole will depend upon the size of the root system to be accommodated: there is little point in making a hole very much larger in diameter than the root spread unless the soil is particularly solid. The hole should be large enough so that the roots are not cramped and buckled when they are inserted. Remove the top soil and position the plant to the same depth as it was before lifting; it is most important that the plant is not set too deeply and you can see the original depth by the soil mark on the stem. Once the hole is dug out the soil at the bottom should be forked over and large stones and other debris removed; do not bring any of the subsoil to the surface. Very heavy subsoil may be improved by forking in a quantity of small stones or sand. Add well rotted farmyard manure, peat, composted bark or garden compost and a sprinkling of general fertilizer to the hole and fork it into the base; fresh manure should not be used as it may rot the roots. Special proprietary planting composts are available which are particularly beneficial when the soil is inclined to be rather heavy and sticky. The subsoil at the base of the hole should now be firmed with the feet to prevent it sinking as the ground settles after planting.

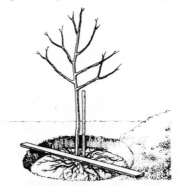

Planting a bare root tree.

Bare roots benefit from being placed on a small mound of soil at the base of the hole. This prevents an air space developing below the roots and acts as a cushion should the subsoil settle later. Now place the plant in the hole, first cutting away any damaged roots with a sharp knife or secateurs. Bare roots should be spread out evenly and then be covered with top soil to which a sprinkling of general fertilizer and bulky organic material have been added. Carefully joggle the plant up and down so that the soil trickles between the roots and firm the soil with the feet as filling proceeds.

Certain plants, particularly evergreens and conifers, will be purchased as 'balled' plants. These will have been lifted from the nursery with a good fibrous root system which is then enclosed in a wrapping of sacking. On no account should the sacking be removed until the plant has been placed in the planting hole, otherwise much of the surrounding soil may fall away and disturb the roots. Once the root ball has been placed in position the sacking is carefully cut away and removed except for the piece below the roots which will eventually rot away. The root ball should be moist at the time of planting so, if necessary, soak the roots complete with sacking in water before planting.

The same rule applies to plants growing in other types of container like whalehide and polythene pots, particularly when they are in peat compost which can be very difficult to moisten when once planted. Rigid plastic containers should be tapped away before planting, whereas polythene or whalehide pots should be carefully slit up either side with a knife before removing the root ball. Any roots that are girdling the ball may be gently eased away before planting so that they will establish more easily. The surface of the root ball should be at or just slightly below the finished soil

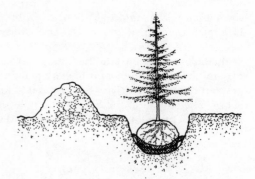

Method of planting a balled or
container grown shrub.

level, the soil being firmed as the hole is filled up. Firm soil around the roots
is really essential so that the plant will establish properly and, should it
become loosened by frost, refirming with the feet will be necessary.

When planting is complete, rake the soil surface level to provide an attractive finish and then, unless rain is imminent, give the planting area a
good soaking. Finally apply a surface mulch of bulky organic material or a
sheet of black polythene well anchored down. This will help to conserve soil
moisture and suppress subsequent weed growth. Both of these items are
most important for the proper establishment of the plant. Evergreens, in
particular, will need protecting from drying winds and this is best achieved
by draping polythene or sacking around the windward side supported by
posts driven into the ground. It may also be worthwhile spraying the leaves
with S.600 plastic solution to reduce transpiration.

Stake trees Trees should be supported by a stake at planting time. It is well
worth obtaining a good quality strong stake not less than 2½in (6cm) in
diameter which has been treated with wood preserving liquid; ash, chestnut,
oak or spruce stakes are suitable and should be driven 1½ to 2ft (45 to 60cm)
into the ground on the windward side. The stake should, of course, be
placed in the ground before the tree is planted otherwise root damage may
result. The height of the stake is important so that it gives the tree sufficient
support and yet it must not be so long that it rubs against the branches:
ideally the top of the stake should be 3in (7.5cm) below the point where the
lowest branch grows out from the main stem.

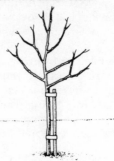

A newly planted tree securely
staked.

Special tree ties are available for fastening trees to the stake. These are usually made from plastic material, one end of the strip being nailed to the stake; a distance piece is placed between the stake and tree and then the strip is wrapped around the tree trunk to return to the stake. It is important that the loose end remains intact because, as the tree girth increases, the strip is loosened and then reattached to avoid strangling the tree. Two such ties are usually sufficient, one placed near the top of the stake, the other approximately 2ft (60cm) above the ground.

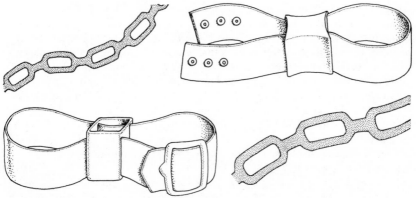

A range of tree ties.

Planting depth of 'worked' trees Fruit trees and some ornamental trees have been grafted on to special rootstocks. It is important that the union where the stem joins the rootstock is kept above soil level, otherwise roots which develop from above the union will grow and nullify the effect of grafting. The union can often be seen as a slight swelling or scar at the base of the main stem. Generally, provided the tree is planted at the same depth as it was in the nursery, all will be well and the union will be well above ground to avoid scion rooting. An exception to this general rule is when rose bushes are planted and this case the union should be at soil level.

Tree spacing Ornamental trees come in all shapes and sizes which makes it impractical to suggest a standard planting distance between one specimen and another. Soil type and climate has a bearing on the rate of tree growth, particularly in the early years of a plant's life and it is worthwhile visiting established gardens in the vicinity not only to see the plants that flourish but to try to find out their rate of growth. Good nurseymen's catalogues give the height and spread of each plant at maturity and it would be prudent to consult such references before making a choice of plant for any particular spot.

The same applies to shrubs, which vary enormously in height and spread; and although plants like to grow near to one another, they will require drastic thinning after two or three years when they are planted too close. It all depends on the final result to be achieved: mixed borders made up of a collection of different kinds of plants like herbaceous perennials interplanted with other subjects would require shrubs to be spaced widely, whereas a border containing shrubs alone would require the plants to be set closer together.

Hedge plant spacing There are relatively few trees and shrubs which are generally used for hedges and these are planted close together so that an effective barrier is made in as short a time as possible.

FAST-GROWING HEDGE PLANTS. X *Cupressocyparis leylandii* (Leyland cypress) planted 2 to 2½ft (60 to 75cm) apart will make a dense hedge at least 6ft (1.8m) high within three to five years and once the required height and spread is reached will require clipping once or twice each year. *Lonicera nitida* 'Ernest Wilson' has small ovate leaves and responds well to regular clipping when it makes a dense hedge. Set out the plants 1½ft (45cm) apart. *Prunus cerasifera* 'Pissardii' (purple-leaved plum) is a deciduous plant that makes an excellent hedge when the plants are spaced 2ft (60cm) apart.

SLOWER-GROWING EVERGREEN HEDGE PLANTS. *Chamaecyparis lawsoniana* (Lawson's cypress) is excellent for an exposed or shady situation and should be planted 2ft (60cm) apart. *Ilex aquifolium* (holly) makes an impenetrable hedge when planted 1½ to 2ft (45 to 60cm) apart. *Taxus baccata* (yew) is one of the best evergreen hedges and is not so slow growing as is generally believed. This plant does, however, need well drained soil and should be set out 1½ to 2ft (45 to 60cm) apart.

SLOWER-GROWING DECIDUOUS HEDGE PLANTS. *Berberis thunbergii* 'Erecta' is an excellent compact shrub for a low hedge providing very good autumn tints and requiring little clipping; space the plants 1½ft (45cm) apart. *Carpinus betulus* (common hornbeam) resembles *Fagus sylvatica* (common beech) and both should be planted 1½ to 2ft (45 to 60cm) apart.

FLOWERING HEDGES. These hedges are particularly effective when space is available for them to spread beyond 3ft (1m) and any clipping necessary should be done after flowering. *Berberis darwinii* has small holly-like leaves and bright orange-yellow flowers; plant 2ft (60cm) apart. *Cotoneaster lacteus* has large leathery leaves and white flowers; plant 3ft (90cm) apart. *Pyracantha rogersiana*, also white flowered, plant 1½ft (45cm) apart. *Rosa rugosa* with purplish-pink flowers makes an excellent hedge when the plants are set out 3ft (1m) apart.

Rose spacing Different rose cultivars vary in vigour and habit especially when comparing one locality with another; however, approximate plant spacing under average conditions would be 1ft (30cm) apart for miniatures; dwarf floribundas and hybrid teas 14in (35cm); average hybrid teas and floribundas 2ft (60cm); shrub roses are spaced at two-thirds of their expected height, which would give a planting distance from 3 to 9ft (1 to 2.7m); standards 6ft (1.8m); climbers and ramblers 9ft (2.7m).

Hybrid teas and floribundas of average vigour should be planted at least 1½ft (45cm) from the edge of the bed and they are at their most effective

This hedge of the rose 'Roseraie de l'Hay' is underplanted with *Geranium* 'Johnson's Blue'.

when restricted to one cultivar to each bed, although this is often not feasible in smaller gardens when groups of three of five of the same cultivar look attractive.

PLANT SUPPORTS. Standard roses will need the support of a stake and ties as recommended for trees; when this type of plant is mixed with shrub roses, it is usually easier to plant the standards first, followed by the bushy types.

Climbing roses are best trained with their stems attached horizontally along wires fixed to the wall or fence; alternatively they may be tied to a framework of rustic poles. These plants are very effective when they are allowed to ramble through a large tree. When roses are planted alongside a wall, it is most important to allow a space of at least 15in (38cm) between wall and plant to prevent the roots from drying out through lack of moisture.

Fruiting plants Most gardens can accommodate some fruit and the quantity and diversity of plants grown is usually only limited by space. Even apple and pear trees can be grown in the smallest of gardens because the plants may be grown in restricted form.

Bush apple trees are grown by the nurseryman on dwarfing or semi-dwarfing rootstocks so that the tree grows within an easily managed form. Cultivars on M9 rootstocks may be planted 8 to 10ft (2.4 to 3m) apart, those on M26 10 to 15ft (3 to 4.5m) and MM106 12 to 18ft (3.5 to 5.5m) apart.

The dwarf pyramid is an excellent form of tree because it is, as its name

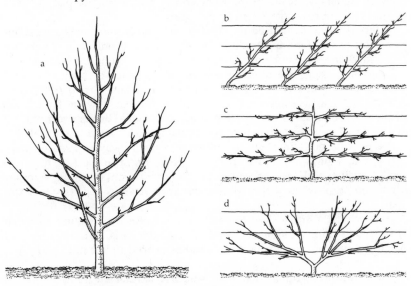

Fruit tree forms: (a) dwarf pyramid (b) cordon (c) espalier (d) fan.

Above: A mixed planting which includes *Stachys lanata*, *Viscaria vulgaris* and iris. *Below: Hydrangea paniculata* 'Grandiflora' and agapanthus.

suggests, low growing to facilitate pruning, spraying and harvesting without the need to climb ladders or steps. The plants are spaced 3½ft (1.05m) apart in rows and supported by two strands of wire fastened to posts at intervals of approximately 15ft (4.5m) along the row. The lower wire is 1½ft (45cm) and the other 3ft (1m) above the ground.

Cordon apples are also grown close together so that a number of different cultivars can be grown in a small area. Space the plants 2½ to 3ft (75cm to 1m) apart in rows not less than 6ft (1.8m) apart. These plants are supported by 3 parallel wires stretched between posts set 12ft (3.5m) apart along the row with 7ft (2.1m) of the post above ground. The bottom wire is attached 2½ft (75cm) above ground level and the other two 4½ft (1.35m) and 6½ft (2m) above ground. Bamboo canes are then fixed at an angle of 45 degrees to which the maiden tree is tied.

Espalier trees make an excellent screen or feature for the garden and may be trained on wires attached to wall or fence or they may be stretched between posts. Set the plants 10ft (3m) apart when grown on M9 rootstock; 10 to 12ft (3 to 3.5m) on M26 and 12 to 15ft (3.5 to 4.5m) apart on MM106.

Pears can be grown in much the same way as apples. Bush trees on Quince C stock are planted 10 to 14ft (3 to 4m) apart and those on Quince A 12 to 15ft (3.5 to 4.5m) apart. The same rootstocks are suitable for cordons which should be spaced 2 to 3ft (60cm to 1m) apart in rows spaced at least 6ft (1.8m) apart.

Dwarf pyramids, again on the same sort of rootstocks, are planted 3½ft (1.05m) apart in rows spaced 7ft (2.1m) apart.

Quince A is normally used for espalier pears when the plants are set out 15 to 20ft (4.5 to 6m) apart, although when trees of only 2 or 3 tiers are required Quince C may be used when growing conditions are favourable.

Plums and gages are often grown as half-standard or bush trees and worked on St Julien A rootstock when they are planted 12 to 15ft (3.5 to 4.5m) apart. In areas subject to late frost, plums may be grown as fan-trained plants against a wall. Where space permits they should be planted 15 to 18ft (4.5 to 5.5m) apart and trained on horizontal wires attached to the wall.

Peaches and nectarines may be grown in a similar way and spaced 18 to 24ft (5.5 to 7.3m) apart. Bush trees are grown on St Julien A, which is a semi-dwarfing stock, and spaced 15 to 18ft (4.5 to 5.5m) or on the vigorous Brompton stock when they require more space at 18 to 24ft (5.5 to 7.3m) apart.

Sweet cherries are seldom planted now because they require so much space and are difficult to manage and protect from birds, however they may be grown as a fan tree when they should be spaced 18 to 24ft (5.5 to 7.3m) apart.

The acid Morello cherry makes an attractive fan-trained tree and may be planted 15 to 18ft (4.5 to 5.5m) apart or it can be grown as a bush at the same spacing.

Figs can be successful provided they are grown in favoured districts; for the best results the plants should have the benefit of a south-facing wall and, where more than one is planted, space them 18 to 20ft (5.5 to 6m) apart.

Cultivated blackberries have much to commend them and where space permits they should be planted 10ft (3m) apart. The same distance applies to loganberries and similar hybrid berries that are trained on wires stretched between posts set along the row. The lowest wire should be fixed 3ft (1m) above ground with 3 more wires each fixed 1ft (30cm) above the other.

Black currants are vigorous-growing plants that require ample space and should be set out at least 5ft (1.5m) apart in rows 6ft (1.8m) apart.

Gooseberries require similar spacing to black currants when grown as bushes, although they may also be grown as cordon plants at 1ft (30cm) apart.

Raspberries are planted 1½ft (45cm) apart in single rows spaced 6ft (1.8m) apart and trained on wires fixed to posts along the row. The lower wire is positioned 2ft (60cm) above the ground with the middle wire 3½ft (1.05m) and the top wire 5ft (1.5m) above the ground. Alternatively, a single wire may be used at 4½ft (1.35m) above the ground so that instead of tying each individual cane to the several wires, the top of the cane is twisted horizontally along the one wire. Yet another method sometimes used for autumn-fruiting cultivars is to run two parallel wires 4ft (1.2m) above the ground so that the canes grow between the wires without being tied in.

Red and white currants should be given the same space as gooseberries except that, when grown as cordons, they are planted 15in (38cm) apart. These plants may also be fan trained at 6ft (1.8m) apart.

Strawberries tend to take up a considerable area of ground for two or three years compared with the crop they produce but are worthwhile where space permits. They should be planted 1½ft (45cm) apart in rows spaced 2½ft (75cm). Well drained soil is needed and the crowns should be level with the soil surface after planting.

Transplanting vegetables The majority of vegetables can be sown in the position where they are to mature. Some plants, however, such as tomatoes and celery, require a long growing season to produce satisfactory crops and should therefore be started indoors early in the year when conditions outside would be unfavourable for satisfactory growth. Other plants like brassicas and leeks respond favourably to transplanting.

Another advantage in transplanting is that the ground can be put to better use in that more crops can be grown in a given area: small plants in a seedbed take up less ground than if they were sown in the space where they are to mature.

Transplanting may, however, cause a check to growth unless it is carefully done. Some plants like tomatoes, cucumbers and sweet corn are best raised in small pots or containers so that when transplanted into the garden the least amount of root disturbance as possible is endured. Similarly other plants when lifted from the seedbed should be removed carefully, first by watering the soil and then lifting the plants with a hand fork. Naturally, the smaller the plant when transplanted, the less the damage caused to its roots and so it will establish more quickly.

Firm planting into moist soil followed by thorough watering in will do much to reduce the transplanting check to growth and, whenever possible, it pays to choose a cloudy day or at least avoiding strong sunshine when transplanting seedlings. Damp over the plants with clear water using a fine rose on the end of the watering can from time to time until they have become established.

The test of good planting, especially with brassicas, is to take hold of a leaf and try to pull the plant out of the soil; if the plant pulls easily from the ground then it was not planted sufficiently firmly; if the tip of the leaf tears away then the plant is firm enough in the soil.

CROP ROTATION

When one particular kind of plant, such as tomato, is grown in the same soil year after year, the crop begins to diminish after about the third year. This is because the soil-borne pests and diseases which favour that particular kind of plant thrive and multiply and 'soil sickness' becomes established, necessitating drastic action if the same sort of plants are to be grown successfully in that area again. Gardeners often remove the border soil from their greenhouse and replace with fresh soil that has not grown the particular crops before; others construct special troughs or purchase containers and growing bags. These methods work well in the greenhouse, although soil replacement to a satisfactory depth is both time consuming and laborious, but they are not always practicable outside.

The practical answer is to rotate the different kinds of plants around the garden from year to year. This will help to avoid a build up of soil pests and diseases and at the same time utilize manures and fertilizers most effectively. Root crops like carrots and parsnips, for example, tend to produce forked roots when they are grown on land that has been freshly manured; but beans, peas, leeks and onions revel in the richness and so it makes sense to grow them on the plot which has been freshly manured.

Although vegetables are the most likely candidates to suffer from soil sickness because the land is intensively cropped, flowers, trees and shrubs are inclined to suffer in the same way. An old rose bed is seldom worth replanting with new rose bushes unless the soil is removed or sterilized. Soil sterilization is difficult for the non-commercial grower due to the lack of suitable facilities although one worthwhile chemical, dazomet, is available to the gardener but only in large commercial size containers.

Fruit trees also suffer from soil sickness and, again, it is seldom worthwhile planting fruit trees on a site where fruit has grown before. Fortunately short-term crops like vegetables can be crop rotated so that any particular kind of plant is not grown on the same area of ground more than once in 3 years or so. It is, of course, important to control weeds because they often belong to the same plant family as the crop plant and would encourage pests and diseases to persist in the same way as crop plants.

Unfortunately the soil-borne disease organisms cannot be seen with the naked eye and so the first sign that the disease is present is when the plant produces the symptoms. One of the main problems in overcropped land is club root disease of brassicas. This causes the roots of cabbages and other plants of the same family to swell considerably and reduces the uptake of

	Plot 1	Plot 2	Plot 3
1st Year	*Double dig and manure* Crops: beans, celery, chicory, cucumbers, leeks, lettuce, marrows, onions, peas, spinach, sweet corn, tomatoes	*Base dressing of fertiliser* Root crops: such as beetroot, carrots, parsnips, swede and turnip Potatoes (this part of the plot can be manured)	*Lime and base fertiliser* Brassicas: such as Brussels sprouts, cabbages, cauliflowers, kale and sprouting broccoli
2nd Year	*Base dressing of fertiliser* Root crops Potatoes (this part of the plot can be manured)	*Lime and base fertiliser* Brassicas	*Double dig and manure* Crops: beans, celery, etc
3rd Year	*Lime and base fertiliser* Brassicas	*Double dig and manure* Crops: beans, celery, etc	*Base dressing of fertiliser* Root crops Potatoes (this part of the plot can be manured)

moisture from the soil, subsequently causing stunted growth and premature death of the plant. Brassicas are also attacked by a minute eelworm which infests the soil when that kind of plant is grown too frequently on the same plot. Another kind of eelworm quickly builds up on land consistently cropped with potatoes or tomatoes. These are not the only plants that are prone to soil sickness, the list is much longer and includes most of the commonly grown vegetables.

A simple but effective crop rotation that would help to discourage soil-borne pests and diseases and make good use of manures and fertilizers consists of dividing the vegetable area into three equal sized plots. In the first year plot 1 is double dug and manure or garden compost is added. This area is used to grow beans, celery, chicory, cucumbers, leeks, lettuce, marrows, onions, peas, spinach, sweet corn and tomatoes.

Plot 2 will be given a base dressing of fertilizer but no manure (as the crop rotation system becomes established plot 2 will have been manured the previous year) because root crops like beetroot, carrots, parsnips, swede and turnip will be grown here this year and fresh manure causes forked roots. Potatoes will also be grown and since they benefit from ample bulky organic manure, fresh manure may, if available, be dug into their part of the plot.

Plot 3 will accommodate the brassicas like Brussels sprouts, cabbage, cauliflower, kale and sprouting broccoli to mature during late autumn, winter and spring. Lime is particularly important for brassicas and any deficiency should be corrected before planting them; base fertilizer will also be required but the application of this may be kept separate from that of lime. It will be seen from the rotation that potatoes, which become prone to scab disease when lime is present, will not be grown on this plot for another two years, by which time the lime content should have decreased considerably.

Next year crops and cultivations move one plot anti-clockwise: root crops and fertilizer move to plot 1; brassicas, lime and fertilizer move to plot 2; beans etc., double digging and manuring move to plot 3.

The following year all again move anti-clockwise one plot so that brassicas and lime move to plot 1; beans etc., double digging and manure to plot 2; root crops and fertilizer to plot 3.

In the fourth year all crops and treatments are back to the original year when beans etc., are in plot 1; roots in plot 2 and brassicas in plot 3. The plots have been planned so that ample time exists between each crop to enable cultivations to be carried out; in some cases there is also time to grow a quick maturing catch crop before and after the main crop.

PROPAGATION

One of the most interesting and satisfying aspects of gardening must surely be the art and craft of raising new plants by the various techniques of propagation. Plants have, of course, been reproducing themselves successfully for millions of years and much can be learned from their methods: viable seed can be produced by the majority of garden plants and this is then dispersed by various means so that it germinates to grow on and reproduce again. However, not all of those seeds will necessarily grow to produce plants identical with the parent: when seed is taken from hybrid plants and germinates, the resulting offspring are usually quite different from their parent. This calls for a different method of propagation to keep the type of such plants and most can easily be reproduced by cuttings, division of the root or by other means. Another advantage of vegetative propagation is that the 'new' plant usually matures faster than the same sort grown from seed.

To be successful with plant propagation, as with other aspects of gardening, really amounts to paying attention to detail: all the implements and equipment used such as seed trays, pots, knife and labels should be clean, otherwise diseases and some pests may be spread throughout the plants. The parent plants themselves, from which cuttings are taken, should be healthy and free from pests and diseases otherwise the infection will be propagated as well as the plant. Seed and cutting compost should also be free from pests and diseases and a fresh batch should be used each time avoiding any that has already been used for raising plants. Suitable ready mixed compost may be purchased like John Innes seed compost which contains sterilized loam, peat and sand; or one of the proprietary peat-based composts may be used to fill seed trays and pots.

These composts have been mixed thoroughly using ingredients which have been chosen with great care so that they blend to provide the essential requirements for seeds to germinate or cuttings to produce root. For example, the compost particles must be of the correct size so that they provide air spaces and yet they should be capable of retaining sufficient moisture without becoming waterlogged.

Similar conditions will benefit seeds and cuttings placed in the ground out of doors. Sandy soils warm up quickly in the spring time but are inclined to dry out quickly and since moisture is essential for germination, the addition of peat, garden compost or composted tree bark raked into the soil before sowing or planting will help. The same material may be used to open up sticky clay and it may also be necessary to add grit or coarse sand to the base of the drill for cuttings or seed when the soil is poorly drained.

SEED SOWING IN THE GARDEN The vast majority of plants we grow can be raised from sowing seed out of doors. These include vegetables, flowers for border decoration or cutting and even some shrubs and trees. In certain cases, for example with hardy annual flowers and some vegetables like radish, carrots and parsnips, the seed will be sown where the resulting plants will remain until they are mature. With some other plants, like biennial flowers such as wallflowers and vegetables like cabbages and kale, the seed will be sown and then the small seedlings transplanted when they are large enough to handle. The main reason for transplanting in this case is that the permanent planting site can be used for another crop whilst the seed is germinating and growing on. Another reason for transplanting certain kinds is that the resulting plants will be superior to those sown direct: a good example is the leek which when planted in a comparatively deep hole will produce a longer blanched stem for eating.

Soil preparation Generally, seeds require a good tilth to germinate properly so that the soil particles come into contact with the seed. The fineness of the soil particles depends on the size of the seed to be sown: small seed like carrot requires a very fine tilth not only so that good contact will be made but also so that they may be sown shallowly, because it is far easier to sow seeds close to the surface in a fine soil than one which is lumpy. Seeds sown too deep in the soil are unlikely to germinate and even if germination did take place the resulting seedlings are likely to be spindly and weak.

Provided the soil is not too wet, that is when the surface dries off within half an hour of raking, a suitable tilth can be produced by raking, although too much surface raking is likely to impair the structure of the soil and only sufficient raking should be done to level the soil and create a tilth. Stones and other debris including weeds should be removed during this final preparation. At the same time, base fertilizer may be raked into the soil to provide nourishment for the young plants.

Sowing depth Different kinds of seeds vary in the depth they are sown depending on their size. Small seeds like carrot, leek, lettuce and parsnip should be sown no deeper than ¾in (19mm) otherwise their stored food reserve would be used up before the leaves emerged from the soil surface. Slightly larger seeds such as those of brassicas, radish, cucumber and marrow may be sown 1in (2.5cm) deep. Seed the size of a pea can be up to 1½in (38mm) deep and very large seed like the various beans up to 2in (5cm) deep.

The seeds of plants that are to remain where they are sown are usually sown in drills. These are 'V' shaped grooves in the ground which are made

Sowing seeds in a drill.

by drawing a hoe or stick along a straight edge or garden line. Stout string attached to sticks makes an ideal line; one stick is pushed into the ground at one end of the row and the other stick is pushed in at the opposite end. The string should be pulled taught so that a really straight drill can be drawn. Uneven germination will result if some of the seeds are sown more deeply than the others and so it is most important that the base of the drill is kept level. This is facilitated by lightly treading over the area with a shuffling motion before the final raking.

Sow seeds thinly Germination rate is usually high and so to avoid spindly seedlings seed should always be sown thinly; in the case of plants which mature where they are sown, space sowing is often worthwhile. This consists of sowing 3 or 4 of the smaller seeds at each station along the row: lettuce for example may be sown in small groups spaced 8in (20cm) apart. Once the seed is sown, the line is removed and the soil taken out to make the drill is returned to cover the seed. The most convenient way to do this is to lightly drag the back of the rake along the soil surface. The soil is then lightly tamped down with the head of the rake.

Since warmth and moisture are both necessary for germination, a good rule of thumb is to wait for weed seedlings to germinate in spring before sowing crop plant seeds. Should the soil be dry during the summer months, the base of the drill may be watered with a can before sowing the seed.

Fluid sowing Some seed like parsnip is very slow to germinate, especially in a late spring when the soil takes a considerable time to warm up. Germination can, if necessary, be speeded up by an artificial technique indoors. It is most important to avoid causing damage to the germinating seeds and so they are placed in a jelly.

A plastic container such as a sandwich box may be used. Line the base of the box with absorbent, unmedicated tissue paper and cover that layer with kitchen towel paper. Then sprinkle water on the paper until it is saturated and pour away any excess water. Now sprinkle the seeds thinly and evenly over the surface of the paper. Replace the lid on the container and stand the box in a temperature of approximately 70°F (21°C). Certain seeds like celery and some lettuce cultivars require light to germinate, otherwise most others would be happy in an airing cupboard.

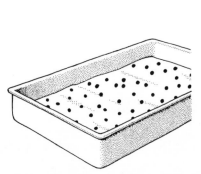
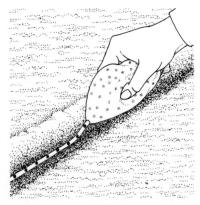

Fluid sowing: germinate the seeds first and then sow them in a jelly.

The container should be inspected daily and as soon as the small white root is seen emerging from most of the seeds, they may be sown. Should the soil out of doors be unfit, or the seeds are unable to be sown for some other reason, the container with seeds may be placed in the cool part of a refrigerator for 1 or 2 days. It is most important that the seeds do not become frozen and some germinated seeds like beans, sweet corn and tomato should not be stored below 42°F (6°C).

Germinated seeds are best removed from the container by washing them into a fine plastic mesh kitchen strainer. The next stage is to mix the seeds with jelly. This can be made by mixing half strength wallpaper paste, provided the cellulose based powder does not contain a fungicide. When the liquid has thickened, divide the volume into two and carefully sprinkle the seeds into one half, mixing them in with the fingers. The other half of the jelly may now be added and again mixed evenly with the fingers.

A polythene bag may be used to hold the jelly; tie the top to avoid spillage and then cut off one corner. The jelly containing germinated seed may now be squeezed into the drill opened up in the garden soil. Cover the drill with soil in the normal way or, preferably, with moist peat. It is important that the soil is moist at the time of sowing otherwise the jelly will solidify and impede further growth of the seedlings.

Broadcast seed sowing Instead of sowing seeds in a drill they may be scattered over the soil surface and then covered by raking or by sifting soil over them. This method is often employed when the resulting plants are to be pricked out and transplanted later.

SEED SOWING INDOORS Some plants and particularly those that are tender, may be sown in pots or trays indoors so that they make growth before the weather is favourable outside. John Innes seed compost or a proprietary peat-based compost is normally used. The container is filled to the top and then the surplus compost struck off with a straight edge. Give the base of the pot or tray 2 or 3 taps on a solid surface to settle the compost and then gently press the compost with the base of an empty flower pot or

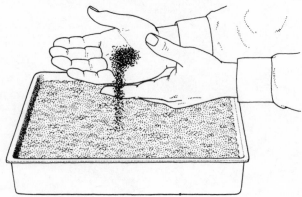

Sowing seeds in a seed tray.

flat presser. The compost should be moistened by standing the pot or tray in a container of water rather than soaking overhead with a watering can, as this tends to float the peat on the surface.

Very small seeds may be mixed with a quantity of fine dry silver sand to facilitate sowing, otherwise the seed may be sprinkled directly from a packet. Alternatively, tip a small number of seeds into the palm of one hand, hold the hand approximately 6in (15cm) from the surface of the compost and gently tap the side of the hand with the fingers of the other hand. Scatter the seeds evenly across the compost so that they do not fall too closely together.

The seeds may now be covered with sifted compost to a depth approximately 1½ times their diameter. Very small seeds should be left uncovered or they may be pressed gently into the compost.

Cover the container with a sheet of clean glass or polythene and then a sheet of newspaper to exclude strong sunlight. Globules of moisture will collect on the cover and this should be turned over each day to remove the condensation.

Place the container in a suitable temperature for germination according to the kind of plant being grown and as soon as germination takes place, the paper and glass or polythene should be removed.

Seedlings should be pricked out as soon as they can be handled to give them space to grow.

DIVISION Instead of raising them from seed, some plants can be propagated by division. Many herbaceous perennials like Michaelmas daises can be lifted from the ground and divided up by splitting the root system down the middle. This is best done by pushing two garden forks back to back into the centre of the root clump and easing the tines apart. Each portion may be planted separately to grow on in its allotted space.

Plants producing fleshy roots and rhizomes like rhubarb and certain irises may be divided by cutting up the rootstock. The best plants often result from the portions retained from the perimeter of the parent clump.

RUNNERS Perhaps the easiest method of propagation is simply to remove

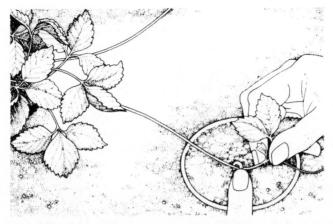

Pegging a strawberry runner into a pot of soil to encourage it to form roots.

a daughter plant from the parent. Strawberry plants, for example, produce stems which form small plants at the tip. These small plants send out roots of their own and then the young plant may be removed from the parent by cutting through the adjoining stem.

LAYERING There are a number of plants, particularly certain woody specimens like rhododendrons and magnolias, which are rather difficult to propagate for one reason or another. These can often be increased by selecting a low-growing stem and embedding it into the soil. The soil should be well drained and yet moisture retentive and the addition of a handful or two of peat and/or grit should improve conditions. Really shy rooters will respond to stem slitting which is carried out by cutting a small slanting slit half way through the lower side of the stem to be layered. Insert the slit portion into the ground and then insert a garden cane or stake vertically alongside to

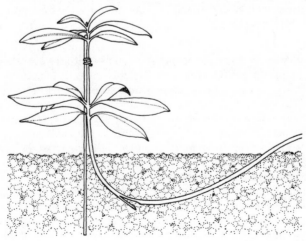

Layering a shrub.

which the tip of the stem is attached. Roots will eventually grow from the slit and then the stem between the new plant and parent may be severed. Once established on its own roots, the new plant may be lifted and planted elsewhere.

The main advantage of layering is that the parent plant is providing nourishment for the stem undergoing propagation, until such time as the new plant is able to fend for itself.

Plants which naturally layer themselves include blackberries, when the tip of a stem falls to the ground and takes root. Loganberries may be layered in the same way by covering the tip of the stem with 6in (15cm) of soil.

CUTTINGS The majority of plants may be increased by taking a portion of stem or leaf and inserting the 'slip', as it is sometimes called, into a rooting medium. The type of cutting taken and rooting medium used depends on the kind of plant to be propagated. Woody plants growing out of doors can be propagated at certain times of the year by simply inserting suitable material into the soil, whilst soft green shoots of shrubs and plants normally growing indoors require more sophisticated conditions.

Hardwood cuttings Fruit bushes, shrubs and trees can often be propagated by firm woody stems taken from the plant after leaf fall in late autumn. Current season's wood should be selected which is neither too fat nor too thin for the kind of plant in question. The majority of hardwood cuttings should be approximately 1ft (30cm) long after cutting away the unripened tip. The base of the cutting should be trimmed just below a bud and the top cut just above a bud without leaving a snag.

Prepared cuttings are inserted to at least half their length in well drained soil by opening a small slit trench with a spade. The cuttings are placed upright against the vertical side of the trench and the soil is then replaced and made firm by pressing with the foot.

The cuttings will be encouraged to root more readily by dipping the lower end into rooting hormone powder, available from garden centres and garden shops.

Softwood cuttings As the name suggests, these cuttings are taken from soft stems and plants easily propagated by this method include houseplants, alpines, many herbaceous perennials and shrubs. Tips of shoots approximately 2½in long (or shorter for some alpines) are snapped or cut from the parent plant. The majority of cuttings root better when the snap or cut is made just below a leaf joint. The cut end is dipped in rooting hormone powder and then inserted in John Innes seed compost or a proprietary peat-based seed and cutting compost. The cutting should not be inserted too deeply but just sufficient to stand without toppling over.

Softwood cuttings root more readily when they remain turgid at all times and so it is usually advisable to remove the lower leaves to reduce transpiration and enclose them in a polythene bag or propagating case indoors. Spring and summer are usually the best seasons to take softwood cuttings when the plants are making vigorous growth.

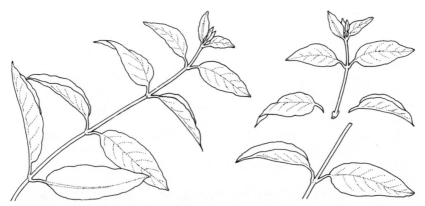

Preparing a softwood cutting.

Semi-ripe cuttings Certain plants, notably conifers and some deciduous plants, are difficult to root unless the base of the stem is maturing although the top is still soft. This stage is usually reached during mid to late summer and the cutting is prepared in the same way as other stem cuttings. An exception to this rule is made when the cutting is prepared with a sliver of old wood in the form of a 'heel'. This heel is taken by pulling the side shoot from the parent plant and then reducing the length of the heel to approximately ¼in (6mm) with a sharp knife.

Leaf cuttings Some house plants like streptocarpus, African violets and begonias can be propagated by leaf cuttings. A healthy semi-mature leaf is taken from the plant and cut into strips. These strips are then inserted vertically into a container of moist seed and cutting compost which is then enclosed in a polythene bag. Provided a temperature of at least 68°F (20°C) is maintained, roots will grow from the severed veins and small plants will appear from the same area. When these small plants are large enough, they

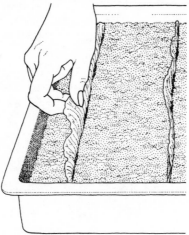

Increasing streptocarpus by means of leaf cuttings.

may be potted up singly. Alternatively the African violet leaf with stalk intact may simply be placed in a glass of water so that the lower half of the stalk is immersed in the water.

Root cuttings Although above ground growing stems are normally associated with cuttings, certain plants with fleshy roots can be increased by root cuttings. Herbaceous plants that may be increased in this way include *Phlox paniculata*, anchusa, oriental poppy and eryngium. Root cuttings are prepared simply by cutting the stronger growing roots into approximately 2in (5cm) lengths and inserting them vertically in well drained compost in a seed tray; the tops of the roots are then covered with ½in (13mm) of similar compost and kept moist indoors or in a cold frame.

BUDDING AND GRAFTING Some plants that are propagated by cuttings may subsequently perform in such a way that they become undesirable as subjects for the garden; apple trees increased by cuttings would normally be too vigorous and roses tend to be rather short lived. Other plants may be very difficult to propagate by cuttings or, as in the case of top fruit trees, it may be necessary to change the cropping cultivar for some reason or other and yet retain the main framework of the tree to maintain the size of harvest.

In all of these cases it would be necessary to take some of the shoot (scion) of the desired flowering plant or fruit cultivar and join it on to a special rootstock (stock) to form a single plant. The scion may consist of more than one bud on a short stem or it may consist of one bud.

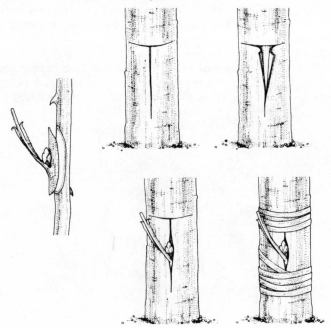

Budding a rose: the bud is removed as shown on the left and inserted in a T-shaped cut in the rootstock.

Budding Budding is carried out during the summer months when the rind of the rootstock plant lifts easily from the wood. This is important because the shield of stem containing the bud is inserted between the rind and wood of the stock. The stock is prepared by cutting a 1in (2.5cm) vertical slit in the rind to penetrate as far as the wood. A transverse cut is then made across the top to form a 'T'. A bud is then cut from the scion plant by inserting the budding knife ½in (13mm) below the bud and cutting upwards just into the wood behind the bud; the knife should come out of the stem ½in (13mm) above the bud. The scion now consists of the bud and a shield-shaped piece of rind together with the wood behind it; the leaf stalk may be used as a handle although the leaf blade should be removed. Next carefully remove the tough wood behind the bud and then insert the shield between the rind and wood of the rootstock stem. Raffia or soft plastic tape is then wrapped around the stem to keep the bud in place. When the bud is growing, the portion of rootstock stem above the scion may be cut away close to the bud.

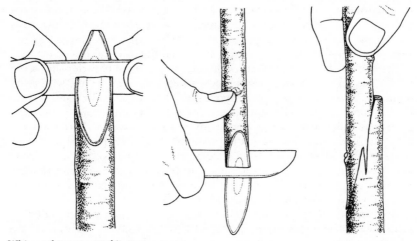

Whip and tongue grafting.

Grafting Grafting usually takes place in the garden during spring when the sap is beginning to rise within the rootstock plant. The technique is most successful, however, when the scion bud development is slightly behind that of the rootstock and so best results are achieved when the scions are taken during the winter when buds are dormant. For grafting the scions are prepared from lengths of stem about ⅜in (10mm) in diameter. The scion wood is cut from the current season's growth, tied in a bundle and then inserted in a sheltered spot in the garden. Stems should be of sufficient length to provide prepared scions 4 to 6in (10 to 15cm) long for grafting.

Various methods of grafting are used and the type suitable for most plants is known as whip and tongue. As with all grafting, it is most important that the cambium (the layer of cells beneath the bark) of the scion makes good contact with the cambium of the stock and so it is desirable to use a large surface area of both pieces.

The stock is first cut down to approximately 6in (15cm) from the ground.

A long sloping cut is then made through the stem of the scion; a mirror image of this cut being made towards the top of the stock. A second cut, like a tongue, is made in the scion halfway up the slope of the first and into the wood. A second cut is also made in the sloping top of the stock so that when the scion is placed on the top of the stock the two slits join together and are held in place by the overlapping tongues. When the scion is of smaller diameter than the stock, it should be placed to one side so that the cambium of each match up.

Finally, the scion and stock are bound with grafting tape, or bound with raffia which is then painted over with grafting wax.

When mature trees are grafted, suitably sized branches up in the tree should, of course, be selected for working.

POTTING COMPOST INGREDIENTS

Plants growing in containers like flower pots require special compost to grow well. Ordinary garden soil may produce perfectly good plants in the open garden but when used for potting, it often becomes waterlogged or too compact and results in stunted growth or even the death of the plant.

There is no one compost that would ideally suit every type of plant: some plants like a moisture-retentive compost whilst others prefer one with acute drainage. However, a good compromise could be achieved by using a standard potting compost like John Innes. The formula for the John Innes composts was published in 1934 after many years of research. It satisfies the main requirements of a good potting compost which may be summarised as: providing the plant with nutrients, being free from pests, diseases, weeds and toxic substances, sufficiently heavy to provide anchorage and stability for the plant, well drained but capable of retaining sufficient moisture and air over a reasonable period for the plant's needs.

John Innes potting compost No 1 consists of 7 parts by volume sterilised loam, 3 of sphagnum peat and 2 of sand together with 4oz (113g) J. I. base fertilizer and ¾oz (21g) ground limestone per bushel. J.I. base fertilizer can be purchased ready made or mixed at home by adding 2 parts by weight of hoof and horn ⅛in (3mm) grist, 2 parts superphosphate and 1 part sulphate of potash. This gives 5.1 per cent nitrogen, 7.2 per cent phosphoric acid and 9.7 per cent potash.

John Innes potting compost No 2 contains the same volume of loam, peat and sand but twice the amount of J.I. base fertilizer and ground limestone. John Innes potting compost No 3 is used for more mature plants. It contains the same volume of loam, peat and sand but three times the amount of J.I. base fertilizer and ground limestone.

Seed sowing compost was developed at the John Innes Research Institute alongside potting compost and the J.I. seed compost consists of 2 parts by volume loam, 1 of peat and 1 of sand plus 1½oz (42g) superphosphate of lime and ¾oz (21g) ground limestone per bushel.

Ready mixed John Innes composts are available from garden centres for those who do not have the necessary facilities to prepare and mix at home.

Due to the lack of suitable loam, other types of compost have been developed and used with success for a considerable time. These loamless composts usually contain sphagnum peat alone or mixed with some other inert material together with slow-release fertilizers. Again, suitable proprietary loamless composts are available or they may be made up at home using such ingredients as medium grade sphagnum peat with a pH of between 3.5 and 4.5; lime-free sand with particle sizes between 0.5 and 0.05mm. This is slightly coarser than builders' sand which is inclined to cake. Perlite is a sterile white crumb structure material processed by firing a volcanic glass; it has excellent drainage properties when incorporated in compost.

Vermiculite is an exfoliated mica that has small particles resembling miniature plates; drainage; aeration and moisture-holding capacity are all good. It is similar to perlite in that it is very light and so density is low. Composted tree bark has been used for a number of years and provided the bark has been milled reasonably fine with particles down to 1mm size it provides a useful addition to the range. Drainage and aeration are very good and moisture-holding capacity moderate so that it should, preferably, be mixed with peat. Since the pH of composted bark is often close to neutral it may be mixed with acid peat without the addition of extra lime, although a pH test should be carried out to be sure and base fertilizer should be added.

Polystyrene granules or chips mixed with peat has given good results. Polystyrene is sterile and gives porosity to the compost which, as a result, tends to dry out more quickly and the plants are more likely to topple over due to the lack of density.

Provided base fertilizer is added, the loamless compost is suitable for making growing bags and filling other containers for growing plants.

CONTAINER GROWING

Growing plants in containers adds a new dimension to gardening and there are almost as many different types of containers to choose from as there are plants to go in them. Virtually anything that will hold compost would do, from sophisticated urns on pedestals to an old worn-out car tyre and in between the two extremes will be found tubs and barrels, clay pots, troughs made from various materials including stone, iron, clay and polystyrene; sinks, old cooking pots, kettles, baskets and others.

Growing bags So convenient and popular is container growing now that manufacturers produce special bags filled with compost to lay on their sides so that holes are made in the top to accommodate plants. These growing bags can be placed in the greenhouse to grow a wide range of plants including tomatoes, cucumbers, lettuce, peppers and aubergines; the bags can be placed on the patio or balcony to grow similar crops or decorative bedding plants.

The bag should be set on a level surface to facilitate even watering otherwise water will drain down to the lower part and either swamp the roots or seep out of the drainage holes. Before planting, it is advisable to loosen the compost within the bag which may have become compacted during transit; the best way to do this is to prod and pat the sides of the bag until the compost is loose and level.

Next, cut slits or holes in the top side of the bag and make small holes in the compost with the fingers. The majority of bags will accommodate 3 tomato plants or 2 cucumbers; when smaller fruits but more of them are required then plant 4 tomato plants instead but the overall crop weight will be just the same.

Although the compost in the bag may feel moist, the plants should, never-the-less, be given a good watering to settle them in. From then on watering should be done with care until the plants are well established and then up to ½ gal (2.2l) per plant per day may be needed by mature tomatoes during a long bright day in summer. If there is any doubt about over watering during the early stages, small slits may be cut in the side of the bag so that excess water can drain away.

Salad crops and vegetables can also be grown in other containers filled with potting composts. An old bucket or large flower pot is ideal for growing such crops as dwarf-growing broad beans, peas, sweet peppers and a crop of new potatoes may be harvested for Christmas dinner by planting a tuber in such a container during the first few days of August.

GROW FRUIT Various types of fruit can be grown in containers. These include soft fruits like strawberries which may be grown in single 6in (15cm) clay or plastic pots filled with John Innes potting compost, or they may be grown in tubs or 'tower pots' which stand upright with the plants set in the side. Gooseberries and currants are other examples of soft fruit which can be successful.

Apples, apricots, peaches, pears and nectarines are all worthwhile and figs are traditionally planted in containers sunk into the ground to restrict root action and subsequent shoot growth.

John Innes potting compost No 2 should be used for bushes and trees, young plants establish well and the size of container should be chosen which will accommodate the roots without cramping. When the existing container is full of roots, pot on into one slightly larger. The best time to repot is when the leaves begin to fall in autumn.

Do not let the compost dry out completely at any time, it needs to be just moist even in mid-winter. During late spring and summer, more water will be needed to keep the plant happy; add liquid feed to the water every 10 days during the growing season.

CONTAINER-GROWN FLOWERS AND SHRUBS Decorative plants too numerous to mention make excellent subjects for container growing. Apart from the fact that they are mobile and can be moved around and replaced as necessary, plants can be grown which would not normally thrive in the garden. For example, rhododendrons and other plants requiring an acid soil can be grown in a container whereas they would not tolerate a soil which is alkaline and could not therefore be grown in the open ground on chalk.

HYPERTUFA SINK GARDENS Natural stone troughs are delightful but scarce and hence rather expensive. Very good immitations can be made, however, by obtaining an old glazed sink.

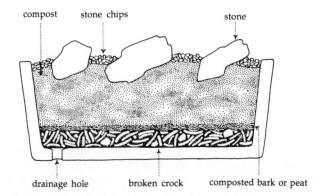

compost   stone chips   stone

drainage hole   broken crock   composted bark or peat

Sectional view of a sink garden.

The shiny white glaze can be covered by a mixture of cement, sand and peat (hypertufa) and made to look just like the genuine article. First cut away the waste pipe leaving the strainer in position for drainage; should the strainer be missing, the hole may be covered over with wire netting. Next thoroughly clean the sink inside and out and then place the sink where it is to stand permanently. The container should be stood on blocks so that excess water from the compost can drain away.

An adhesive like 'Unibond' or 'Polybond' is necessary to ensure that the hypertufa mix stays attached to the sides of the sink. This is applied by a brush and allowed to go tacky before applying the cement mix. Even so the mix has a tendency to slide off from the vertical sides and so it is advisable to fix wire netting around the sink to prevent the hypertufa from slipping before it has had a chance to set.

Measure out 1 part cement, 3 parts sand and 1 part fine peat by volume and add sufficient water to make a stiff mix.

Starting at one corner a small amount about the size of a chicken's egg is pressed onto the surface of the container so that it is reduced to approximately ½in (13mm) thick. Proceed along the top and inside down to where the compost surface will finish (there is no need to cover the inside completely) then continue over the external surface.

After a day or two the surface can be marked to simulate chisel grooves if desired and then left to dry completely before planting up. Mellowness will come with time and can be hastened by painting the hypertufa with liquid manure or boiled rice water to attract algal growth and moss.

Troughs and sinks of various shapes and sizes can be made using the same mix but using cardboard boxes or plastic containers as moulds. Allow the hypertufa to set before tearing away the cardboard and then smooth any sharp edges with a piece of wood.

Good drainage is important Whatever the type of container used, good drainage is essential for the well being of plants being grown. Provided John Innes or a good proprietary loamless compost is used, no extra drainage material is normally required for containers up to 10in (25cm) in diameter.

Containers larger than that, however, should be supplied with drainage material in the form of coarse gravel or broken clay pots placed at least 1in (2.5cm) deep over the drainage holes. A layer of coarse peat or composted tree bark is then placed over the drainage material to help retain moisture and plant foods and stop the compost from blocking it.

HANGING BASKETS Containers that can be suspended make an attractive feature. They may consist of almost any type of material provided it will retain compost and moisture. An open-sided basket made from plastic-covered wire has an advantage in that not only may plants be grown in the open top but small plants can also be tucked through the sides.

Open-sided containers will need to be lined to retain water as well as the compost. Traditionally, moss has been used and can be purchased or gathered from damp banks; polythene sheet is convenient and easy to handle, the green sheet blending well with the plants.

Stand the basket in an empty bucket so that it does not roll about as work proceeds. First line the basket with moistened moss or polythene. Potting compost is filled in gradually so that when plants are inserted through the side of the container, their roots can be covered as filling takes place. Finally set the last plants in the surface of the compost at the top of the basket. Trailing plants look effective planted at the edge with a 'dot' plant such as petunia or zonal perlargonium set in the middle.

Plants already growing in small pots should be watered so that the root ball is moist, then turn the plant upside down and gently tap the edge of the pot on a solid surface to dislodge the root ball. Potting compost is tucked around the roots in the basket and lightly pressed with the fingers. Finally give the compost a thorough watering and hang the basket from a substantial support in a sheltered position protected from strong wind. Hanging baskets containing mature plants can dry out quickly during the summer and so regular watering is necessary, with a liquid feed added to the water every 7 to 10 days.

LAWN TURFING AND SEEDING

There can be no doubt that a good lawn can really enhance a garden. Site preparation is all important and should not be skimped in any way, although it is often thought that a short cut can be taken in this respect when laying turves.

Turfing certainly gives an immediate effect once site preparation has been completed and the lawn can be used more or less straight away, whereas several weeks or months must elapse before the lawn can be used after sowing seed. Turves can be laid during winter if necessary, in fact the best time is from October to February provided soil conditions permit; March and April are good months too although turfing can take place during summer as well when irrigation is available. Seed sowing, on the other hand, is often restricted to mid-August through September and then again in April. Seed is, however, cheaper than turf and a selection of different grasses can be chosen to suit the soil type, site and use to which the lawn is to be put.

Damage is more likely to occur in the early stages of seed establishment, particularly with regard to birds and cats. There is also less chance of importing weeds when grass seed is sown than when buying turves.

INSPECT TURF SOURCE Before buying turf it is advisable to see the product if possible. The turf should be relatively free from perennial weeds but avoid any that has been recently sprayed with herbicides to control weeds. The reason for this is that grass roots may not yet have replaced weeds that have rotted away and the resulting holes will make lifting difficult without causing further damage. The turves should be cut from suitable soil which is not too heavy, light or stony. Thickness of the turf is important for subsequent establishment and anything thinner than 1¼in (3cm) should be rejected. Turves cut to a size of 3ft by 1ft (1m x 30cm) are convenient to handle, anything larger being rather heavy and cumbersome.

SELECTING GRASS SEED Various mixtures are available and some care is needed when choosing a particular mixture. Basically two sorts are available for domestic lawns: those containing rye grass, which are often cheaper and hard wearing, and those without rye grass and which consist of fine grasses to give a quality lawn. Rye grass is often coarse and vigorous but, recently, new cultivars have been introduced by seedsmen which are less vigorous and produce a finer sward and yet are comparatively hard wearing with a good root system – some will even tolerate shade.

Site preparation The first thing to do is to clear the surface of the site of large stones and other debris. Any weeds present should be treated with a fast-acting contact weedkiller that becomes inactivated as soon as it touches the soil. Deep-rooted perennial weeds like dock should be dug out by using a digging fork. Couch grass and bindweed should also be forked out and disposed of.

Undulating sites should be levelled to make a good manageable surface. This is done by first removing the topsoil then cultivating the subsoil and levelling, then returning the topsoil. Poorly drained soils will need attention, they seldom provide good growing conditions: it may simply be a case of cracking a subsoil pan, or tile drains may be installed. Alternatively clinker or stone rubble may be spread over the subsoil before returning the topsoil.

Provided no levelling or drainage work is necessary, basic cultivations consist of forking over the ground by hand, or turning it over with a mechanical cultivator; any large stones and other debris should be removed as work proceeds. Bulky organic material like peat, composted bark or garden compost should be incorporated at the same time to add humus. Heavy clay soil will also benefit from the addition of grit or coarse sand.

The next stage is to rake over the soil to break down any large lumps. Small undulations will soon appear as raking progresses. Tread the soil firm by shuffling over the surface; although rolling may appear to be the obvious treatment, it really is unsatisfactory because the surface often compacts leaving the lower layers loose.

A general fertilizer should be broadcast over the site at the rate of 2oz per sq yd (68g per m²) and raked into the surface of the soil. Finally, walk over the site and pick off any stones and other debris that have come to the surface. The site is now ready for laying turves or sowing seed.

Laying turves Turves should be laid as soon as possible after delivery otherwise the grass will begin to turn yellow. First put a line down one side of the site and set the first row of turves against it from one end to the other. Start the next row so that the end of the first turf comes mid-way along the first turf in the first row and continue laying the turves to the end keeping

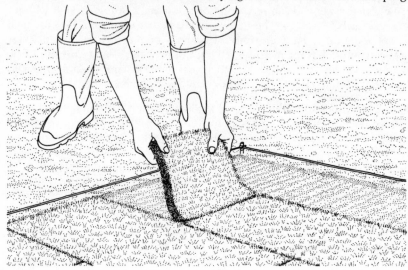

Laying turves: stagger the turves so that they bond well together.

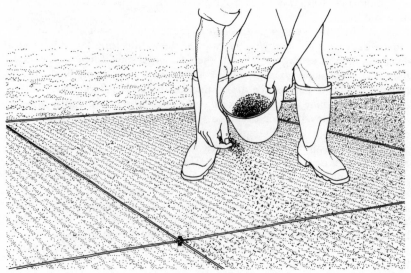

When sowing lawn seed, mark out the area in yard squares and sow the correct measure in each.

each turf pushed close to the next. The pattern of turves will now begin to resemble a bonded brick wall.

After the last turf is positioned, go over the site tapping the turves down with the back of a spade; on a large site a flat bottomed tamper will be more convenient to use.

Finally, broadcast a liberal amount of sifted loam over the area and brush it into the cracks. This will help the turves to establish and avoid curling up by the edges drying out.

Seed sowing Basic cultivation and fertilizer application is similar to that for laying turves except that the soil surface should be brought to a finer tilth. Broadcast the seed evenly at the rate of 1 to 1½oz per sq yd (34 to 50g per m²); special seed distributors are available from garden centres or the seed may be broadcast by hand. Half the seed should be sown in one direction with the other half sown across the other way. This will help to distribute the seed more uniformly and it is prudent to choose a still day for the job.

Finally lightly rake the seed into the surface but do not roll afterwards otherwise the soil surface may pan and give poor germination. Most seed is treated with bird repellent but black cotton should, never-the-less, be cross-crossed over the site to prevent birds from dust bathing and it will also help to keep cats away from the area.

PRUNING

Pruning is a well established technique that has been carried out by gardeners for centuries, and by Nature long before that: consider the removal of branches by wind and snow, twigs by rabbits, leaves by caterpillars and developing fruit by maggots – to name but a few examples. The plant will respond to that cut and the removal of its growth in various ways; should the cut have been made in winter when the growth is dormant, much more growth is likely to be made during the following year than had no cut been made at all. Strange and difficult to believe perhaps, for those not familiar with the ways in which plants react. Look at the piece of wood cut off and count up the buds that would have grown out as shoots the following year and it can be seen that all the energy available is divided up between only those buds left on the plant. After all, the roots are the same size and they are foraging for plant foods and soil moisture just the same. On the other hand, if a rough cut is made, the branch may die right back or should the pruning be carried out at the wrong time of the year, flowers and fruit may not be forthcoming during the season. In these cases pruning will not have had a good effect on the plant.

Then why not let the plant grow without pruning as might be the case in its natural surroundings? First of all the overall appearance of many shrubs and trees can be improved by judicious, pruning; flowering and fruiting plants are made more prolific by the removal of unwanted shoots and there are some, like the rose, which produce far better flowers on new wood. The appearance of an overgrown shrub border with each specimen encroaching upon the next is not a pleasant sight.

Fruit bud development is often encouraged by pruning at certain times of the year or perhaps by pruning the roots. With care and understanding, the plants become much more rewarding and useful; however we do need to have a clear idea of what we want to achieve and whether the plant can respond accordingly.

Pruning is one of the most important operations in the garden. And yet it is safe to say that it is the one activity more abused through lack of understanding than any other. The reasons for this phenomenon are manifold when you consider the number of different sorts of plants that are candidates for the pruning knife. We may be inclined to think of fruit trees like apples, pears or plums and bushes such as gooseberry, black or red currants or perhaps ornamental shrubs and roses as the obvious plants; we should not lose sight of the improvements to be made in privet and other hedges screening the garden, vines and even soft-stemmed plants like annual bedding, which start the year as seeds in a packet and complete their life cycle from seed to flower in one year. Cucumbers and tomatoes growing outside in the garden or in the greenhouse produce much better crops when they are pruned regularly and houseplants – both flowering and foliage – growing in pots deserve a mention as well. Not all garden plants need pruning and those that do may require only spasmodic attention: perhaps a shaping once in a while every other year or so. And yet there are a number of plants all the better for pruning in the summer and again in the winter, or even more frequently than that.

In general there are five objectives to consider when pruning any plant: to direct growth into the branches and shoots where it is desired; to prevent overcrowded growth; to prevent invasion by pests and diseases; to regulate the number and position of flower buds, and to control vigour.

First of all, walk round the plant and get to know it; ponder awhile on its function in life. The overall shape is important, not only during the summer when the leaves are present but in the winter too, when deciduous plants will have shed their leaves. The idea is to try to create a balance between growth and productivity which may result in fruit, flowers, effect or all of these things. In addition to improving the appearance of the plant, its size can be controlled to a certain extent and very old plants can often be rejuvenated by the skillful use of the pruning tool.

Next, consider how to use the plant in such a way so as to reap the most benefit from it within the space allotted. This applies just as much to a cordon apple tree with short confined branches growing in a confined space, as it does to a large standard crab apple reaching tall with spreading branches to provide shade during hot summer days, or the slender fastigiate form of an ornamental tree to enhance the appearance of a group. Regrettably, plants are at times seen with lop-sided growth. This may have come about by the close proximity of a neighbouring plant restricting light; a strong prevailing wind often causes much the same problem, especially when the plant is growing near to the sea when salt-laden breezes scorch the developing soft shoots and buds.

There may be an inclination here to cut back the side with strong growth to balance the stunted side. Unfortunately this would only lead to yet more vigorous growth of that side, especially when the pruning was carried out during winter or spring. The real answer is to prune the side which lacks vigour, so that growth is stimulated and within a year or more, depending on the size of the specimen, a more uniform shape will emerge.

A plant happy in its surroundings is less prone to disease. There is also no doubt that infection can have a bearing on the shape of a plant. Canker, which attacks apple trees for example, can be very limiting: growth is likely to be stunted or even non existent beyond the portion of stem girdled by the disease. This often gains entry through a wound made by sucking insects like woolly aphid or through pruning cuts. Some diseases gain entry through healthy tissue, for example blossom wilt of plums attacks the flower and then grows through the stalk to infect the remainder of the shoot. Apple tree mildew does much the same by causing the leaves to turn silver, then brown and finally to die and fall from the tree, although before that stage is reached, buds and shoots are infected.

All of these symptoms lead to a reduction of vigour and less fruit; unless checked, the disease will spread throughout the tree and attack others too. Ornamental plants are subject to disease attack, an example being the rose, which tends to be very susceptible to a leaf disease known as black spot. This is very troublesome in areas subject to an atmosphere with high relative humidity and it causes the leaves to fall prematurely, which leads to a reduction in extension growth and inferior blooms. When the disease has spread into the shoot, it is necessary to remove the infected part by cutting back into wood that is free from the disease and shows no sign of spotting. Dead wood should always be disposed of, otherwise there is a risk of coral spot fungus spreading to healthy tissue from the dead area.

Plants suffering from mechanical damage caused by careless handling, wind, snow or even lightning are subject to disease attack and the damaged branch should be cut back to another branch or the main trunk. Animals, both large and small, may graze on plants – deer are very partial to rose bushes in some areas. Damaged shoots should be cut back to a bud and branches to the main stem or a shoot. Squirrels have a habit of tearing down the bark from trees and rabbits are notorious for chewing young shoots and bark. When bark is removed completely from around a branch, the shoot usually dies and is better removed as soon as possible.

Damage caused when branches rub together is also a common reason for the onslaught of disease. Crossing branches are inclined to rub and it is often surprising how much movement there is in shrubs and trees with only a light breeze blowing. Fruit trees are particularly susceptible to crossing branches: inspection at pruning time during winter does not always reveal trouble ahead to the inexperienced eye, because one branch crossing the other looks too far away. However, during the growing season, fruit develops and weighs the branch down so that contact is made with the one below and trouble sets in. Pruning away those troublesome parts will put strength into growth elsewhere. In fact, it is true to say that weak growth often results from a lack of pruning at the right time: the aim is to create a balance between the production of wood and flowers, when flower or fruit production is required.

In the case of plants being grown for their leaf shape and colour, bark or other non-flowering attributes, then good strong healthy growth is still to be encouraged. Spindly, weak stems are of no use because they are unable to contribute to the welfare of the plant and they tend to be prone to attack by pests and diseases; seldom, if ever, does a weak shoot that is simply short-ened back give rise to acceptable growth and so it is best removed altogether. The answer, then, is to encourage the plant to produce the kind of growth we wish it to make, by directing the development of the buds so that they are regulated to exploit the area allotted to them. The relative position of one shoot to another is determined by training the plant at an early stage in its life, and continues by correct pruning for the remainder of its existence.

A young plant usually consists of one single stem with a number of buds developing between the leaf stalks and main stem. These buds can be en-couraged to grow out by removing the growing point at the apex of the plant. This is known as 'stopping' and is a routine operation carried out with plants like chrysanthemums to encourage the buds to grow into shoots to form a bushy habit. The same practice is applied to a young fruit tree by cutting away part of the maiden stem to form a bush. It should be noted that hard pruning, that is the removal of a large portion of that stem, will promote stronger growth of the remaining buds; whereas light pruning, or the removal of fewer buds, usually results in less extension growth of the remaining buds. The subsequent shoots are often 'stopped' yet again to stimulate growth of their buds and a good example here is when a ridge cucumber is grown in the garden to sprawl over the ground: the tip of the stem is pinched out to encourage lateral shoots to develop, then in turn each of these is pinched and sub-laterals grow to be trained away from the main stem in all directions.

Growth can be directed to expand in a certain direction by the selection of a particular bud. Stems cut back to an outward-facing bud or shoot, will cause the resulting growth to proceed in that outward direction – a principle adopted in building up the framework of different sorts of plants.

Controlled growth, then, can be directed in such a way that the plant becomes more effective in producing better fruit or flowers and it is likely to be more attractive than when it is left unpruned. Not only that but consider-ation should be given to air movement around the plant, particularly in the central area which tends to be rather susceptible to attack by diseases. Light transmission into the middle region is important, too, so that wood ripens properly and remains healthy. Well placed branches allowing air and light to penetrate will aid the application of insecticides and fungicides so that the spray will make good contact with the innermost branches.

The underlying principles of pruning are common to most plants and it is worth noting at this stage, that the removal of wood during winter gives rise to vigour and stimulates growth in the following summer; whereas summer pruning removes leaves together with the shoots and therefore reduces vigour. This is a method often employed with, for example, certain kinds of tree fruit to restrict the growth.

Making the cut A good craftsman deserves good tools and there is a very

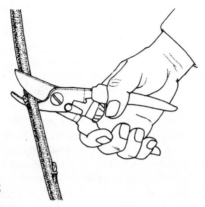

When pruning make a sloping
cut immediately above a bud.

wide range of pruning implements to choose from. When choosing and
buying tools it does not necessarily follow that the most expensive tools are
best, but it does pay to buy the best quality that can be afforded.

Whenever a stem is severed, it is most important to make the cut just
above a growth bud. These are usually more pointed and slimmer than a
flower bud, although they do vary from species to species and descriptions
of the various plants are dealt with in their respective sections. The reason
for cutting back to a shoot bud is that extension growth will subsequently
take place, whereas a flower bud would produce just a flower and possibly
fruit to follow but then growth would stop and the twig would possibly die
back. On no account should a cut be made so far away from the bud as to
leave a long portion of bare stem. The snag of stem above a bud invariably
dies back necessitating further pruning and perhaps more drastic treatment
should the disease go unnoticed for any length of time.

Some professional pruners still use a knife for the job. It should be em-
phasised that the blade needs to be very sharp and needless to say that
every care should be taken for that reason, one slip could cause a very nasty
accident. Keep an oil stone handy to tone up the blade from time to time,
even the best of steel loses its razor-like edge with use. Take hold of the
shoot to be pruned approximately 2in (5cm) below the proposed cut with
the bud facing you. The thumb of the knife hand should be folded over the
fore finger and not in front of the sharp edge of the blade. Place the sharp
edge of the knife on the far side of the stem away from the bud in line just
below the bud tip. The operation is carried out by one stroke of the knife
slanting slightly upwards, so that the blade cuts through the shoot just above
the bud. In the case where a shoot is growing close to the one to be pruned,
and especially when it is growing between you and the shoot to be pruned,
it is usually safer to use secateurs to avoid damaging the remaining stem by
the follow through action of the knife blade.

Always keep the face well away from the knife and it is as well to kneel
rather than to bend when dealing with a pruning cut well down. Due to the
skill required and possible hazard involved in using a knife for pruning, the
majority of people prefer to use secateurs and there are basically two types

available for stems measuring up to ¾in (19mm) in diameter: the anvil type consists of a blade which makes contact with a flat strip of brass; the so-called parrot bill type derive their name from the curved shape of the blades. Whichever type is used, the cut made just above the selected bud should be made so that it slopes away from that bud. Long-handled secateurs often called 'loppers' are available and are more convenient to use for bush pruning when stems need to be removed from soil level. They also come into their own when shoots are just out of arm's reach when using small hand tools.

Large branches may need to be removed from time to time and great care is needed to avoid ripping the bark as the branch falls away. It often pays to begin removing the branch by first making a cut underneath, then proceed with the downward cut so that a clean surface results. Large limbs may be tied to the one above for temporary support until they are cut through, or they may be removed gradually by cutting back from the far end in manageable lengths. In any case, before making the final cut of a large heavy branch, it is better to first make a cut underneath, approximately 6in (15cm) from the trunk, then remove the saw and begin to cut into the branch from the top approximately 1in (25mm) outwards from the underneath cut. The branch is then removed.

Advice is often given to cut off large branches flush to the main stem or trunk. Recent research has suggested that diseases are more likely to attack the tissue and progress further into the tree when that method is used. The correct pruning position is at an angle to the main branch or trunk. Close inspection of the tree will show a ridge of tissue where the branch joins the main branch or trunk. This is known as the 'branch bark ridge'. The top of the pruning cut should be made just on the lopped branch side of the ridge and it should be angled away from the main stem to form a mirror image of the angle of the ridge. With this method the wound heals over much faster than when the cut is made flush with the main stem or when a stub is left. Unfortunately wound dressings and sealing paints are of little use in preventing infection because diseases are often found growing beneath them, the spores having been sucked into the tissue at the time of wounding.

Safety is of paramount importance at all times and a little forethought before starting work may prevent a nasty accident. We do on occasion hear of young boys, and older ones too, being electrocuted by flying a kite near power lines. The same could apply by cutting through an unseen cable camouflaged by leaves and branches, especially when working from a metal ladder.

Ladders and steps should be placed firmly on the ground before stepping on them. Tie the top of the ladder to the tree and have someone stand on the bottom if there is any chance of the ladder slipping. Beware of falling branches and never leave a partially severed branch or tools up above.

ROOT PRUNING Over-vigorous trees are often less productive than those with balanced growth. One way of regulating the problem is to remove part of the root system of the plant so that a slight check to growth follows. Small trees and bushes may be simply dug up and then immediately replanted after lightly trimming the roots. Larger specimens may be treated in much

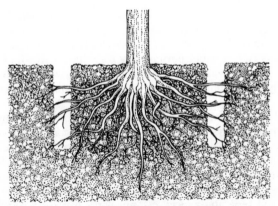

Root pruning checks the growth of an over-vigorous tree.

the same way except that it is impracticable to replant them. Instead a trench is dug around the root zone approximately 2ft (60cm) away from the main stems or trunk (or directly below the circumference of the canopy of branches of a large tree) and the roots are cut through as the trench is dug. Remove the root debris and then replace the soil treading firmly. Only half of the root zone should be treated in any one year to avoid a severe check to growth.

BARK RINGING Another method often employed to restrict the uptake of water and soluble nutrients into the tree from the roots is to remove a small portion of tree bark from the trunk. The main reason, however, for bark ringing – as it is called – is to reduce the amount of food travelling from the leaves down to the roots, again helping to control growth. The best time to carry out the operation is when the bark lifts easily in late spring and it is achieved by inserting the point of a sharp knife into the bark so that it penetrates to the hard wood. Make a cut half way round the trunk and remove the knife. Insert the point of your knife again ½in (13mm) away from the original incision and make a similar cut. The strip of bark is then completely removed. A similar half circle is then removed on the opposite

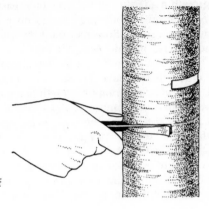

Bark ringing: another way of checking growth.

side of the tree trunk approximately 6in (15cm) below the first. Both wounds are then painted over with wound sealing paint so that they heal over satisfactorily. Care should be taken to remove only the recommended width of bark from the tree, a wider portion may result in the death of the tree as can often be witnessed when rabbits or deer graze on tree bark. Bark ringing of cherries or plums is not desirable due to their tendency to bleed.

SHRUB PRUNING Pruning in itself is unlikely to compensate for the poor choice of plant in the first instance: an over-vigorous specimen outgrowing its allotted space will never be complementary to the overall scene, especially when it receives the all-too-frequent short back and sides to try to keep the growth within bounds. Careful consideration given to the choice of plant to allow ample garden space so that the plant develops properly is just as important as soil type and aspect; certain plants like rhododendrons need acid soil to grow properly and others are rather tender and so look for shelter from cold wind to avoid die back of branches and stem.

Weather damage is a form of natural pruning; unfortunately many shrubs may be cut back by frost and cold wind at a time when flower buds are developing, consequently the anticipated flowers will not be forthcoming. The same could be said about pruning a shrub at the wrong time of the year. This occurs all too frequently, because questions are often asked why this or that shrub does not flower regularly but, on further questioning, the real answer is only too evident.

It would be wrong to suggest that all shrubs need pruning every year and yet the majority of them could be improved by pruning from time to time; there are examples like the *Cornus* with brightly coloured stems which look much more attractive when pruned back to within a few buds of the mature wood during the spring of each year. Old plants can often be rejuvenated by careful pruning so that they again become attractive and productive. In some cases the removal of dead and weak growth may be sufficient for the first stage of renovation, leaving further treatment to the following year by way of the normal technique for that particular kind of plant.

Established shrubs are pruned at different times of the year and by different methods, according to when they flower and whether they produce flowers on growth made during the previous season, or during the current season's shoots. Shrubs producing flowers on growth made the previous year are those that usually flower in the first few months of the year and early summer. These include *Forsythia intermedia*, *Philadelphus*, *Pieris* and *Weigela*; they should be pruned immediately after flowering by cutting away the majority of shoots that have flowered to within two or three buds of the old wood. The shrubs flowering on growth made during the current season usually flower from mid-summer or later including *Buddleia davidii*, *Hibiscus syriacus* and *Potentilla fruticosa*: these are pruned after the turn of the year just before the buds burst in spring.

Evergreen shrubs like *Elæagnus* and *Aucuba*, grown mainly for their interesting leaves, require only occasional pruning to keep them within bounds. This is best carried out before new growth starts in spring so that winter damage is removed at the same time. These large-leaved evergreens should always be pruned with secateurs, otherwise when hedge clippers or shears are used, much damage is caused by cutting the leaves resulting in an unsightly appearance and infection.

Dead-heading Although natural for some plants to produce seed heads after flowering, the energy used is often to the detriment of next season's flower display. Large-flowered roses often produce their blooms in flushes, no doubt many of them will be cut fresh for indoor decoration, those remaining on the plant, however, will eventually fade; they are then better removed by cutting back the faded flower to a shoot below so that it will develop more quickly to produce a replacement bloom. Great care is needed when removing faded flower heads from plants such as *Hydrangea* and *Rhododendron* because next year's flowers develop from buds just below the old flower.

FRUIT The various types of fruit trees and bushes generally require different pruning methods due to their peculiar growth habit. Some kinds, like the autumn-fruiting raspberry, bear fruit on the current season's growth whereas others, for example the black currant, produce fruit on the previous season's wood; certain apple cultivars do not fruit until the wood is two or even three years old and these factors should be considered before pruning is started.

Loganberry and blackberry These plants produce their fruit on long shoots arising as suckers from the root. The shoot growth is made during one year to fruit the next so that at a certain time of the year the plant supports both old and new stems. Since the individual stems can grow up to 10ft (3m) long they need to be trained by tying them to wires stretched between posts. Three wires usually suffice, the first 3ft (1m) above the ground, the next 5ft (1.5m) and the top wire 6ft (1.8m) high. The easiest method of training is to tie in the new growth to one side of the plant leaving the other side free for next year's new stems, otherwise the vigorous stems can easily become a tangled mass making pruning more difficult than it should be.

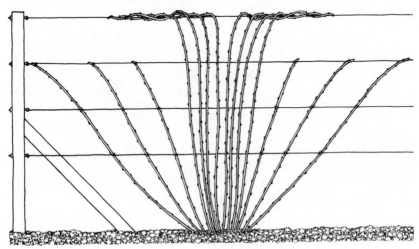

Pruning and training a blackberry: the young canes are tied in the middle.

When fruiting is finished the spent stems should be cut away at ground level leaving the space free for next year's suckers to be tied in for fruiting the following year. No doubt more stems will arise from the stool than are necessary and the weakest may be cut away as they appear, to leave six of the best for cropping.

Raspberry These plants produce canes each year from the root in the same way as loganberries and blackberries. The canes do not grow so long but should, never-the-less, be tied to similar supporting wires to keep them tidy and avoid congested growth and chafing. Again, no more than six canes should be allowed to develop from each stool, the surplus being removed early so that energy will be conserved for the remaining shoots.

Cultivars fruiting during summer will produce the fruit on canes made during the previous year. After fruit has been gathered, the old canes should be completely cut away at ground level to leave no more than six new canes to each plant to bear next year's crop. During the following March the soft curved tip of each cane may be cut away so that the buds down the length of the cane will develop more uniformly.

Autumn-fruiting raspberries require different treatment because they produce fruit on the young current season's growth. In this case all growth is cut away to approximately 4in (10cm) from the ground during March of each year.

Black currant This plant produces fruit on wood made the previous year so that pruning is done to encourage strong new growth to crop the next year. The best time to prune the bush is when fruiting has finished; fruit harvesting

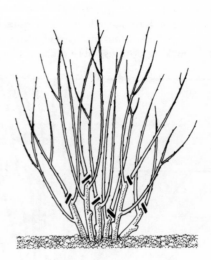

Pruning a black currant.

Apple variety 'Sunrise'.

can be somewhat tedious and for that reason some of the fruiting wood can be cut away when the fruit is ripe in order that the crop may be gathered more easily.

Some cultivars send up a good deal of new shoots from soil level so that much of the old wood can be cut away at that point; others, however, make side shoots from existing stems in which case the spent wood should be cut back to that new shoot. It may be necessary to retain two or three new shoots to each old one so that sufficient wood is available for next year's crop. Generally, at least one-third of the existing wood is cut away after fruiting each year to make room for new shoots.

Blueberry The cropping pattern is very similar to black currants and so the same pruning technique may be employed.

Red and white currants The bushes consist of leading main shoots which give rise to side shoots. Each year during winter the leading shoots should be cut back by one-half of the growth made during the previous season; the cut being made close to a healthy outward-facing bud. The side shoots are pruned during summer, the best time is when the fruit is beginning to ripen, and each side shoot is cut back to leave only five or six leaves. These side shoots are then cut back during winter to within ½in (13mm) of the leading shoot.

Before mature plants become congested, some old wood may be cut away during winter to allow younger growth to establish.

Gooseberry Culinary cultivars may be pruned during winter by thinning out

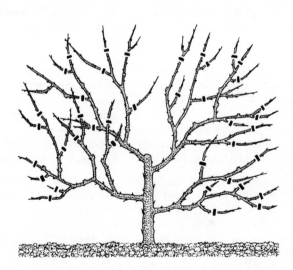

Pruning a gooseberry.

Two crops for the greenhouse. Above: The grape 'Foster's Seedling'.
Below: *Chrysanthemum* 'Buckland'.

up to one-third of the mature wood. The only other treatment necessary being to remove one-half of the extension growth made during the previous season from each leader.

Dessert cultivars require pruning during winter by cutting back the leading shoots by one-half of the growth made the previous season. When the bushes become mature after 3 or 4 years the leaders should be reduced by two-thirds of the previous year's growth. The leaders of cultivars with a drooping habit should be cut back to an upward-facing bud. Side shoots should be cut back each winter to within 2in (5cm) from the older wood.

Some cultivars are inclined to produce strong suckers from the base of the plant and it is important to remove them as they appear.

Grape vine (outdoor) During the first year after planting, after leaf fall and before January, the growth is cut back to firm wood leaving two to three buds. One of the resulting shoots should be selected during the following year to be tied vertically on to the supporting wires strained between posts. These wires are spaced 9in (23cm) apart up to 4ft (1.2m). The other shoots should be tied in horizontally and when 3ft (1m) of growth has been made the growing point should be pinched out. During the following autumn after leaf fall, these side shoots are cut back close to the main stem. The main leading shoot is at the same time cut back to a bud 3ft (1m) from the ground.

Several buds will develop during the following growing season and the uppermost shoot is tied vertically to the wire support and the growing points of all remaining shoots are pinched when 1ft (30cm) of growth has been made. Subsequent shoots (sub-laterals) that arise should be stopped when they have produced one leaf.

During the following autumn after leaf fall the main vertical rod should again be cut back to firm ripe wood. The side shoots are cut back to two buds.

One of the two buds will be selected during the following spring to be tied to the wires and allowed to produce fruit although no more than six bunches should be allowed to develop during the third year after planting, otherwise no fruit will be forthcoming during the following year.

Pruning during subsequent years follows the same pattern and where space permits side shoots may be trained horizontally to mature when sub-laterals will develop to be trained vertically. These vertical rods are then cut back to two buds each autumn and one of the resulting shoots being selected to crop.

Grape vine (greenhouse) During the first year after planting, only the main shoot should be allowed to grow. Any side shoots that develop are stopped by pinching out the growing point after two leaves. The main stem is cut back to firm ripe wood during December and the small side shoots cut back to two buds.

The following year will see the main rod growing to the apex of the roof where it should be stopped by pinching out the growing point. Side shoots developing from old wood should be tied into the supporting wires spaced 9in (23cm) apart. Each winter these lateral shoots are cut back to two buds, one of which is selected to grow on the following spring.

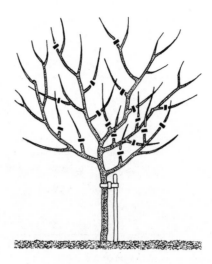

Pruning a bush apple tree.

When the small grapes begin to swell, each green shoot is cut back to two leaves, subsequent shoots from that stem are stopped at one leaf.

In greenhouses where only one grape vine is to be grown, one lateral shoot either side of the main rod should be tied in horizontally and allowed to mature. Sub-laterals then develop vertically spaced 4ft (1.2m) apart along the house and each of these vertical rods is then treated as if it were an individual plant.

Apple and pear (bush) Starting with a maiden, that is a young tree with a single upright stem, during the first winter after planting that stem should be cut back to 2ft (60cm) from the ground. Dormant buds will produce several side shoots during the following growing season and four of the strongest should be selected during the following winter to be cut back by half to an outward-facing bud.

It is at this stage that plants are often purchased from a nursery or garden centre and during the following season further growth will be made. During the next winter the leading shoots are cut back by two-thirds of the new wood whilst lateral shoots are cut back to leave three buds. The basic framework of the tree has now been established and the following winter will see the leaders cut back by one-third and the lateral shoots again cut back to leave three buds.

Trees producing upright-growing leaders should be pruned to an outward-facing bud whereas those with a relaxed spreading habit should be cut to an inward-facing bud.

Subsequent pruning of an established bush consists of cutting out branches that cross over one another, winter pruning lateral shoots and reducing the length of some leaders each year. Any shoots girdled by canker disease should, of course, be removed first. Overcrowded branches may also be thinned out to permit entry of light, air and to facilitate spraying with fungicide and insecticide as necessary.

Apple and pear (cordon) Cordon trees provide the opportunity to plant

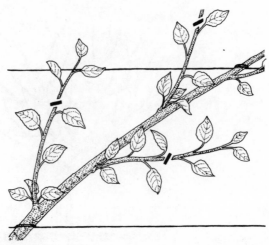

Summer pruning a cordon apple.

several different cultivars in a small space. The pruning method is somewhat different from the normal so that growth is confined to the small area.

No pruning is necessary during the winter following planting of a maiden except that when lateral shoots are present, they should be shortened to three buds. After this initial winter pruning, laterals should always be pruned during late summer.

During the first week of August in southern England and rather later in the north, all lateral shoots should be cut back to leave three leaves beyond the basal cluster. Soft green shoots should be left until mid-summer otherwise regrowth would occur necessitating repeat pruning to one leaf on the regrowth shoot.

If the tree lacks vigour and satisfactory growth is not being made, the leader should be cut back by one-third of the new growth during mid-winter. Other than that no winter pruning is necessary.

REJUVENATING OLD TREES (APPLES AND PEARS) Trees that have outgrown their situation are really best grubbed out because they are usually difficult to manage. Should a tree be worth keeping for some reason then the first thing to do is to remove all dead and diseased wood. This may be sufficient to open up the head, otherwise further thinning will be necessary by cutting out crossing branches and those growing through the centre of the tree. Tall branches may be reduced in height by 'de-horning'. A method used by cutting back to a horizontal branch.

Trees that are still reasonably vigorous should be renovated over a period of two or three winters otherwise unbalanced vigorous growth may be encouraged which leads to biennial bearing. Large wounds should always be pared smooth.

Plums and gages These plants should always be pruned in spring just as growth starts or immediately after fruiting in late summer or early autumn so that the wounds heal quickly thus avoiding silver leaf disease.

During the first spring after planting, maidens should be cut back to 4½ft

(1.4m) for half-standard and 3ft (1m) for a bush; any laterals present should be thinned out so that the remainder are spaced 3in (7.5cm) apart. Lateral shoots growing below the desired lowest shoot should be cut back to four leaves during the summer.

Trees other than maidens when planted should be left unpruned until they have been established for one year. The laterals may then be thinned out to leave four uniform well spaced shoots and these are cut back by half during the spring. Further pruning is usually unnecessary except for vigorous spreading cultivars like 'Victoria', when it is often desirable to shorten the leading shoots for up to two more years.

Dead wood and branches crossing over each other should be removed as necessary during summer and should the growth become too dense, thinning is carried out at the same time.

Cherry Sweet cherries are not usually grown in gardens due to their attractiveness to birds and the fact that at least two different cultivars need to be grown to fertilise each other. Considerable space is therefore taken up which could be available for more effective subjects.

Young trees purchased from nurserymen will already consist of a framework and little pruning is necessary, or desirable due to the susceptibility to silver leaf disease. However, dead branches and those crossing each other should be removed during August so that the wound heals quickly.

Space permitting, wall fan-trained sweet cherries tend to be more easily managed than standards. During the summer after planting the young tree is cut back to 2ft (60cm) above the ground to the nearest lateral shoot growing parallel to the wall (or fence). All other shoots are removed except one growing in the opposite direction by cutting them clean away from the main stem.

The two shoots are tied to canes at an angle of 45 degrees and during the following summer the shoot growing from the end of the cut laterals is tied to the cane. Two shoots from the top side and one from the underside of each lateral should be tied to the horizontal wires.

During the following late spring each of the eight shoots is cut back to leave 30in (75cm) of stem. The main framework is now formed and no further pruning should be required except for the removal of any shoots growing out from the wall or growing inwards. Tie in the new shoots to fill a vacant space. Others that are not required for that purpose can be pinched by removing the tip when they have made six leaves.

Remove any dead wood in August and shorten pinched back shoots to four buds. When the tree reaches the top of the wall, bend over the leaders and tie them down. The leaders can be cut back to a weak lateral the following August.

Sour or acid cherries like the 'Morello' are more usually grown in gardens as a free-standing bush or as wall-trained trees. The tree is self fertile and is suitable for growing on a north-facing wall or in the shade.

The framework may be built up as for the wall-trained sweet cherry although side shoots can be left closer together since new growth should be encouraged each year. Mature trees require hard pruning each early autumn

Summer pruning a fan-trained peach: after harvesting, the branch which has fruited is cut back to its replacement lateral.

by removing whole branches so that sufficient new shoots grow to maintain cropping.

Peach Fruit is borne on shoots made the previous year. Young wall fan trees can be trained in the same way as sweet cherries and it is important to know that a fruit bud is round and a shoot bud is pointed. A shoot bud is often accompanied by two fruit buds, one either side.

In order to maintain a succession of shoots to fruit the following year, it is necessary to allow a shoot bud at the base of the fruiting stem to grow so that it will replace the fruiting stem after harvesting the crop.

A mature fruiting tree is best pruned by first 'disbudding' (that is pinching out the top of the green shoot when it is no more than 1in [2.5cm] long) all of the shoots growing outwards, or inwards to the wall. When those shoots have been attended to, the idea is to leave shoots at 6in (15cm) spacing along the fruiting stem; these are pinched at 4 leaves. All other shoots should be disbudded except the one growing at the base of the stem bearing fruit. This is the replacement shoot which is tied in to produce fruit the following year. The extension shoot should not be allowed to grow beyond 18in (45cm) and when vacant wall space is limited this replacement shoot may be pinched at five leaves.

When a young tree has fruited and there is sufficient wall space available, the replacement shoot can be tied in alongside the old fruited stem. When space is limited, however, the fruited stem should be pruned away to make room for the new replacement shoot to be tied in place for fruiting next year.

Fig Fig trees need warmth and sun to crop satisfactorily and are best fan trained on a warm wall. The young tree may be formed as described for sweet cherry although a much simplified method may be employed by training the young lateral shoots fan-wise without any pruning during the first year.

As growth is made during each spring and, no later than June, the new shoot is pinched out at the fifth leaf. Subsequent shoots which develop during the summer should be tied in so that they are each given sufficient room to benefit from the sun and next year's fruit will then develop on these ripened shoots.

Any winter pruning necessary should be restricted to the removal of dead wood and crossing branches. Care should be taken to avoid damaging the small fruits at the end of the previous year's wood.

Medlar Once the tree has been trained in the same way as described for apples, little pruning is necessary other than thinning out overcrowded wood and crossing branches.

Quince Both bush and standard trees tend to produce much twiggy straggling growth and the only pruning necessary is the removal of dead and congested growth and crossing branches. Standard trees tend to produce vigorous vertical shoots and these should be pruned back during summer.

STORING VEGETABLES AND FRUIT, DRYING FLOWERS

Certain vegetables store perfectly well in the open ground where they have grown. These include celeriac, Chinese radish, Jerusalem artichoke and parsnip; although it is prudent to cover the surface of the soil with bracken or straw to keep the ground free from snow and to a certain extent frost. When severe frost is forecast, however, it is better to lift a supply of roots beforehand.

Potatoes, provided the tubers are dry and without pest, disease or mechanical damage, can be stored in sacks placed in frost-free, dry conditions.

Beetroot, carrots, swedes and turnips are lifted when they are ready in autumn, the tops being twisted off – especially with beetroot to avoid bleeding – and then stored in boxes between layers of moist but not wet peat or sand to avoid dehydration.

Shallots are usually lifted during summer and dried off before placing them in a net bag hung up in a dry position. Onions are ripened off somewhat later, usually during September and October when they may be tied up into strings, or placed in old nylon stockings and hung up. This eliminates

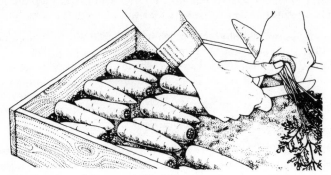

Storing carrots in a box of peat or sand.

the somewhat tedious task of tying onion strings since each individual onion is kept separate by tying the stocking between each one. Onions should be well ripened before storing and it is usually better to use the largest, which do not store so well, first of all.

When any amount of root vegetables need to be stored they may be placed in a clamp. This will free ground for cultivations and dispense with a number of boxes that may be used for other purposes like storing flower tubers and corms. To make a clamp, first spread a 2in (5cm) layer of straw on the ground then place the dry and sound root vegetables on this to make a pyramid. This pyramid is covered by a 2in (5cm) layer of straw and then a 2in (5cm) layer of soil tamped down with the back of a spade. An air vent should be provided at the top of the pyramid by leaving a small tuft of straw uncovered.

It is most important that only sound vegetables are stored otherwise disease will very quickly spread through the crop.

FRUIT Ideally, fruit should be stored in a vermin-free, frost proof but cool dark room which can be ventilated if necessary. During the first two to three weeks of storage apples and pears will need ample ventilation and after that only on dry days when the air in the store has a strong smell.

Apples and pears Fruit soon deteriorates unless it is stored carefully. Long-term storage usually means loosely wrapping each fruit in oiled or wax paper but for medium storage open polythene bags may be used provided all of the fruit in each bag is the same cultivar and at the same stage of maturity; no more than 5lb (2.2kg) of fruit should be stored in each bag and the bags should be perforated with small holes for ventilation. Individual fruits may also be placed on shelves or racks or in shallow boxes. Only sound fruit free from blemish should be stored and even then the stored fruit should be inspected every 10 to 14 days so that any deteriorated fruit may be removed. Pears require very frequent inspection because they tend to rot quickly when they become over ripe.

Cobnuts and filberts The nuts should be left on the tree until fully ripe and then harvested on a dry day. Remove the husk and lay the nuts out to dry. Traditionally the nuts were then packed into glazed earthen jars, the last layer of nuts sprinkled with salt and the jar was then tied down with brown paper and placed in a cool but frost-free room. Should glazed jars not be available, biscuit tins or a large sweet jar would serve the same purpose.

Grapes The bunch should be completely ripe and then cut with a handle to include the stem and 9in (23cm) of the supporting lateral. Fill a wine bottle two-thirds full of clean cold water to which 2 or 3 lumps of charcoal have been added to keep it fresh. Place the bottles in a wire or similar rack and insert the handle of the bunch so that the grapes hang as if they were still on the vine. Provided the store is kept cool and dark with sufficient ventilation, the grapes will keep for many weeks.

DRYING FLOWERS A number of different sorts of flower heads can be dried and used for floral decoration during the winter months. These include the so-called everlasting flowers like *Helichrysum bracteatum* with its vast range of different coloured papery petalled heads, *Statice bonduellii* and many others. Hydrangea heads and many grasses and ears of corn can also be dried. Seed heads like poppy and others are well worth drying.

Everlasting flowers should be cut on a dry day when the flower is almost completely mature but not quite. The stems are simply tied together after removing the leaves and then hung upside down in a cool airy place. Grasses are treated in the same way except that they should be cut somewhat less mature and it is not necessary to remove the leaves.

Flowers which do not dry well by themselves like *Celosia cristata* (cockscomb), larkspur, salvia and *Buddleia davidii* may be encouraged by hanging them upside down in the airing cupboard. Alternatively they can be dried by placing them in an air-tight box and covering them in borax. It usually takes from one to five days to dry the flowers, when they may be removed and then kept in a dry atmosphere.

Some flowers belonging to the daisy family tend to shatter easily after drying unless the base of the stem has been sealed with gum arabic before drying.

Trees and shrubs Mature one-year-old branches from evergreens, or deciduous branches cut just before the leaves change colour, can be stood in a vessel containing a 3in (7.5cm) depth of boiled liquid made up from 1 part glycerine and 2 parts water. The branches should be stood in the solution whilst it is still hot and it does help to bruise the lower end of the stem so that the liquid is more easily absorbed. They should remain until evergreen leaves have almost completely changed to an attractive brown colour. Deciduous branches should remain for approximately two weeks until the glycerine has spread over each leaf.

The branches may then be removed and arranged in a dry vase or stored in boxes or plastic bags until they are required.

INSECTICIDES AND FUNGICIDES

Various pests and diseases attack crop plants from time to time causing damage which more or less affects the plant. In some cases the damage caused is minimal and hardly warrants the use of a pesticide; on the other hand, certain pests and diseases are so active that unless precautions are taken at an early stage, the plant will be severely checked or even die.

Generally it is better to wait until the pest is seen before applying an insecticide whereas prevention is always better than cure so far as diseases are concerned.

Some pests and diseases are common to many plants and these will be found under the 'General' heading in the tables which follow. Those pests and diseases more likely to attack particular crops will be found under the name of that plant.

It is most important to read carefully the container label before using a pesticide: in some cases there is an interval between application and harvesting and certain chemicals, although recommended for some plants, are harmful to others.

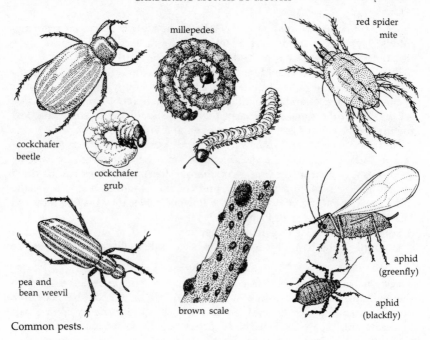

Common pests.

MAJOR PESTS AND THEIR CONTROL

Pest	Damage	Chemical	Product
GENERAL			
Chafer beetle	Eat irregular shaped holes in leaves	Permethrin Dimethoate and permethrin	Picket Bio Long-Last
Ants	Plants wilt due to root disturbance.	Pyrethrum Gamma-HCH Phoxim Pirimiphos-methyl	Anti-Ant Duster Boots Ant Destroyer Fisons Ant Killer ICI Antkiller
Aphids (greenfly and blackfly)	Suck sap causing distortion and loss of vigour.	Pirimicarb Malathion	Rapid Greenfly Killer
Cutworms	Moth caterpillars which attack plants at ground level.	Carbaryl Trichlorphon Permethrin	Garden Insect Powder Caterpillar Killer Picket
Caterpillars	Holes in leaves and flowers.	see Cutworms	
Leatherjackets	Larvae of crane flies feed on plant roots.	Bromophos Carbaryl	Bromophos Garden Insect Powder
Thrips	Feed on leaves and petals causing flecks	Permethrin Dimethoate	Picket Bio Systemic Insecticide
Millipedes	Feed on plants at soil level.	Diazinon Pirimiphos-methyl	Root Guard Sybol 2

Pest	Damage	Chemical	Product
Red spider mite	Sucks sap from leaves causing spotting and discoloration.	Dimethoate Pirimiphos-methyl	Systemic Insecticide Sybol 2
Slugs and snails	Feed on leaves and stems.	Metaldehyde Methiocarb	Slug Pellets Slug Gard
Whitefly	Suck sap and secrete honey dew causing sooty moulds.	Permethrin Dimethoate	Picket Systemic Insecticide
Earwigs	Feed on petals.	Permethrin Phoxim	Picket Fisons Ant Killer
Woodlice	Chew small jagged holes in leaves	Gamma-HCH Phoxim Pirimiphos-methyl	Boots Ant Destroyer Fisons Ant Killer ICI Antkiller
Wasps	Feed on fruit	Pirimiphos-methyl Pyrethrum and resmethrin	Sybol 2 House/Garden Plant Pest Killer
Wireworm	Feeds on roots. Holes can be seen in large roots.	Carbaryl Bromophos	Garden Insect Powder Bromophos
Mice and rats	Eat seeds and seedlings.	Coumatetralyl Difenacoum	Racumin Rat Bait Ratak
ASPARAGUS			
Asparagus beetle	Adult and maggot feed on leaves and young shoots.	Permethrin Gamma-HCH, rotenone	Picket Hexyl
BEETROOT			
Mangold fly	Tunnels in leaf.	Dimethoate and permethrin Pirimiphos-methyl	Bio Long-Last Sybol 2
BROAD BEAN			
Weevil	Maggots feed on roots of broad beans. Adults feed on leaf margins.	Permethrin and heptenophos Pirimiphos-methyl	Tumblebug Sybol 2
BRASSICAS			
Mealy aphids	Sucks sap reducing vigour and distorts growth	Permethrin and heptenophos Pirimiphos-methyl	Tumblebug Sybol 2
Cabbage root fly	White maggots burrow into root and stem	Carbaryl and rotenone Diazinon	Garden Insect Powder Root Guard
Flea beetle	Maggots feed on roots. Adults make small holes in young plants' leaves.	Rotenone Gamma-HCH	Derris Dust Gamma-BHC Dust
Gall weevil	Grubs cause galls to form on roots.	Diazinon Carbaryl	Root Guard Garden Insect Powder
CARROT			
Root aphid	Feed on roots causing severe splitting.	Pirimiphos-methyl Diazinon	Sybol 2 Root Guard

Pest	Damage	Chemical	Product
Carrot fly	Maggots tunnel into roots causing decay.	Diazinon Pirimiphos-methyl	Root Guard Sybol 2
CELERY			
Carrot fly	see Carrot		
Celery fly	Maggots tunnel into leaves causing brown blotches.	Permethrin Malathion	Picket Malathion
LEEK			
Leek moth	Caterpillars feed on leaves causing shot-hole effect.	Permethrin Fenitrothion	Picket Fentro
LETTUCE			
Root aphid	Appears as woolly patches on roots. Sucks sap restricting growth.	Pirimiphos-methyl Gamma-HCH, rotenone	Sybol 2 Hexyl
ONION			
Thrips	Feeds on leaf area causing silver flecks.	Permethrin Malathion	Picket Malathion
PARSNIP			
Root aphid	see Carrot		
Carrot fly	see Carrot		
PEA			
Midge	Maggots feed on flower buds and distort pods.	Permethrin Rotenone	Picket Derris
Pea moth	Maggots bore into pods and feed on seed.	Fenitrothion Permethrin	Fentro Picket
Thrips	see Onion thrips		
Weevils	see Broad beans		
SPINACH			
Leaf miner (Mangold fly)	see Beetroot		
SWEETCORN			
Frit fly	Maggots burrow into shoot resulting in stunted and twisted leaves.	Permethrin Malathion	Picket Malathion
APPLE AND PEAR			
Apple blossom weevil	Maggots eat holes in blossom buds.	Fenitrothion Permethrin	Fentro Picket
Capsid	Sucks sap from leaves causing distortion; and from fruitlets which develop bumps.	Permethrin Fenitrothion	Picket Fentro
Chafer	Beetles feed on blossom and skin of fruit.	Permethrin Fenitrothion	Picket Fentro
Codling moth	Caterpillar eats its way into core of fruit.	Fenitrothion Permethrin	Fentro Picket
Leaf hopper	Feeds on surface of leaf causing mottling.	Permethrin Malathion	Picket Malathion
Pear midge	Maggots feed on developing fruit causing swollen, discoloured fruitlets.	Fenitrothion Permethrin	Fentro Picket

Pest	Damage	Chemical	Product
Sawfly	Maggots feed on fruit skin causing scars and bore into fruit.	Permethrin Fenitrothion	Picket Fentro
Sucker	Eggs overwinter on trees and on hatching immature sucker damages flower bud.	Tar oil Bromophos	Clean Up Spring Spray
Tortrix moth	Caterpillars feed on leaves which are spun together. Later stages bore into fruit.	Fenitrothion Permethrin	Fentro Picket
Weevils	Larvae feed inside blossom buds and cause petals to turn brown.	Bromophos Permethrin Bromophos	Spring Spray Picket Spring Spray
Winter moth	Caterpillars feed on buds, leaves and young fruit.	Permethrin	Picket
Woolly aphid	Overwinter in crevices. White waxy clusters feed on sap often giving rise to canker.	Tar oil Bromophos	Clean Up Spring Spray

PLUM AND CHERRY

Pest	Damage	Chemical	Product
Capsid	see Apple		
Cherry fruit moth	Feeds on buds and flowers. Fruitlets are tunnelled.	Bromophos Permethrin	Spring Spray Picket
Pear slug sawfly (on cherry)	Black slug-like maggots feed on upper surface of leaf.	Permethrin Fenitrothion	Picket Fentro
Plum fruit moth	Maggot burrows into fruit and feeds near stone.	Permethrin Rotenone	Picket Derris
Plum sawfly	Maggots tunnel into fruitlets.	Bromophos Permethrin	Spring Spray Picket
Scale insects	Suck sap reducing vigour of new shoots.	Malathion Pirimiphos-methyl	Malathion Sybol 2
Tortrix moth	see Apple		
Winter moth	see Apple		

APRICOT, NECTARINE AND PEACH

Pest	Damage	Chemical	Product
Capsid	see Plum		
Scale insect	see Plum		
Winter moth	see Apple		

BLACKBERRY, LOGANBERRY AND RASPBERRY

Pest	Damage	Chemical	Product
Bramble shoot webber	Caterpillar feeds on leaves spinning them together.	Fenitrothion Permethrin	Fentro Picket
Cane midge	Adult punctures rind of cane. Maggots feed just below surface of cane causing bark to peel. Cane spot often follows.	Permethrin Fenitrothion	Picket Fentro
Leaf hopper	Feeds on blackberry leaves causing mottling.	Permethrin Malathion	Picket Malathion

Pest	Damage	Chemical	Product
Blackberry beetle	Adults feed on flowers. Maggots feed on fruit.	Permethrin Rotenone	Picket Liquid Derris
Blackberry shoot moth	Caterpillars bore into fruit which wither.	Permethrin Tar oil	Picket Clean Up Mortegg

CURRANTS AND GOOSEBERRY

Pest	Damage	Chemical	Product
Black currant leaf midge	Maggots feed on young leaves causing them and young shoots to curl, pucker and twist then turn black.	Permethrin Formothion	Picket Topgard Systemic Liquid
Capsid	Feed on leaves which develop spots then develop into holes. Leaves also pucker.	Permethrin Fenitrothion	Picket Fentro
Currant sawfly	Larvae feed on leaves.	Permethrin Malathion	Picket Malathion
Gall mite	Produces 'big bud' in blackcurrants. Infected buds are enlarged and rounded. Pick off distorted buds. In severe cases grub plant and destroy.	Benomyl	Benlate
Gooseberry sawfly	Larvae feed on leaves, causes rapid defoliation.	Permethrin Malathion	Picket Malathion
Scale insect	see Plum		
Weevils	see Apple		
Strawberry blossom weevil	Flower buds wither and die.	Rotenone Permethrin	Liquid Derris Picket
Strawberry seed beetle	Removes seeds causing fruits to shrivel.	Rotenone Permethrin	Liquid Derris Picket

CHRYSANTHEMUM (Outdoor)

Pest	Damage	Chemical	Product
Gall midge	Maggots feed inside leaf causing galls.	Gamma HCH Malathion	Hexyl Malathion
Leaf miner	Maggots tunnel in leaf.	Trichlorphon Permethrin	Caterpillar Killer Picket

NARCISSUS

Pest	Damage	Chemical	Product
Bulb scale mite	Yellow brown streaks and distorted leaves	Expose dormant bulbs to frost. Avoid planting on infected ground.	
Narcissus fly	Maggots feed inside bulb.	Dip bulbs before planting. Dust over soil in June.	Gamma HCH Gamma HCH Dust
Stem eelworm	Dark rings inside bulb.	Burn infected bulbs. Avoid planting in infected ground.	

Pest	Damage	Chemical	Product
TULIP			
Stem eelworm	Greyish-brown soft area on bulb. Distorted streaked leaves.	Burn infected bulbs. Avoid planting on infected ground.	
TURF			
Chafer grub	Yellow patches.	Diazinon	Root Guard
		Bromophos	Bromophos
Earthworm	Casts.	Rotenone	Liquid Derris
Leatherjacket	Yellow patches.	HCH	Gamma BHC Dust
		Diazinon	Root Guard
Wireworm	Yellow patches.	Diazinon	Root Guard
		Pirimiphos-methyl	Sybol 2
ROSE			
Rose leaf-rolling sawfly	Young leaves roll downwards.	Pirimiphos-methyl	Sybol 2
		Fenitrothion	Fentro
Scale insect	Scurfy flecks on shoots.	Pirimiphos-methyl	Sybol 2
		Malathion	Malathion
Slug sawfly	Black maggots feed on lower surface of leaf.	Permethrin	Picket
		Malathion	Malathion
GREENHOUSE AND FRAME			
Tortrix	Caterpillars feed on flower buds. Leaves often joined together by web.	Permethrin	Picket
		Rotenone	Derris
Capsid	see Chrysanthemum		
Gall midge	see Chrysanthemum		
Leaf miner	see Chrysanthemum		
Symphylid	Feed on roots causing plants to wilt.	Pirimiphos-methyl	Sybol 2
		Gamma HCH	Hexyl
CUCUMBER			
French fly	Small holes in leaf which enlarge as leaf grows.	Permethrin	Picket
		Malathion	Malathion
Fungus gnat (Sciarid fly)	Maggots feed on root causing plant to wilt and die.	Pirimiphos-methyl	Sybol 2
		Malathion	Malathion
Millipede	Feed on stem at soil level and lower leaves.	Permethrin	Picket
		Gamma HCH	Gamma BHC Dust
Root knot eelworm	Swollen roots. Plants wilt and die.	Remove and destroy infected plants.	
Springtail	Feed on roots. Also bore holes in seedlings.	Pirimiphos-methyl	Sybol 2
Symphylid	see Tomatoes		
CYCLAMEN			
Tarsonemid mite	Distorted growth.	Burn infected plants.	
Vine weevil	Grubs feed on roots and corm causing plant to wilt.	Pirimiphos-methyl	Sybol 2
		Gamma HCH	Hexyl

Pest	Damage	Chemical	Product
GRAPE VINE			
Mealy bug	Waxy masses covering bugs which suck sap.	Pirimiphos-methyl	Sybol 2
		Malathion	Malathion
Scale insect	Small scales protect insect which sucks sap.	Pirimiphos-methyl	Sybol 2
		Malathion	Malathion
LETTUCE (See Lettuce Outdoor)			
POT PLANTS			
Capsid	Distorted growth.	Permethrin	Picket
		Fenitrothion	Fentro
Leaf miner	White tunnels in leaf.	Permethrin	Picket
		Gamma HCH	Hexyl
Mealy bug	see Grape Vine		
Scale insect	see Grape Vine		
Sciarid fly	Maggots eat germinating seedlings and attack roots.	Pirimiphos-methyl	Sybol 2
Symphylids	see Tomatoes		
Tarsonemid mite	Distorted growth.	Burn infected plants.	
Vine weevil	see Cyclamen		
TOMATO			
Leaf hopper	Yellow/white flecks on underside of leaf.	Permethrin	Picket
		Malathion	Malathion
Leaf miner	see Pot Plants		
Potato cyst eelworm	see Outdoor Tomato		
Root knot eelworm	see Cucumber		
Springtail	see Cucumber		
Symphylid	Small white insects feed on roots causing plants to wilt.	Pirimiphos-methyl	Sybol 2
		Gamma HCH	Hexyl
Tomato moth caterpillar	Holes in stem, leaves and fruit.	Permethrin	Picket
		Rotenone	Liquid Derris

Above: Autumn tints of *Smilacina racemosa* with *Hebe* x *franciscana* 'Variegata'. *Below*: Brilliant winter shoots of *Salix alba* 'Vitellina'.

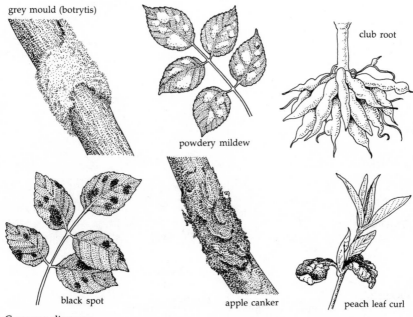

grey mould (botrytis)

powdery mildew

club root

black spot

apple canker

peach leaf curl

Common diseases.

MAJOR DISEASES AND THEIR CONTROL

Disease	Damage	Chemical	Product
GENERAL			
Grey mould (Botrytis)	Grey fluffy mould.	Benomyl Thiophanate-methyl	Benlate Systemic Fungicide
Powdery mildew	White powder on leaves and stem.	Bupirimate plus triforine Benomyl	Nimrod T Benlate
Foot rot	Dark lesions on stem at soil level.	Copper sulphate plus ammonium carbonate	Cheshunt Compound
Black leg	Seedling stems turn black.	Benomyl Thiophanate-methyl	Benlate Systemic Fungicide
Downy mildew	Velvety mould on leaves which turns yellow.	Mancozeb	Dithane 945
Wire stem	Base of stem shrivels.	Benomyl	Benlate
Rust	Orange spots on leaves.	Propiconazole Mancozeb	Tumbleblite Dithane 945
BEANS			
Chocolate spot	Brown spots on leaves.	Benomyl	Benlate

Elaeagnus pungens 'Maculata'.

Disease	Damage	Chemical	Product
Halo blight	Pale spots on leaves.	Destroy infected plants and avoid soaking French bean seeds prior to sowing.	
BRASSICAS			
Club root	Malformed roots.	Mercurous chloride	Club Root Control
		Thiophanate-methyl	Systemic Fungicide
CELERY			
Leaf spot	Brown spots on leaf.	Benomyl	Benlate
LEEK			
White tip	Silver flecks unite and leaves turn white.	Mancozeb	Dithane 945
ONION			
Neck rot	Soft rot at neck of plant.	Benomyl	Benlate
White rot	Base of bulb rots causing leaves to turn yellow.	Mercurous chloride	Calomel
		Benomyl	Benlate
PARSNIP			
Canker	Brown lesions on root.	Control carrot fly.	
PEA			
Leaf and pod spot	Pale spots with dark brown margins.	Burn infected plants.	
TOMATO (Outdoor)			
Blight	Brown patches on leaf, stem and fruit.	Mancozeb	Dithane 945
APPLE AND PEAR			
Blossom wilt	Blossom wilts and turns brown. Disease grows back down shoot.	Tar oil	Clean Up
		Benomyl	Benlate
Apple brown rot	Brown spots on fruit coalesce and cause fruit to turn brown.	Tar oil	Clean Up
		Thiophanate-methyl	Systemic Fungicide
Canker	Brown lesions on bark.	Thiophanate-methyl	Seal and Heal Pruning Paint
Moss and Lichen	Grey/green growth on bark.	Tar oil	Clean Up
			Mortegg
Scab	Dark green/brown/black spots on leaves and fruit.	Bupirimate plus triforine	Nimrod T
		Thiophanate-methyl	Systemic Fungicide
PLUM AND CHERRY			
Bacterial canker	Pale spots on leaves turn brown and centre falls away.	Copper	Liquid Copper Fungicide
Blossom wilt	see Apple		
Brown rot	see Apple		

Disease	Damage	Chemical	Product
APRICOT, NECTARINE AND PEACH			
Peach leaf curl	Puckering and puffy growth on leaves.	Prevent tree from getting wet during winter if possible.	
		Copper	Liquid Copper Fungicide
Scab	Brown spots on leaves. Fruit cracked with gummy exudation.	Copper	Liquid Copper Fungicide
BLACKBERRY, LOGANBERRY AND RASPBERRY			
Cane spot	Brown spots with purple margins on leaves and stem.	Benomyl	Benlate
Spur blight	Purple patches on canes. Brown spots on leaves. Axillary buds shrivel and die.	Benomyl	Benlate
CURRANT AND GOOSEBERRY			
American gooseberry mildew	Dense white growth on fruit and shoots.	Bupirimate plus triforine	Nimrod T
		Benomyl	Benlate
Black currant leaf spot	Brown spots on leaves causing premature leaf loss.	Bupirimate plus triforine	Nimrod T
		Mancozeb	Dithane 945
Black currant rust	Brown marks on leaf	Mancozeb	Dithane 945
STRAWBERRY			
Leaf spot	Red spots on leaf	Benomyl	Benlate
Red core	Red discoloration on roots and crown.	Destroy infected plants. Avoid planting on infected ground. Plant in containers or growing bags.	
Verticillium wilt	Plants wilt during day. Pink discoloration in crown and leaf stalk.	Destroy infected plants. Avoid planting on infected ground.	
BORDER CARNATION			
Leaf spot	Dark rings on leaves and stem.	Mancozeb	Dithane 945
Ring spot	Pale spots with darker margins on leaves and flowers.	Mancozeb	Dithane 945
CHRYSANTHEMUM (Outdoor)			
Leaf spot	Brown spots with darker margin on leaf.	Mancozeb	Dithane 945
Petal blight	Pink spots on florets develop into water-soaked area.	Control pests. Mancozeb	Dithane 945

Disease	Damage	Chemical	Product
Ray blight	Centre of flower and leaf turns brown.	Mancozeb	Dithane 945
White rust	Pale green/yellow sunken areas in upper surface of leaf which turn brown in centre. Pale yellow/pink pustules on underside of leaf which turn pale brown.	Inform local office of Ministry of Agriculture then burn plants after inspection.	
GLADIOLUS			
Dry rot	Black lesions on corm. Leaves turn yellow. Stem rot causes plant to topple.	Benomyl Thiophanate-methyl	Benlate Systemic Fungicide
Core rot	Corm decays to soft rot. Leaves turn yellow.	Benomyl Thiophanate-methyl	Benlate Systemic Fungicide
NARCISSUS			
Root Rot	Brown rotting of bulb and roots.	Benomyl Thiophanate-methyl	Benlate Systemic Fungicide
Leaf scorch	Brown tipping of leaves.	Benomyl Copper	Benlate Liquid Copper Fungicide
Fire	Premature leaf death and flower spotting.	Benomyl bulb dip.	Benlate
TULIP			
Grey bulb rot	Shoots fail to grow or die before flower shows. Bulb appears dry with grey discoloration.	Benomyl bulb dip.	Benlate
Fire	Small water-soaked areas leading to scorched patches on leaves. Blooms rot.	Benomyl	Benlate
ROSE			
Black spot	Dark purple spots on leaves.	Bupirimate plus triforine Propiconazole	Nimrod T Tumbleblite
Late spring	Downward rolling of leaves. (See Rose leaf-rolling sawfly).	Physiological disorder caused by cold nights.	
GREENHOUSE AND FRAMES			
Damping off	Water-soaked areas on stem cause plant to topple.	Benomyl	Benlate
CARNATION			
Bud rot	Rotting flower buds.	Ventilate to reduce humidity. Remove infected buds.	
Wilt	Leaves wilt and turn yellow.	Destroy infected plants.	

Disease	Damage	Chemical	Product
CHRYSANTHEMUM			
Petal blight	see Chrysanthemum (Outdoor)		
Ray blight	see Chrysanthemum (Outdoor)		
White rust	see Chrysanthemum (Outdoor)		
CUCUMBER			
Mycosphaerella	Young fruits wither.	Ventilate. Remove infected fruit.	
TOMATO			
Brown root rot	Roots turn brown and corky causing plant to wilt and die.	Isolate roots from infected soil when next planting. Grow in containers.	
Leaf mould	Brown velvety patches on underside of leaf which coalesce and cause leaves to shrivel. Often incorrectly called 'mildew'.	Mancozeb Thiophanate-methyl	Dithane 945 Systemic Fungicide
Potato blight	see Tomato (Outdoor)		
Wilt	Root disease causing leaves to wilt and turn yellow. Internal dark ring to stem when cut across.	Shade house. Damp down to keep humid.	

HERBICIDES

Weedkillers have an important role to play in garden upkeep and maintenance because weeds can soon spoil the effect and give the area an untidy appearance. Not only that but weeds compete with crop plants for light, nutrient, soil moisture and reduce air circulation around the plant to such an extent that plant diseases may gain a foothold.

The application of bulky organic mulches around plants to suppress weeds, and the use of a hoe or hand weeding will do much to control them but time does not always permit the use of these measures; disturbance of the soil or path surface may bring fresh seeds to the surface so that they germinate to produce another flush of weed growth and the hand removal of weeds from the lawn presents an awesome task.

Weeds can be controlled to a certain extent by the cultural technique of planting crop or ornamental plants close together: ground-hugging shrubs and conifers soon cover the ground and make life difficult for the weeds. Another good example is lawn fertilizer application, or rather the lack of it, when clover often invades a lawn with low nitrogen content, especially when phosphates are relatively high in the soil.

Although the majority of weeds can be controlled by the use of herbicides, not all weedkillers can be used everywhere in the garden: some are selective in that they control a certain type of plant growing amongst others and it is worth remembering that a herbicide does not select a weed growing amongst crop plants just because we consider it to be a 'weed'; however it can select, for example, broad-leaved weeds growing amongst grasses in a lawn. *The instruction label must be read carefully before even opening the container for use.* Herbicides can be divided into several different groups:

Leaf acting, contact herbicides These are herbicides that are applied to the leaves and kill off the top growth; they may be non-selective so far as plants are concerned, that is total weedkillers, or selective by killing broad-leaved weeds in a lawn, for example.

Leaf acting, translocated herbicides These are applied to the leaves and the active material passes through the leaves into the root to kill the whole plant. They may be non-selective (total) plant killers or selective.

Soil acting, residual herbicides These are applied to the soil and remain active for a considerable time depending on quantity used and soil type. They may be selective or non-selective (total) weedkillers.

Mixtures of different kinds of weedkillers are available particularly for use on the lawn as this often contains so many different kinds of weeds; some lawn weedkillers are mixed by the manufacturer with fertilizer so that the two jobs can be done at once. Weedkillers are often applied mixed with water, whereas others may be applied as granules or powder.

Herbicides often have two names: the common chemical name, which is usually an abbreviated form of the very long chemical name, and the product name. The common chemical name is often referred to but since the product brand name is the one printed boldly on the container, both are given below for convenience.

Common Chemical Name	Product Name
LAWN WEEDKILLERS (and mosskillers)	
chloroxuron/ferric sulphate/urea	Tumblemoss
2,4-D/dicamba	Lawn Spot Weeder
2,4-D/dicamba/ioxynil	Bio Lawn Weedkiller
	Super Verdone
	Super Verdone Spot Weeder
2,4-D/dichlorprop	Murphy Lawn Weedkiller
2,4-D/fenoprop	New 4-50 Lawn Weed Spray
2,4-D/mecoprop	Boots Lawn Weedkiller
	Supertox
dichlorophen	Bio Mosskiller
	Super Mosskiller and Lawn Fungicide
	Mosstox – Plus
ioxynil	Actrilawn
ioxynil/mecoprop	New Clovercide Extra Lawn Weedspray
	New Clovotox
MCPA/dicamba	Fisons Lawn Weedkiller
tar oil	Clean-Up
PATHS, DRIVES AND WASTE LAND	
aminotriazole/2,4-D/diuron/simazine	Hytrol
aminotriazole/MCPA	Path Spot Weeder
aminotriazole/simazine	Super Weedex

Common Chemical Name	Product Name
aminotriazole/MCPA/simazine	Path Weedkiller
2,4-D/2,4,5 – T	Kilnet
	New SBK Brushwood Killer
dichlobenil	Casoron G
glyphosate	Tumbleweed
paraquat/diquat	Weedol
paraquat/diquat/simazine/aminotriazole	New Pathclear
sodium chlorate	Sodium Chlorate
sodium chlorate/atrazine	Atlacide Extra Dusting Powder

FLOWER BORDERS

2,4-DES/simazine	Herbon Blue
CIPC/diuron/IPC	Herbon Garden Herbicide
dalapon	Dalapon
glyphosate	Tumbleweed
paraquat/diquat	Weedol
Alloxydim sodium	Weed Out

TREE AND SHRUB BORDERS

2,4-DES/simazine	Herbon Blue
dalapon	Dalapon
dichlobenil	Casoron G
glyphosate	Tumbleweed
paraquat/diquat	Weedol
simazine	Weedex

VEGETABLES

paraquat/diquat	Weedol
propachlor	Covershield
simazine	Weedex

FRUIT

dalapon	Dalapon
glyphosate	Tumbleweed
paraquat/diquat	Weedol
propachlor (strawberries)	Covershield
simazine	Weedex

GROWTH REGULATORS

The use of special chemicals to stunt or elongate growth of garden plants is not essential for the plant's survival but, after all, gardening is a hobby and there is no doubt that the use of growth regulators is both fascinating and in certain cases rewarding.

Growth regulators can be used to help promote rooting in cuttings, reduce the height of houseplants, retard the extension growth of trees, hedges, shrubs and grass plants, reduce lawn mowing, enhance fruiting in plants, cause plants to grow many times larger than normal and, in certain cases, growth regulators are also used as herbicides. They are used by commercial growers and farmers to shorten the length of straw on cereals, to increase tree fruit harvest by encouraging blossom to set, especially when apple blossom has been frosted. Harvested fruit can be stored for longer periods and ripening can be retarded in certain cases – to give but a few examples. Growth regulators are natural constituents of plants.

Commercial pineapple growers noticed that flowering of the plants was stimulated when smoke from burning vegetation was blown over the plants, but it was not until the late 1920s that it was discovered that growth-regulant gases like ethylene in the smoke were responsible for this. Since then a chemical has been developed and marketed to do the same job and many other regulators have also been discovered including the 'hormone' type weedkillers 2,4-D and MCPA during the 1940s.

Maleic hydrazide is used as a retardant to suppress the growth of hedge plants and turf and to prevent sprouting of onions and potatoes in store. This is a very old retardant and was first discovered in 1895. It is not at the moment available in small retail packs.

Chlormequat chloride known as Cycocel or CCC is used by farmers to reduce the stem length and increase yield in cereals; its use on garden plants is confined to certain cultivars of Indian azalea to initiate early flower buds and cause compact growth; it is used for the same purpose in pelargoniums and it also reduces the height of poinsettias.

Daminozide is available in small garden size packs under the product name of 'Gro-Slo' and in larger packs as 'Alar'. This is used on azalea, pot chrysanthemum, chrysanthemums for cutting to strengthen the stem neck, hydrangea, poinsettia and various bedding plants to retard growth.

Dikegulac-sodium is sold under the brand name of 'Cutlass' and is sprayed onto certain hedge type and shrubby plants after clipping them over in spring. The chemical inhibits apical dominance of the shoots so that side branching occurs and yet the hedge remains at the same height as when it was cut. Only those parts of the hedge treated will be effected so that if only one side or top is required to be held at that length, the other side will grow as usual. The same material is also used to 'pinch' the apical growth of potted shrubs including fuchsias to keep them compact.

Paclobutrazol is a growth retardant still in the research stage at the time of writing but should be available shortly for use on a wide range of plants including trees, shrubs and houseplants where it will retard growth and provide the opportunity to grow various kinds of plants which could not be grown before due to lack of space. One of the main uses in the garden will be to control grass growth that often gets out of hand during holidays.

Gibberillins were first isolated in Japan in 1938 but it was not until the late 1950s that they were considered seriously to alter the growth of plants. Commercial growers use them to increase the yield and quality of seedless grapes, increase fruit set of pears and enhance the yield of hops. Giant-sized plants can be grown by using gibberillic acid to elongate the plant's cell tissue; seeds of some plants belonging to the rose family, certain trees and vegetables including celery are notoriously difficult to germinate unless treated with gibberillins.

Indol-3-ylacetic acid (IAA), 4-indol-3-ylbutyric acid (IBA) and 1-naphthylacetic acid (NAA) are formulated under various rooting hormone product brand names for use in plant propagation to promote callus and root formation in cuttings. The active ingredient is usually purchased ready for use having been mixed with talc and a fungicide by the manufacturer. A liquid formulation is also available but there is a chance of spreading virus and bacterial diseases from one cutting to another whilst soaking in the same container. Only the base of the cutting is dipped into the hormone and any excess is shaken off before inserting the cutting into rooting medium.

INDEX